TEACHERS' READING/TEACHERS' LIVES

SUNY Series, Urban Voices, Urban Visions

Diane DuBose Brunner and Rashidah Jaamí Muhammad, Editors

Teachers' Reading/Teachers' Lives

Mary Kay Rummel

AND

Elizabeth P. Quintero

State University of New York Press

Published by
State University of New York Press, Albany

© 1997 State University of New York

For information, address State University of New York Press,
State University Plaza, Albany, N.Y. 12246

Production by M. R. Mulholland
Marketing by Dana E. Yanulavich

Library of Congress Cataloging-in-Publication Data
[info to come]
10 9 8 7 6 5 4 3 2 1

Rummel, Mary Kay.
    Teachers' reading/teachers' lives / Mary Kay Rummel, Elizabeth P.
Quintero.
        p.   cm. — (SUNY series, urban voices, urban visions)
    Includes bibliographical references and index.
    ISBN 0-7914-3485-0 (hardcover : alk. paper). — ISBN 0-7914-3486-9
(pbk. : alk. paper)
    1. Education—Biographical methods. 2. Teachers—United States—
Books and reading. 3. Teachers—United States—Biography.
4. Teaching—United States—Case studies. I. Quintero, Elizabeth
P. II. Title. III. Series.
LB1029.B55R86   1997
371.1'0092'2—dc21   96-36918
                                                               CIP

CONTENTS

FOREWORD

Beyond seeing order in randomness, by being aware of the detailed make-up of chaos, teachers may be "open to new ways of intellectual processing." In *Teachers' Reading/Teachers' Lives*, Rummel and Quintero open such a space for educators to examine the challenges that they face on the eve of the twenty-first century. Advocating a critical pedagogy, the authors echo Paulo Freire, Henry Giroux, bell hooks, and others who insist that teachers have the power to change the direction of their students' lives. *Teachers' Reading/Teachers' Lives* reminds educators to act on something James Baldwin said many years ago, "The world changes according to the way people see it, and if you alter, even by a millimeter, the way people look at reality, then you can change it."

By merging autobiographical and theoretical modes of discourse *Teachers' Reading/Teachers' Lives* invites educators into a conversation that focuses on becoming more "effective authors" of our own lives as a way of being more in touch with the lives of students. Long have educators sought ways to "empower" students, to show them that their stories—their meaning-making processes—are a very valid part of the learning experience. Now in this study, Rummel and Quintero open the question: Are teachers who read literature and who read their own lives reflectively in a more sensitive and enlightened position to create a more democratic learning environment? Here we find answers in the story of Bill, a special education teacher who reads adventure/travel books and creates outdoor programs for his students. Examples of his reading range from the story of an American family exiled for generations in Russia to Barry Lopez's *Arctic Dreams*. We find answers in the story of Pamela, a writer and a dancer. This Brooklyn elementary teacher combines art, dance, and literature to encourage her students to create their own poetry books. In the words of bell hooks, Pamela's students are "learning that writing is a way to capture speech, hold on to it, and keep it close."

While readily acknowledging that there is never one "correct" pedagogy or one "correct" teaching method, Rummel and Quintero encourage educators to re-see their practice as the interrelationship of life with teaching in a continuum. Because *Teachers' Reading/Teachers'*

Lives provides space for teachers to inventory—for innovative pedagogical tools—their own lives, their own reading, their own teaching, it is a valuable and important contribution.

Rashidah Jaamí Muhammad
Governors States University
University Park, Illinois

ACKNOWLEDGMENTS

Teacher's Reading/Teachers' Lives has grown out of many years of passionate teaching practice and many years of dear, committed relationships among students, teachers, family, and community members. We would like to thank especially our families; Christine Hendrickson, Ann Green, and Jamie Madsen, students from the Department of Education at the University of Minnesota, Duluth, who through the Undergraduate Research Opportunities program were able to help conduct some of the interviews and give insights from their perspectives about this work; Maureen Lally; and the muses of Lake Superior.

PART I

INTRODUCTION AND VOICE MATTERS: AUTOBIOGRAPHICAL SKETCHES OF TEACHER-AUTHORS

1

Introduction: Sensitive Dependence on Initial Conditions

We contend that the goal of education is personal and political empowerment both of teachers and of their students. June Jordan (1987) speaks of this empowerment through language, "If we lived in a democratic state our language would have to hurtle, fly, curse, and sing, in all the common American names, all the undeniable and representative participating voices of everybody here" (30). Thus, we began this teacher interview study with the following question in mind: Is the ability to deconstruct personal experience, both actual and metaphorical, through both personal literacy and literacy instruction what makes teachers sensitive to and able to empower children?

We, as does Lorenz (Gleick, 1987), believe that by paying attention to the sensitive dependence on initial conditions—in this case teachers' reading—we can learn from the teachers with whom we collaborated in this study. Our methods for this research study involved auto-biographical cultural criticism. Through autobiographical cultural criticism, this study explores critical issues in teaching—specifically the influence of reading upon the lives of teachers who are sensitive to diversity. We investigated the effects of this reading on teachers' lives and explore how reading affects our becoming effective authors of our own lives. This study emulates a new academic genre which integrates two modes of discourse usually kept sharply separate: the auto-biographical and the theoretical.

Resisting readers and thinkers have always interpreted text based on their own experience. An example of this is Jamaica Kinkaid's (1990) Lucy who was made, by her English schoolteachers, to memorize and recite "Daffodils": "I was then at the height of my two-facedness: that is, outside I seemed one way, inside I was another; outside false, inside true. And so I made pleasant little noises that showed both modesty and appreciation, but inside I was making a vow to erase from my mind, line by line, every word of that poem" (1990, 19).

We, the authors, are teacher-researchers with our own stories and our own experiences, both metaphorical from literature and actual from life experiences, woven together making us who we are as teachers. In this research, as we looked into our collaborating teachers' stories, we became aware of the influence of reading in their development of personal metaphors for life which, in turn, influences their teaching in many ways. We have used various methods to "listen to" the stories of teachers. We listened to teachers' family histories—to find the origins of the stories—in the interviews and for underlying metaphor as a continuing pervasive influence on teachers' work.

As we interviewed, we, as did Rogers (1993), realized that we hope to change not only the voice of research through teachers' voices, but also its practice. Through this process, we expanded our initial question to include the following dimensions: Is it teachers who personally experience power of fantasy in their own lives who are able to respect the importance of fantasy in the development of young children? Is it the relationship between literacy and art that helps us get at the complexities of life? Does the fact that metaphorical experience involved in art, including cultural traditions and ceremonies, has been tied to action as a concrete expression of itself relate to teacher development? What are the metaphors constructed by resisting readers? What are their metaphors for teaching? How do they personally deconstruct culture in relation to their own experience? How do teachers get nourishment for the soul?

Theoretical Framework

She's was always there when I went outside . . . flashes of yellow on purple as she flew in and out of the bougainvillea blossoms. Her name was Juliana. I remember going to the rooftop of the tiny pink house overlooking the village when I was happy and she seemed to be hopping around reflecting my spirits. I remember when I was sad or upset and I wanted to hide in the vines and plants in the courtyard, she hovered near as if to say "I'm here with you." She first joined me in Chapala, a small village in Mexico and followed my uprooted family to San Antonio, Texas and then finally to Florida. At some point in this journey, she was joined by her friend, a white butterfly named Juanita. My fantasy world and spiritual world were alive in these two butterflies. I still think of them today when I see a yellow or white butterfly.

—Elizabeth Quintero

In connection with our study, we thought of these yellow and white butterfly companions when we looked at the design for our study. We had been influenced by the work of Lorenz (Gleick, 1987) and his study of chaos theory, a theory that has become an elaborate study of natural phenomena. Lorenz elucidated the principles of that theory with the Lorenz attractor which reflects the pattern on butterflies' wings and around the eyes of the owl and other designs in nature. Lorenz's perceptive ability to see order in apparent randomness and "sensitive dependence on initial conditions" (Gleick, 1987, 29) left him open to new ways of intellectual processing. We felt inspired by his risk-taking and have used as our metaphor for research his figure, "Lorenz attractor" sometimes labeled the "Lorenz butterfly," described here:

> This magical image, resembling an owl's mask or butterfly's wings, became an emblem for the early explorers of chaos. It revealed the fine structure hidden within a disorderly stream of data . . . To show the changing relationships among three variables required a different technique. At any instant in time, the three variables fix the location of a point in three-dimensional space; as the system changes, the motion of the point represents the continuously changing variables . . . Because the system never exactly repeats itself, the trajectory never intersects itself. Instead it loops around and around forever. (Gleick, 1987, 29)

Our choice of the Lorenz butterfly as our metaphor, borrowed from chaos theory, is in part due to its vivid illustration of overlaps of phenomena—overlaps, not intersections. After interviewing the teachers, we saw, as Lorenz (Gleick, 1987) saw, order in apparent experiential randomness of the teachers' lives and "sensitive dependence on initial conditions" (Gleick, 1987, 29). We use this metaphor, not as a thoughtless application of one area of science to another, but as a metaphor to structure our conversation about a complex qualitative study.

The point of our research is that effective teaching is a continuum. There is never one finding as a result of this research about effective teachers; there is never one pedagogy; there is never one teaching style that is right. Effective teaching is the interrelationship of life and teaching in a continuum looping around forever. This is what makes these teachers "artisans" as described by Casey, implying the possibility of changing the world through work. These teacher artisans create curricula which weave their knowledge with the needs and interests of their students. Their commitment to students is part of the fabric of their total lives.

We see through the teachers' experience a fine structure which shows the changing relationships among our three variables (theoretical perspectives). And as in the Lorenz butterfly, the system (the data) never exactly repeats itself, the trajectory never intersects itself. Instead it loops around and around forever and illustrates information we can learn from our informants' lives. The three fixed points are for us the three theoretical perspectives through which we view the data. The system that changes is the interaction of the four themes changing constantly according to the individuals and the contexts. In other words, theory changes in light of different teachers and contexts.

We use as our theoretical/philosophical framework critical theory (Freire, 1973), feminist theory (Rogers, 1993), and relational, social theory (Rogers, 1993). The first variable in our "butterfly" metaphor of research and teaching is critical theory. Critical theory is embraced as it applies to the process of conscientization as Freire (1985) envisioned for adults and as it applies to children. Freire (1985) defines conscientization (based on the Brazilian conscientização), as "the process by which human beings participate critically in a transforming act" (106). He goes on to say that "conscientization thus involves a constant clarification of that which remains hidden within us while we move about in the world, though we are not necessarily regarding the world as the object of our critical reflection" (Freire, 1985, 107).

> A critical pedagogy can only be correctly discussed from within a particular "point of practice"; from within a specific time and place and within a particular theme. This means doing critical pedagogy is a strategic, practical task not a scientific one. It arises not against a background of psychological, sociological, or anthropological universals as does much educational theory related to pedagogy—but from such questions as: *"how is human possibility being diminished here?"* (Simon, 1988, 2)

Giroux (1988) and other advocates of critical pedagogy (Freire and Macedo, 1987; Shor, 1987) advocate the fruition of "teacher as intellectual." Giroux (1988) states, "I want to argue that one way to rethink and restructure the nature of teacher work, is to view teachers as transformative intellectuals" (25). Giroux (1988) maintains that this quest of the intellectual is helpful for three reasons. First, it defines teachers' work as an intellectual endeavor as opposed to a mere technical one. Second, it brings to light the conditions necessary for teachers to combine ideological and practical issues. Third, it legitimizes teachers' roles in combining political, economic, and social interests through daily pedagogy. We maintain that the most effective teachers are in fact intellectuals who not only combine political, economic and social issues in daily pedagogy, but who also are critical theorists in the sense of "resisting readers." In some cases, we feel our data indicate that these teachers are born as resisting readers; in other cases, it seems that the teachers' journey through life has caused them to develop into resisting readers. Resisting reader/teachers, it seems from our research, make critically based decisions, not only in terms of classroom context, but also in terms of curriculum choices. Trueba (1989) writes that one of the dilemmas teachers typically face in schools is "whether to abide by curriculum requirements or simply to decide on their own what is best for students" (111). They often are forced to make the painful choice of abiding by the constraints set on them even though they recognize that what they are being asked to do in the classroom is not the best for their children.

Feminist epistemology, the second variable in our research metaphor, which is theory about the nature of knowledge, has challenged many tenets of traditional knowledge as it is male defined and practiced in Western patriarchal cultures. Feminist methodology is "a set of guidelines about how to conduct research in the face of disbelief in such" (Rogers, 1993, 266) forms of knowledge. It is through this feminist methodology that the researcher seeks to include, rather than exclude, the researcher in the research and interpretation. As Shannon (1993) points out, "Feminist theory looks not for what has been excluded, but for what has been silenced" (124). We use feminist literary theory in order to provide a framework to document risk taking and ask, as ethnographer Behar (1993) did: "Ultimately, Esperanza's transgressions against patriarchal ideology are tied up in paradoxes . . . Of course, the question remains: From whose perspective, whose absolute scale of feminist perfection, are her attitudes and actions being measured? (296–97).

We use feminist theory as a way to pay attention to varied perspectives in teaching. We are guided by feminist theory in action through the work of notable women writers. Maxine Greene (1992b) mentors us in our work, "Think of American culture as a conversation among different voices. . . . The purpose of education is to recognize the voices" (13). She speaks of her personal metaphorical development: "If it weren't for Jo March in *Little Women*, I wouldn't be where I am today" (Greene, 1995, 91).

Likewise, Maxine Hong Kingston tells of personal historical influences: "When my second grade class did a play, the whole class went to the auditorium except the Chinese girls . . . our voices were too soft or nonexistent" (Hong Kingston, 1989, 167).

Thus, we come to the third variable in our framework, the relational, voice-centered approach of autobiography. As previously stated, we, the authors, are a subjective presence in the collection, analysis, and dissemination of research stories. Bloch (1991) explains that this type of symbolic science "focuses on intersubjectivities that are created through interactions between people, their discourse, and the interpretations of meaning within specific contexts" (97). This relational theory uses experience as central to theorizing and to understanding practice and, as Clandinin and Connelly (1994) maintain, "For us, keeping experience in foreground comes about by periodic returns to the works of Dewey (1916, 1934, 1938). For Dewey, education, experience, and life are inextricably intertwined" (5).

> Situation, the central term in Dewey's theory of experience, is specified by two criteria, interaction and continuity. Interaction refers to the intersection of internal and existential conditions. . . . Continuity refers to the temporal positioning of every situation. Situations don't just happen; they are historical and temporally directional according to the intentionality of the organism undergoing experience. (Clandinin and Connelly, 1994, 6)

We have seen through the process and content of our research that in the construction of narratives of experience, there is a relationship between living a life story and telling a life story. This telling a life story often is made in the language of metaphor. Clandinin (1986) found that verbal imagery of teachers often clusters around metaphors such as *planting a seed* or *making a home* and that these metaphors reveal the "complex coalescence of personal and professional experience and of theory and practice. In an exploration of the relationships between teachers' reading histories, the historical context in which they move and the broader patterns which release our educational imaginations, metaphor takes on central importance. Metaphor often provides the possibility of communicating what cannot be expressed literally. We make the world familiar with metaphor, Maxine Greene (1992b) says, "We feel less powerless when we can name and explain." This empowerment is the essence of critical transformation.

Methodology

As we asked teachers to participate in this study, we used Casey's (1993) concept of teacher as 'artisan' implying the possibility of changing the world through work. These teacher artisans create curricula which weave their knowledge with the needs and interests of their students. Their commitment to students is part of the fabric of their total lives. In most cases, they create or participate in organizations which impact larger systems of school or society. We included teachers from a wide spectrum of racial, class, and gender backgrounds who teach in a variety of contexts.

Autobiographical criticism is used by Pegano (1990) to think differently about experience without repudiating it. The objective of this study, like Pegano's, is not to "desert the old neighborhood," but to revisit old neighborhoods to remember personal experiences of learning to speak and read and write, in order to think differently about how these skills are taught in America's schools where we have been students or teachers.

With previous studies on gender and reading as background, we interviewed teachers at various grade levels and sites to explore what they read as children and how reading relates to their perceptions of their place in society and what they read now as adults. Insights from Gilligan's (1982) interviewing strategies and a combination of strategies described by Patton (1987) as "interview guide" and "informal conversational interviewing" techniques gave our informants' voice in order to relate how reading has affected their values and their decision making. Depth interviewing such as this consists of asking questions, recording the informants' answers, and then following up with more relevant questions. In the interview guide approach, topics and questions to address are decided in advance and documented in outline form. The interviewer decides on the order of questions and specific wording as the interview progresses. In informal conversational interviewing, the questions emerge from the immediate context and are asked in the normal course of events, such as a visit in the teacher-informant's classroom. As Patton (1987) states, "The purpose of interviewing, then, is to allow us to enter the other person's perspective" (109).

We then designed a listening guide that illustrates the relationships among literacy, metaphor, nurturance, family history, and risk-taking in the form of being a resisting reader and teacher. The listening guide was used as we listened to the taped interviews and also as we analyzed information from the transcribed interviews. The listening guide consists of four stages. First, we listened to the teachers' comments in terms of what factual information was being related regarding both personal reading history and familial and relationship history. Second, we listened to voice, which often resonated with realities of race, class, and gender embedded in what the person was saying. Third, we attended to the ways teachers talked about literacy and relationships. Fourth, we listened again to the whole voice with attempts to adhere to guidance from feminist literary critics who have contributed to what Rich (1979) calls "revision . . . the act of looking back, of seeing with fresh eyes, of entering an old test from a new critical direction" (35).

After interviewing thirteen teachers, as Lorenz (Gleick, 1987) saw, we saw order in apparent experiential randomness of the teachers' lives and "sensitive dependence on initial conditions" (29). We saw through the teachers' experience a fine structure which shows the changing relationships among our three variables (theoretical perspectives). And as in the Lorenz butterfly, the system (the data) never exactly repeats itself, the trajectory never intersects itself. Instead, it loops around and around forever and illustrates information we can learn from our informants' lives.

The teachers' stories point to expected and unexpected information. In the category of "Metaphor and Art as Frameworks for Living," we see that the life metaphors described are related in that through reading the teachers used those metaphors to open up wider worlds outside their experience. Teachers in this study actively engage in some art form as a part of their lives. This is clearly a part of these teachers' self-nurturance, which again shows the interrelated nature of our theoretical model and our findings. Reading is a source of ongoing nurturance connecting both personal and professional lives. "Family History" shows a combination of the importance of sociocultural context and images of place in childhood. There was often no bedtime story, but newspapers, mystery novels, and romance novels were important in the lives of family members in most cases. We have found that the resisting reader is a reader and thinker who deconstructs text based on personal experience. All asked critical questions as child readers, and they, through reading, gained confidence and knowledge to take the risks necessary to be critical teachers. Reading these interviews leads us to realize that the lives of teachers are like the lives of artists or spiritual leaders—every moment is a commitment in a recurring pattern of action and interaction.

In order to reflect on the wisdom shown by these teachers, we look at issues related to the four themes. Yet, in light of our belief in the continuum, the stories and the interaction of all themes in different ways in all cases, the reader sees overlapping patterns. For example, in the story of Vicki, we see family history in the passing down of stories from grandmother to mother to daughter. As she tells the story, there is overwhelming evidence of the metaphor of literacy as circle, which through nurturance expands her literacy connections from family to classroom to community. Then we see her classroom built on the synergistic combination of all these forces giving her the strength and creativity to resist financial and bureaucratic barriers to providing positive literacy experiences for the children. Similarly, in Raúl's story, we see the themes overlapping and interacting to synergistically propel an "artisan" teacher. Raúl points out the strengths he felt in his large, farmworker family as they migrated during his childhood. Through the strengths, he could see the holes in stereotypical, mainstream curriculum, and as early as high school he became an activist demanding to study heros from his own background. His illuminated vision and persistence carry over to his activist work with the Migrant Education programs in Minnesota and help him see the strengths in the Hmong students he now teaches in St. Paul. The strengths he is able to see inform him about providing learning experiences that support the students.

This relationship of the themes is not an intersection of categories, but is akin to a gravitational field in which the themes interact. For Vicki, as well as the other teachers, metaphor, nurturance, family history, and resistance are present in the other three categories of themes. By looking at the teachers' stories through the lenses of the four themes, we are informed about the most dynamic issues relating to literacy development. The apparent randomness in the variables is predictable when viewed using a metaphorical framework borrowed from chaos theory and can inform teacher education.

In part 1, we participate as informants by relating glimpses of our stories, perspectives, and dreams for our research and our work. As Lather (1994) suggests, we, the researchers, move beyond referential naivete in a way that does not simply collapse the referent, that does not elide what Cornell West (1990) terms "a reality *that one cannot not know*" (20). We do our research in a Gramscian "historical laboratory" that continually reminds us of our metaphor of the Lorenz butterfly with the combined information from ourselves and our informants looping around forever.

In our presentation of the information from the interviews of the teachers, we intentionally present the words of the informants in their own voice, with limited commentary on our part. As Lather (1994) again guides us, we aim "to grasp both specificity and discontinuity, deploy the space of dispersion . . . to make use of drama, artistry, literary practices" (3). We believe that the complexity, contradiction, ambiguity, and tension which the reader will see in each teacher's story form the vitality of the research findings we have collected. While the teachers' information falls into the four themes, the different life experiences do not repeat themselves, but yield information about teachers' variations on the four themes. Using our visual metaphor of the butterfly's wings, each teacher's story paints different patterns of color on the design of the picture which informs us.

In part 2, the lives of the teachers in this study illuminate many complex issues in education today. Their strength and commitment in diverse contexts provide insight into some difficult questions being asked by those working to meet children's needs through education. In chapter 4, Bill Simpson, a special education teacher in Stillwater, Minnesota, shows how the power of early reading-based metaphor affects both personal life and teaching. Through the language of reading, Bill was able to begin to live adventure and to bring dreams into being for himself and his students. Chapter 5 is the story of Pam Russell, who teaches in Brooklyn, New York. Her early reading nourished a love of art that she continues to use in her literacy-rich classroom. In chapter 6, David Haynes, a middle school teacher who now teaches in Saturn Magnet School in St. Paul, Minnesota, shows us a lively mix of the art of writing, people watching, activism, and teaching. David grew up in St. Louis, Missouri, and is a published writer whose school experiences inform his stories and whose stories help him work with and support his students. In Chapter 7, Lisa Boehlke, a teacher in the St. Paul Public Schools, reveals that her effectiveness is much broader than simply being an expert in English as a Second Language methods. Her global perspectives in a concrete and complex sense, are the twine that bind the academics and affective influences she and her students have on each other. In Chapter 8, Tracy Montero, an elementary teacher in Brooklyn, New York, uses her passion for and training in ethnography to open cultural borders for her students. In Chapter 9, Donn Renee Morson-McKie, an elementary teacher in Brooklyn, New York, uses her art to create community for herself, her family, and her students. In Chapter 10, Wayne Wazouko, speaks as a culturally appointed teacher who came to a teacher education credentialing program to give and to receive information. Chapter 11, Dell Tideman, illustrates the themes of our research as they appear in the life of a teacher brought up in a middle-class, conservative community. She reveals herself as a teacher "artisan" who is able to see embedded artistry in her students and nurture their potential through her reading and her guidance in their reading. Chapter 12 tells the story of Vicki Brathwaite, an elementary teacher in Brooklyn, New York. Vicki nurtures connections involved with literacy among women in the family, teacher mentors such as Lucy Calkins, and peers who meet regularly to share reading and writing. In Chapter 13, Kathryn Mongon speaks of discovering the saving power of literacy as a young child in a traumatic situation and who is commit ted to making this power available to her students. In Chapter 14, Raúl Quintanilla exemplifies two themes in particular. As a young reader he asked critical questions of resistance, and from early childhood he had the artist's ability to perceive visual, emotional beauty in simple, ordinary experience. In Chapter 15, Mary Tacheny, a primary teacher in Franklin Magnet School in St. Paul, Minnesota, works with Southeast Asian immigrant children and their families. In Chapter 16, Judith Borer shows reading as a fuse releasing a teacher from a limiting, male-dominated, rural background to become an advocate for female students and for all women.

In part 3, Chapters 17 through 20, the four themes of metaphor, nurturance, family history, and resistance are explored using a composite of all the teachers' contributions.

Another image used for "The Lorenz Attractor" is the owl's mask (Gleick, 1987, 29). We use it, the recurring patterns, as a bridge to the interviews, the unending circles of family history, resistent voices, art, and reflection.

Whose Hands Are These?

1
The onyx bay
gives me back those years
when my boys, up early,
chose cereal in small packages
to eat on the beach.
Then I had to get up at five
to sit on the dock and watch sunfish
breakfast on moths.

The sun walks slowly here.
It first lights the edge of the island
that blocks the view of the channel,
then steps toward the shore.

Last night my sons took the boat alone.
As the channel turned black I listened
for their motor, my eyes pleading
with the distant water.
My hands twisting
became my mother's hands
She braided her fingers in worry
even as she waited to die
her sons returned for the last time.

As I thought about calling the sheriff
the night for me became a knife edge hung
between the bottomless shadows of pines.
Then the boat entered the channel
and the bay the moon the loon cry
were given back to me.

2

Behind me in the woods
an owl lifts from a tree too small to hold it.
　　　　I see its shadow first
　　　　then I freeze
　　　　in an old dream.
　　　　Wrapped in dark feathers
　　　　ringed eyes
　　　　a soft conspiracy.

　　　　Sail above me
　　　　owl
　　　　each moment now
　　　　is yours

　　　　and I run
　　　　like your small prey
　　　　through the chaos
　　　　that is the pattern of things. (Mary Kay Rummel)

References

Behar, R. (1993). *Translated woman: Crossing the border with Esperanza's story.* Boston, MA: Beacon Press.

Bloch, M. N. (1991). Critical science and the history of child development's influence on early education research. *Early Education and Development, 2* (2), 95–108.

Casey, K. (1993). *I answer with my life: Life histories of women teachers working for social change.* New York: Routledge Press.

Clandinin, D. (1986). *Classroom practices: Teacher images in action.* London: Falmer.

Clandinin, Jean D., and Connelly, F. M. (1994). *Handbook of qualitative research.* London: Sage Publications.

Dewey, J. (1916). *Democracy and education.* New York: Macmillan.

————. (1934). *Art as experience.* New York: Capricorn Books.

————. (1934). *Experience and education.* New York: Collier Books.

Ferguson R., Gever, M., Minh-ha, T. T., & West, C. (Eds.) (1990). *Out there: Marginalization and contemporary cultures.* New York: The New Museum of Contemporary Art and MIT.

Freire, P. (1985). *The politics of education.* Granby, MA: Bergin & Garvey.

————. (1973). *Education for critical consciousness.* New York: Seabury Press.

Freire, P., and Macedo, D. (1987). *Literacy: Reading the word and the world.* South Hadley, MA: Bergin & Garvey.

Gilligan, C. (1982). *In a different voice: Psychological theory and women's development.* Cambridge, MA: Harvard University Press.

Giroux, H. (1991). The politics of postmodernism: Rethinking the boundaries of race and ethnicity. *Journal of Urban and Cultural Studies, 1* (1), 5–38.

Giroux, H. A. (1988). *Teachers as intellectuals: Toward a critical pedagogy of learning.* MA: Bergin & Garvey Publishers, Inc.

Gleick, J. (1987). *Chaos: Making a new science.* New York: Penguin.

Gordon, W. J. (1961). *Synectics: The development of creative capacity.* New York: Harper.

Greene, M. (1992a). Imagination and breakthroughs in the unexpected. Unpublished paper presented to the Association of Supervision and Curriculum Development. New Orleans.

————. (1992b). The passions of pluralism: Multiculturalism and the expanding community. *Educational Researcher, 22* (1), 13–18.

————. (1995). *Releasing the imagination: Essays on education, the arts, and social change.* San Francisco, CA: Jossey-Bass.

Hong-Kingston, M. (1989). *Woman warrior.* New York, NY: Knopf.

Jordan, J. (1987). *On call.* Boston: South End Press.

Khatena, J. (1972). The use of analogy in the production of original verbal images. *Journal of Creative Behavior, 6,* 93–102.

Kincaid, J. (1990). *Lucy.* New York: Plume.

Lather, P. (1994). *Gender issues in methodology: Data analysis in the crisis of representation.* Unpublished paper. New Orleans, LA: AERA National Conference.

Patton, M. Q. (1987). *How to use qualitative methods in evaluation.* Newbury Park: SAGE.

Pegano, J. A. (1990). *Exiles and communities: Teaching in the patriarchal wilderness.* Albany, NY: State University of New York Press.

Rich, A. (1979). *On lies, secrets, and silence.* New York: W. W. Norton.

Rogers, Annie G. (1993). Voice, play, and the practice of ordinary courage in girls' and women's lives. *Harvard Educational Review, 63* (3), 265–295.

Shannon, P. (1993). *Becoming political.* Portsmouth, NH: Heinemann.

Shor, I. (1987). *Freire for the classroom: A sourcebook for liberatory teaching.* Portsmouth, NH. Heinemann.

Simon, R. (1988). For a pedagogy of possibility. *Critical Pedagogy Networker, 1* (February).

Trueba, H. T. (1989). *Raising silent voices: Educating the linguistic minorities for the twenty-first century.* NY: Newbury House.

West, C. (1990). The new cultural politics of difference. In R. Ferguson, M. Gever, T. T. Minh-ha, C. West (Eds.), *Out there: Marginalization and contemporary cultures,* 19–38.

2

Voice Matters: Autobiographical Sketches of Mary Kay Rummel

I am sitting next to the rushing Fall River just outside of Rocky Mountain National Park in Colorado thinking about my own reading history and how the patterns of my life are like the patterns playing upon this river. The rapids seem to be another metaphor for chaos theory, pattern within difference. One rapid never intersects another wave. There is repetition of pattern, but each rapid is different. This trajectory of water loops forever, but I can't see the loop, can't see the arch of water that returns to the peak where it began. These thoughts resulted in a poem:

> In Chaos
> Today be where you stand
> It's midsummer in this place of little summer
> Be blessed Be blessed
> Let the light make you rosy where you stand
>
> If you cannot be where you are
> Then leave in full charge like a glacial river
> Focused as the heron leaving earth for air
> Reject longing if you cannot be where you are
>
> Let death scare you into living
> You are a clay pot made to hold and be held
> The sun has left its marks upon you
> The moon's loneliness will scare you into living
>
> Wings of the butterfly, eyes of the owl
> River spray becomes stars becomes cloud
> You are part of a looping trajectory
> See it in the wings of the butterfly, eyes of the owl

> Loosen the grasp of your fingers, your heart
> The river will teach pattern in chaos
> Today be where you stand
> Loosen the grasp of your fingers, your heart.

One night during winter quarter I turned on the classic movie channel and watched *The Song of Bernadette* as I read student papers. Gradually the papers were put aside and I was rapt, held by the images that had mesmerized me as a child, first in the book and later in the Jennifer Jones film. I became that child again; for a short time the laughing critic in me shut down. The woman who knew that the silent suffering, the obedience to priests was ridiculous was silenced, and I remembered how passionately I had wanted to be a saint. Bernadette in her story and all the women saints in all the stories became saints through suffering, physical pain borne not just in silence but with great enthusiasm. Saints were silent suffering women, but oh how I wanted to be one, and it all came from reading. From the time I was ten, I wanted to read about real women heroines. I searched the old wooden book shelves in St. James School library, and all I could find were hagiographies, biographies of saints.

Bernadette was told by her priest to go into the convent even though she wanted to marry and have children, and she went in grandly with the villagers all weeping and her loved one saying goodby with flowers and a promise of faithful celibacy. And then she was there in cold stone among cold women who wanted to break her. I remembered how I did what Bernadette did—went into the convent— led by all the books I had read, how books led me out again.

The following poem (1995) arose from memories of my youthful experiences with those biographies of the saints:

At the Side Altars

It was the central truth	we were given
in the center of	our souls
the figure bleeding	torn

Instead of the mother	giving birth
we were given the son	dying
over and over	again

Be like him	the priests said
Die everyday to yourself when	it was life
we needed death already	waiting

| *Be like him* they said | but I was a girl |

reading   creating
each woman saint   her own geography.

Therese in her French convent
knew hell on a pin head
all the love she carried for god
ripened as a rose in her
lips parted in song
as his language sunk in her
suffering made her sing

Rose of Lima
lived in silence
was cut by a surgeon
without anodyne
never cried
wore a crown of twisted
metal under her veil
never cried over the killing
in the Peruvian hills

Italian Maria Goretti
was murdered
while fighting a rape
she forgave Allessandro
as he stabbed her
he in prison felt remorse
she of course wasn't there to see it
a model for us the nuns said
but they never talked about
the women in my neighborhood
who said no
who wouldn't forgive
and died anyway

I tried to be like them
a saint of West Seventh
Went to the dentist
who didn't use novocaine
and offered it up.
Put a chinese checker board
under my pillow.
Imagined myself into a frenzy
like the best of penitents

for three hours on Good Friday
then skipped out in relief.
> *My saint now is the Roman Barbara*
> *who broke silence*
> *her head kept talking*
> *as it rolled away from her body*

I have loved to read my whole life. When I was in elementary school and junior high, I read every book I could find about the lives of girls: *Little Women, Ann of Green Gables,* the Betsy-Tacey books. In high school I loved the literature we read—most of it the canon—most of it by men, Greeks and Shakespeare, Eliot and Hopkins, and later I added Yeats to my list of loved literature and the works of Pablo Neruda. These works taught me the ecstasy of language. The two works I loved most in high school were *Murder in the Cathedral,* by Elliot, and *Death Comes to the Archbishop,* by Willa Cather. In college I memorized the whole "Wreck of the Deuschland," by Gerard Manley Hopkins.

Actually, this joy I experienced in language connected much of what came later in my life, determining the kind of work I chose to do and the kind of teacher that I am. I was so hungry for beauty when I was a young woman, and in the world in which I lived, a working-class urban neighborhood, I could find it best in books and religion. Religion created the way I found beauty in the world. Looking back, I see all the misogyny I absorbed along with religion—how I learned "my place." I came from a large family, and we lived in a small house. It wasn't safe for girls to go down to the river or up in the hills alone, so solitude was hard to find for us except in a church or wandering the pages of a book. This is what I did while my brothers spent their days fishing and trapping on the wild banks of the Mississippi River.

I was fortunate to attend a women's college where the literature classes were filled with the works of women, so it wasn't until graduate school, when I was writing and trying to get published, that I realized how difficult it was for women to get their work published. Out of respect and longing, I began to devour books by women.

Now I love books that center on women's experience of spiritual realities underlying their lives, books such as Uruquart's *Away,* Riesler's work about the goddess-centered civilizations, Tony Morrison, Julia Alvarez, Sandra Cisneros. I like books that rewrite myth such as *Myths of Avalon* and love Rudolpho Anaya's *Bless me Ultima.* There are many poets whom I consider mentors.

For many years reading carried with it a sense of rebellion against authority. At home I would end up reading when sent to make beds or

wash dishes, and in school I always had a book hidden behind whatever basal reader or text book we were supposed to be reading or
wedged between my knees and the desk. In high school I read *Gone with
the Wind* and then *Forever Amber* during Higher Algebra until I was
caught.

When I was in training in the convent, my superior was against
literature. She told us how she stopped reading novels. In the middle of
C. S. Lewis's *Perelandra* she became aware of how absorbed she was and
stopped reading right then. She never did learn the ending. We had to
ask permission to read any books that weren't required in our college
classes, and she always said no. Kneeling, I would hold up books I
wanted to read, *Kristin Lavransdatter* (which is my favorite book of all
time), *The Stranger, War and Peace,* and she always took them from my
hands and put them on her desk. Finally, another nun whom I respected
said, "Just read whatever you want, forget about permission," and I did
just that.

I remember running to the college library with snowflakes fleck-
ing my black shawl, piling up on it. The English literature section was
near the windows in the basement stacks. Through them I could see the
slow rise of ground to the powerhouse tower and the ceiling of protec-
tive oaks in the woods around the building.

At first I just peeked at books and then just decided to read. I
copied quotes, planted them like seeds in my mind. Each book, each
quote was a step away from the life that I was living. It took me four
more years to read, copy, and dream my way out of the convent.

The step from reading to writing has always been a natural one for
me. When I was young, I kept journals. When I read language I loved, I
would try to imitate it. Ruth Rosten (1987) describes this experience: "I
write the way I/ learned to speak—I imitate/ go house to house with
an empty/ cup, borrow voices from a dozen poets."

From the time I was in high school I wanted to write poetry. I
believed that it was the best thing anyone could do. I never remember
writing poetry in school. It was something I did in my diary, and I never
shared my poems. I read poetry when I came across it in the library and
loved studying poets in high school English especially Elliot and cum-
mings. But no one ever taught me how to write it. By the time I was in
graduate school I was writing and getting poems published, but I felt
apologetic about them. I knew they weren't good. Finally, in graduate
school I had the opportunity to take advanced poetry writing. Michael
Dennis Browne, poet in residence at the University of Minnesota, is a
very gifted teacher. We met each week in his living room and discussed
each others' work. I still remember the blizzardy Minneapolis day

when in the middle of one of his classes a light went on in my head and I said to myself, "That's how you do it. That's how you write poetry."

I walked out of class that day, and my writing changed. I began to grow as a poet, am still growing. I believe that, without the inspiration of a great teacher, I could have read poetry and tried to write it for many years with no breakthrough. Browne showed me how to follow the associative trail of the contemporary poets we were reading. I learned about the mind's ability to leap quickly from one association to another. He taught me how to leap in my images, to write down all the associations suggested to my imagination when I was writing, instead of staying on a narrow theme or topic, and to move from the familiar into imaginative contexts that were new to me.

The lesson I learned about the relationship between writing and thinking in a particular way has influenced the work I do with children as a writer in the schools. Poetry grows out of a frame of mind, a way of perceiving the universe.

For me poetry has always been an action by which I both come to self-knowledge and affirm that discovery through language. Because I came from a background of silence, it has been a way of breaking that silence. Poetry has always been tied to feeling and personal perception for me and has been a saving gift for me in my life. It meant the loosened tongue to me, prophecy, speaking out.

September 23, 1973, was the day that Pablo Neruda died. His death and the events surrounding it changed my life, my view of language, and the way I see and feel about my country. Allende, the democratically elected Chilean leader, was assassinated, and the military took over, with the assistance of the United States. I found myself at a memorial service for Neruda in Minneapolis, led by Robert Bly and Meridel LeSueur. I began to understand poetry as a revolutionary act and began reading women poets who lived this belief, as Neruda had.

Many years ago I wrote a poem about this writing in my life as a way of connecting all my roles of mother, teacher, writer, and someone who works for change. It was inspired by something I read and is the first poem that I had published in a literary journal. It is also introduces my first poem in my first book of poetry.

> Seamstress
> I remember a sewing machine
> a black Singer with a pedal
> that tapped all afternoon
> beneath my grandmother's foot.
> Her thick fingers pushed cotton

and silk into its snapping mouth
until her eyes darkened from strain.
Parades of bright dresses,
shirts, shawls tumbled from her machine.
On our thin bodies

we wore her eyes.
In the mirror
I see my mother's face
and my grandmother's face
a long parade of Irish Marys
with tunnels for eyes
holes where children crawl
eyes made blind
from too much looking
at the sea.

Afternoons
I feed my typewriter
raw fear and strange words
the cotton pieces of my life.
They step out whole
and walk away on thin legs
solid like mirrors
with eyes wide open. (Rummel, 1989)

I always planned on being a teacher. Tied in with my going into
the convent, it was a given. Always, my greatest interest and talent was
in literature and writing. Under the glass of my desk during my first
year of teaching second grade were printed broadsides of poems that I
wrote during the year. I remember one, a haiku:

To what height do you aspire
aspire, green growing wood weed
in a patch of brown?

I shared my poems and the poetry I loved with my students. I
always strongly believed in the connection of poetry with the body and
the rhythms of our lives. I remember the first snow fall during my first
year of teaching. I recited a poem that ends "the trees are dressed in
silver skirts/ and want to dance around," and my whole class of forty-
two second graders stood up and danced around the room holding
hands without any kind of signal from me—it was pure response.

Encouraging creative response and guiding children in their writing was what I loved about teaching children. Poetry with its ground in feeling, its basis in sensory imagery, its compression and rhythm which children love provides a way of saying things that cannot be said. It is a way of doing what Maxine Greene (1995) suggests when she talks about helping students find language to bring dreams into being, language that introduces them to the experience of going beyond.

I always read to my students sections of what I was reading myself—Shakespeare, Emily Dickinson, Elizabeth Bishop, Pablo Neruda, and James Wright, as well as parts of the work of Adrian Rich, Lucille Clifton, and Nikki Giovanni. I also read poetry specifically written for children.

In 1987 I began the literacy work that I loved the most as a writer in the schools in the Dialogue program. It was a four-year project in the St. Paul Public Schools that brought together professional writers who worked for the COMPAS Writers-in-the-Schools program and teachers from St. Paul Schools. We developed a collaborative long-term relationship designed to enhance writing in the schools both through the teachers writing themselves and through our team teaching writing to students. Through this program I was able to team teach with instructors one week a month for a year in a specific city school. I really got to know the children, and I led a teachers' group that met once a month where they shared their own writing and their teaching writing experiences. It was very satisfying; it brought together everything I love to do, and I could really see the results of my work. There was much excitement in those classrooms around the acts of writing and sharing writing.

Although I have always been struggling to integrate the different parts of my life, my writing feeds my teaching, and in some ways, teaching feeds my writing. Virginia Wolf's *A Room of One's Own* and Tillie Olsen's stories about women breaking the silence of their lives through writing really affected me. It has always been a struggle to find time to do creative writing. Yet I know that work is organic; everything feeds off of everything else.

This struggle and separation were reflected in graduate school. At that time the educational field of reading was kept separate at the University of Minnesota from language arts and children's literature. I specialized in language arts and children's literature as well as in English composition. Naomi Chase, who recruited me to come to the University and work with her, was a wholistic language teacher at a time in the late seventies when everything was becoming more segmented. It was hard to integrate various disciplines of study and to

integrate work in the English department and in the Education Department. I find the same problem teaching on the university level; there is a
separation between creative work and professional writing. One of my
goals is to contribute to the blending of the disciplines.

From the beginning I tried to integrate my life as a teacher of
young children and my life as a writer. Now I must integrate my life as a
teacher educator and as a writer. The butterfly metaphor helps me with
this because the roles are not one. Rather they are two strands not
intersecting but occurring at the same time, feeding each other. I
learned much about the importance of audience for children who are
writing through becoming a public writer myself and publishing my
first book of poetry. I learned about the importance of building a literacy community in the classroom from my twenty years of participation
in Onionskin, a group of highly professional, creative, and productive
women writers. For me, writing feeds teaching far more than teaching
feeds writing. But that is my fault.

I have always had the sense that the writing part of my life is off to
the side of my real life. Actually, my life's work is that of integration.
This is also true in the methods classes that I teach for preservice
teachers. I have the same expressive goals for them that I had for the
children with whom I have worked. I want them to experience the
transforming power both of writing and of responding to literature. I
want them to grow in their love of and ability to use language and then
to pass it on to children.

I think that when I am able to integrate the pieces of my life—
reading, writing, teaching, being a family member and friend—as I live
in the present I will be in some kind of heaven, the kind described in the
poem with which I began this chapter.

The germ of the idea for this book came out of a discussion—a
rumination about my own early reading and the way that it affected my
life. In the service of the word, teacher-readers, what are our stories?
What is mine, and what is yours? I am a poet. You love children's books.
We know how to empower children through language. We do it with
our lives. We swim in a river of language. Reading leads to writing
which leads to reading. We need to hear the poems of the children of the
world, for without those voices, those poems, something vital and deep
and large is missing from our lives.

References

Greene, M. (1995). *Releasing the imagination: Essays on education, the arts and social change.* San Francisco: Jossey-Bass Publishers.

Roston R. (1987) In Moore, J. and Waterman, C. (Eds.), *Minnesota Writes Poetry.* Minneapolis: Milkweed Editions.

Rummel, M. K. (1995). At the side altars. *Sidewalks* (9), 37–38.

———. (1989). *This body she's entered.* Minneapolis: New Rivers Press.

3

Voice Matters: Autobiographical Sketches of Elizabeth Quintero

I see Mary, my sister, now working with different shades of pastel paper, for a graphic arts project for a business client, and I see her as a twelve year old, drawing seventeen versions of a portrait on the back of as match cover. She would display them on the sill of the long screened porch window, and my friends and I would vote on which one she should send in. She created drawings, stories, and plays in which we were the actors. We watched in awe.

This fantasy play, in my family, had much to do with identity and family history. "You're right; it was what we didn't hear rather than what we did. Also, it was the way things were not said that made a difference whether we were interested. If something was not said or hushed up, and we got a hint of it, we tended to make up stories to fit what we thought we didn't hear," my sister said.

And I remember arguing with Mary all summer long—every summer—about which of us got to lie on the old wicker chaise lounge to read our books. Papa's house built during the boom of the twenties (in relative disrepair by the fifties) had a long screened porch on one side. (We moved in with him, my grandfather, in the fifties when my father died.) There was a very old wicker sofa and chaise lounge with a green flowered cover. We read there. Summer after summer. I walked to the library two blocks away, and like my mother and sister, probably read most of the books in the small library. I remember the literal and metaphorical trips the books took me on. I loved the fantasy of magical tales and the believable action and resistance in biographies. I remember reading about Isadora Duncan, the dancer (and rebel, as she seemed to me), Clara Barton, the nurse; Harriet Tubman and the underground railroad; and George Washington Carver. The science topics interested me, but always in the contexts of the human dynamics—the struggles, successes, and barriers. The books helped me ask questions and see some complexities related to those I didn't understand in my environment of the Old South.

But back to Mary, I remember the stories she would tell me, at nap time, at bedtime, or any time we were bored or told to be quiet. She told stories of mythical, fairy-like beings with some of the added in-congruent intrigue of the latest Nancy Drew mystery she happened to be reading at the time. Not only did she tell stories about fairies, but she created them for me. She told me last year when I asked about the years she spent making the fairies and all the realia to go with them: "It was something I think I needed to do because I was bored and because I needed to create a little legend that belonged to you and me alone; I hated my real world so much that I wanted to pretend that there was another, fantasy one out there. With your help I almost convinced my-self! I was always so grateful that you let me do these fairies with you."

Color matters. Culture, race, language—am I expected to talk about those because of my politics, because of my single-parent ad-vocacy, because of my three sons who are Mexican nationals, because of my name? Well, apologies to the expectations. I can't talk about strug-gles of race and culture in a neat, distinct way. Even a few years back when I really wished I could, I couldn't. I can only speak personally of questions. Of information left out.

Carl Grant, at a small early childhood conference in Madison in 1991, asked me if I would tell my story for a book he was preparing (*Educating for Diversity*, a book I now use in one of my classes). He needed a Cuban American perspective of struggle and success. "I can't," I said. "Why not?" He was surprised. Astute observer, he was probably thinking of our ten-minute conversation there in front of the fireplace after Lourdes introduced us. *Florida, Texas, Mexico, the surname. The names of your boys. Your underlying family focus in your work.* "No, I can't," I apologized. "I wasn't raised Cuban American. I wasn't raised anything." *Other than one of two sisters raised by a single mother, dark skinned with green eyes and curly hair, who became bent by the dominance and disapproval of a less intelligent brother, among others.*

I told Carl Grant, "I'm a mongrel who is clearly different from the white mainstream, but with only gotas (drops) of Latina, maybe Creek Indian, maybe black. I don't know. I can really not claim any identity other than me." He looked at me. "You could pass for several," he said with a twinkle in his eyes. "There are more and more mixed ones like you coming up these days." The conference ended. We left it that I would talk to a Cuban friend, Jorge, who came in the Mariel boat lift in the early eighties. I never forgot Carl's comments.

Color matters. In Nuevo Casas Grandes, where I lived when my oldest two sons were born, I took my two babies with me daily to the tortillaria. The oldest looks more like his father. He has beautiful cinnamon skin, black curly hair, and black eyes. Then the second child was born, with skin and hair color light like my sister's and my green eyes. "Mira, che lindo, el huerito" (Look, how cute the blond one is), all the women exclaimed, totally ignoring my twenty-month-old older son. Then when we traveled to El Paso to stay with old friends, many friends (some of whom are Chicanos, some of whom aren't) always ooohed and ahaaaed over the older, darker boy and ignored the lighter one. Color matters. It becomes emotional and blatant when a parent reacts to the potential hurt of her babies.

Color matters. Shortly after we first came to Duluth, I sent my two oldest sons to a small private school because I was so determined that they have Spanish in school. This school was the only school in the community in which a student under grade eight could study Spanish. I was uncomfortable with the lack of children of color, lack of students from working-class and poor families, and lack of children from single-parent families. But Spanish is very important for our family. I found out that language cannot be made more important than dignity.

There were two incidents in which I was called to come to talk to teachers. The first time I was "invited" into the school conference room. Around a huge table sat the entire seventh-grade staff—twelve teachers and counselors. I, who teach both parents and preservice teachers about the complexities of teacher/parent conferences, told myself, "I will not be intimidated by this. I will not waver in my support of my son," as the knots in my stomach grew. I was asked, after a patronizing preface stating that they realized that I was very busy with my work, if I was able to spend much time with my three boys. I explained that during the past nine years of single parenting I had very valuable moments, routines, family customs that make my family very strong in our relationships with each other.

Then I was told about my son's apparent disrespect of two teachers in two different classes and his inappropriate behavior. I made a comment about disrespect not being tolerated in our family and asked what they had interpreted as disrespect and inappropriate behavior. I was then told that Memo's disrespect was his habit of breaking eye contact and looking down when being reprimanded by one of these two teachers and sometimes not answering when they knew he disagreed with them. I went briefly into the human diversity 101 lecture about cultural differences in terms of eye contact and in terms of whether it is appropriate to outwardly argue with an elder. The Spanish teacher and the earth science teacher then spoke up and said they had seen nothing but cooperation and positive interactions of this same student, my son, in their classes. Social context.

Then there was the bus incident. I was called at the office mid-afternoon. The dean of the middle school told me there had been a serious incident of misbehavior on the bus the previous day as reported by the bus driver. The dean said she had no choice but to suspend my son from school for two days and from the bus for two weeks, but (patronizingly again) since I am a single parent, she knew I would need to make logistical arrangements for my children. I incredulously asked what the incident was, and when it was explained to me, I asked if she had talked with my son or other students on the bus to hear their side of the story. "No," she answered. I replied, "I demand a meeting with you, the bus driver, my son, and me before any of these actions are taken." She agreed, somewhat surprised, to set up a meeting the following day. I went home to talk to my son, and acknowledging raucous behavior to some extent, he explained the incident to my satisfaction. It was not what the bus driver claimed.

The next day as I approached the office for the meeting I was met by four of my son's friends who also ride the same bus. "It wasn't just Memo; it was all of us. And we were goofing on each other—nobody said anything to the bus driver." I was touched by their support for their friend, my son. We entered the meeting, but the bus driver was not able to attend. So the dean explained what the bus driver had said and then asked my son his side of the story. The dean acknowledged that there were very big differences in the two versions, but that since the bus driver had filed a formal complaint according to her impressions, disciplinary action must be taken. I asked how the bus driver had singled out Memo. "Well, she didn't know his name, but knew it was a funny, different name. Then we showed her school pictures of all the kids on that bus." A lineup. "And she picked out Memo right away." I was beginning to get the picture. I said that I felt for anyone who drove a bus full of thirteen year olds, but, "What is their training?" I asked. "Oh, they don't have much training except a workshop about gangs." Oh, I was really getting the picture. I said, "I am going to ask you something that I want to get out on the table right now with Memo here. Do you think Memo was singled out by this woman who has seen videos of gang members because he looks different?" Memo piped up, "I don't look any different from my friends, Mom." I replied, "Mi amor, you don't except you don't look like you are from Minnesota—Duluth anyway. You have gorgeous black curly hair and dark skin . . . and an earring." I asked the Dean, "What do you suppose the students in the gang video training tape looked like?"

The dean shifted in her seat and responded, "Memo, what your Mom is talking about is that both you and I [she is Japanese American] would blend right in if we lived in Los Angeles. In Duluth we look different." Then she went on to say that essentially, if one is not white, middle class, in Duluth, one must work harder, dress better, make better grades, make more money to be equal. I was incredulous. I wanted to make sure that my son knew that her opinions were not acceptable ones for a responsible adult to have—according to my value system. So I pushed it. I asked her a few more questions about equality, respect, and dignity. At which point she put her elbows on her desk, put her chin in her hands, and said, "I know, it's not right. But that's just the way things are, and I don't think we can do anything to change it." Angrily, I asked that if any people have any hopes of affecting change, isn't it those of us who are in education. I added that I couldn't get up in the morning and go to work if I thought there was nothing I was able to do throughout the day to make a tiny positive change. To make her final point, she looked at my son and said, "You know when I saw you and your friend at the university soccer game last week and said hello to you? My friends I was with asked how I knew you because you didn't look like a student who would go to my school. You know the earring, the baggy pants." Infuriated, I looked at him and said, "You are well groomed and clean, and your choice of style is yours to make—it's fine." We left, and the next day I withdrew both sons who had gone to school there.

Dance class. It was a forty-five-minute drive each Saturday. "Miss Jackie" spoke some English; some of the girls in the class didn't. Everyone spoke Spanish. The studio was next door to Jackie's house where she lived with her mother, her husband, and her daughter. I remember hanging out at their house eating fried egg plant and fried plantains and listening to Abuela's (Grandmother's) advice and stories for her nieta (grandaughter). Jackie's family wasn't different from many families I was close to and didn't seem that different from mine (even though I later learned they tried to be like Papa's white Charleston family). We danced flamenco, modern jazz, and classical. We made (mostly our mothers made) costumes of shiny green and purple lamé. I sometimes thought the conversations in Spanish went by not understood by my mother. Later I knew.

As a child, I never understood the unquestioned practice of separation of the races. What was my race? My mother and I were as dark, darker than many Cubans I knew, while my father and sister were very light with light blue eyes. "White, of course," my Mother always replied and looked away.

What's left out? I tell students to always ask the questions about whose stories and opinions are left out of every text book, every re-search study, every news report. What did Papa, my grandfather, do in Havana? Why didn't my aunt tell me when my father died? Why did my mother know nothing about my father's family? Where were they from? Who was my father's father? A dark, high cheek-boned man in a photo? Was it his face I inherited—a different face from my light-skinned, blue-eyed father. Did he belong to a tribe? Who was the grand-father on the other side of the family related to besides the Welch and Scotch stone mason? Who was the wild woman from Wales who lived with drunks in New Hampshire?

There was the talk of Papa's (my mother's father) family in Charleston, so wealthy and prominent. We lived with Papa after my dad died when I was seven. The house was a modest house, with holes in the floor that were highways for roaches in the summer and damp, cold winds in the winter. We weren't wealthy or prominent. The only family members of his I ever met were his two sisters, Aunt Ethel and Aunt Edith. Aunt Ethel was an elementary teacher and lived her life with her friend Louise. (My sister and I still wonder if they were both still alive, would they let us use the word *partner*.) On her deathbed in Charleston, Aunt Ethel told my sister who was trying to find out some family history to go to search for family in a cemetery at a certain location. Excited, my sister called a cab. When he came and she gave him the location. He turned and looked at her. "Why would you want to go there? That's just the old slave cemetery."

I have tried to not feel anger and shame that my family (the few I knew) communicated through secrets and things not said. I keep Lorde's words close, "For in order to survive, those of us for whom oppression is as american as apple pie have always had to be watchers, to become familiar with the language and manners of the oppressor, even sometimes adopting them for some illusion of protection" (Lorde, in West, et. al., 1990, 281).

I began traveling to new places early in my life. My father was in the navy, so before I was five I knew that the waves of the Atlantic at Virginia Beach were very different from those of southern California on the Pacific. When my father was diagnosed with cancer, we moved to Guadalajara, Jalisco, Mexico, in hopes that the climate would help his health. I loved the huge, ancient hotel where we first lived in our new city. It was the first house I'd ever lived in with stairs. It had 143. My sister and I counted. And it was our "home" for a while. It didn't matter that we had two small rooms that were really our family's. I had never seen tiles with paintings on them, centuries-old furniture, or pig brains served on a platter. Sometime right before my sixth birthday we moved to Chapala, a smaller town of about four thousand people, about sixty miles from Guadalajara. Here we lived in a small pink adobe house with a flat roof with a tiny flower garden on top. I could see Lake Chapala in one direction and the dirt and cobblestone streets and tiny adobe houses in all other directions. One day I remember going to Miranda's house. She was the woman who came over once a week to do the ironing. Miranda had six younger brothers and sisters and an aunt and a grandma living with her and her mother and father. Their house was two rooms and seemed much smaller than our four-roomed one. What I remember most was the family pig who lived in the house with them. I wasn't surprised by the chickens who came and went at will in and out of the glassless windows and pecked on the dirt floors. But I had never seen a pig indoors. I didn't even notice until I got back home when my mother asked whether I understood everyone's talk in the family. I knew a little bit of Cuban Spanish from early, early years in Tampa, Florida, and we had been in Mexico probably six weeks.

Later, in high school in the rural central Florida town we lived in after my father died, I read many of the classics of the canon. I read *To Kill a Mockingbird*, *The Red Pony*, *Grapes of Wrath*, plays by Ibsen; I read Ann Frank, Faulkner, and Hemingway. I was reading *Gone with the Wind* hidden behind my advanced algebra book when Mr. Smith discovered me, threw the chalkboard eraser at me, and suspended me from class for the week. I remember being caught up in the lives of the characters. I was there with them. I was nurtured by the resistance they taught me. I later read, in college and after, books by Alice Walker, Rudolfo Anaya, Sandra Cisneros, Isabel Allende, and especially Gloria Anzaldúa. I wished as I read and reread these authors that I had known about their works when I was growing up.

My fascination with travel, as I became older, began to be connected with writing. I was entranced with *The Day on Fire* both because of the story told about the journey through Africa and because of the character of Rimbeaud. I admired Margaret Mead as she traveled and wrote and tried to contribute to a more just and complete understanding of human interaction. Travel and write. Beauty and hope— necessities for my nourishment. "The world doesn't seem smaller because of my traveling; it seems bigger and broader in ideas, opportunity and values." Not very profound of a statement, but from a twenty-year-old kid, who grew up in the Old South sandwiched between early childhood traveling in Latin America, in a family that rigidly attempted assimilation into white, middle America, it was a beginning. I traveled as a poor student with not much of a conscious cause other than my own education. Besides an education in facts and ascetics that hadn't passed my way until then, I also picked up a perspective that I didn't want to lose.

Once, I was on my way hitchhiking with a roommate to Rome (I was on a study grant in Florence, Italy, and twenty years old) to see the Leroi Jones play *Slave Ship*. I was expecting to be moved to passion—the several years I had spent in the deep South in the fifties and sixties were etched in my soul as painful memories of inequities. What I didn't expect was walking into the heart of an angry Communist demonstration against Nixon's announced invasion of Cambodia. The people marching spread for five or six big city blocks carrying red signs—some with a hammer and sickle, some with Mao, some "Nixon go home" and "US Aggressors go away." Those people HATED Americans. I hated the war in Vietnam. But this. Learning complexities. There was no sugar coating here. We are imperialists, Nazis, and very despicable.

On different kinds of learning notes that same year, I learned from Maria and Vittorio, an elderly Italian couple who spoke no English. I often went to their modest Florentine apartment for luscious dinners and involved discussions about Dante. I met a couple from Kenya on a train and we exchanged letters for years, but I never saw them again.

Later, after graduating with an English degree and working as a waitress in Red Lobster, I decided early childhood education was what I would do. I spent literally every cent on a plane ticket to visit the British Infant Schools and Summerhill. I had so little money, I was questioned strictly before I was allowed to enter Great Britain. With luck, I found a room (a large closet, really) for about ten dollars a week. The apartment belonged to Mrs. Roth, who stayed in the next room. She was an invalid who had escaped from the concentration camp at Dachau. She was always in pain, and yet each time she saw me she wanted to talk about Goethe. Fairly soon I learned about a training program for preschool teachers that involved much practical experience in various inner-city neighborhood preschools. I plunged in, and to my delight I was placed in a school in a Middle Eastern immigrant neighborhood. During those months, I visited a school based on Summerhill philosophy located in Castle Douglas, Scotland.

Later, back in north Florida, I found work in a small preschool for three- and four-year-old children. After I finished my master's, I expanded my work to kindergarten teaching. I still use the story of how my supervising teacher knew about, and condoned, my using Spiderman comics to encourage and teach a student to read. He had refused even to try to learn, and his parents were worried. He read after three weeks. A five year old girl insisted that I read *The Red Pony* to the whole class. It was during this chapter of my life that Mary, my sister, sent me a box of used books she'd finished with and I was introduced to Achebe by *Things Fall Apart*.

Years later in the Southwest, after more work in different settings, as I observed the communication of monolingual English-speaking children, of African American children both in rural schools and in inner-city schools, of monolingual Spanish-speaking children in Mexico, and of Spanish-English bilingual children in Texas and New Mexico I saw the "roots of literacy" as an integral part of what children do as they understand and take part in their world. It was exciting to see literacy develop through a child's painting about "una piñata" (a birthday party which included a huge number of family and friends and activities—where as a part of the activity, a piñata is broken), through a collaborated effort of Lego building for the purpose of replicating the space craft *Discovery*, through the teaching and learning of a rap song, and through the practice of the songs for a Posada (a Christmas ceremony in Mexico). Literacy was spreading roots across and through the cultures of children in my world. I knew that I was witnessing the roots of *literacies*.

During these times of observation and reflection about these developing literacies, I had the opportunity to work with the many parents of many young children as we collaborated about the task and pleasure of positively affecting the children's lives. Children come to early childhood programs straight from the influence and "cariño" of their parents' arms. Every parent I had met—from a diversity of circumstances, from difficulty to comfort—cared deeply about his or her child that was being entrusted in my care.

As I came to know more and more parents, I read with skepticism the research that implied that parents who lacked formal education would negatively affect the education of their children (Stitch and McDonald, 1989) because I had met numerous parents with only three to five years of formal schooling who had raised intelligent, successful children who are now attending the country's most prestigious universities (Quintero and Velarde, 1991). I had begun to see the social context in relationships between parents and children, as in child development in general, as the important factor for a child's learning success.

So, in the process of addressing these issues in my work, I collected ideas, assumptions, and hypotheses about multilingual children's roots of literacy and the effect that their parents and early teachers could have on this development. I had the opportunity to design an intergenerational program, which became Project FIEL in El Paso, Texas, so I could use what I was sure about. I knew the strength of the child/parent relationship. I knew that the innate enthusiasm of every child to learn and flourish in a secure and meaningful social context would make a literacy class, in which parents studied alongside their children, dynamic and interesting. And I felt more and more certain that the family bond and the opportunity to engage in appropriately flexible and meaningful activities would make it possible to transcend difficulties such as different patterns of language dominance, different literacy abilities, and different learning needs.

I see my experiences in family literacy as tangible evidence of what Maxine Greene (1992) was touching upon when she made the following comment: "It seems clear the more continuous and authentic personal encounters can be, the less likely will it be for categorizing and distancing to take place. People are less likely to be treated instrumentally, to be made Other by those around."

This collage of experiences has fed my two-decade commitment to using literature in my teaching. I am not a literature teacher or a writing teacher. Yet I believe that the voices and experiences expressed through literature are the authentic teachers about culture learning and life—spoken by the artists living the experiences. I ask students in my early childhood classes, my nonnative-language teaching methods classes, and my human diversity classes to listen to and to speak with through reflection these authors.

Who I am is in part what I do. My friend Carlos tells me the Azteca meaning of the term *chicana* is "human being, relative to all." I like that. Like Edwin Bustillos, founder and director of a human-rights and environmental organization called CASMAC (Advisory Council of the Sierra Madre) in the state of Chihuahua in Mexico, "I think the objective of being on this earth is to be useful." Identity and action are always intertwined and always complex. Struggle is always involved, and it is the fuel to continue. "Hope makes part of me just like the air that I breathe" (Freire and Godotti, 1995, 48).

References

Brunner, Diane B. (1994). *Inquiry and reflection: Framing narrative practice in education*. New York: State University of New York Press.

Freire, P. and Godotti, M. (1995). We can reinvent the world. *Taboo*. New York: Peter Lang Publishing. Gadotti.

Greene, M. (1992). The passion of pluralism: Education and the expanding community. Unpublished paper presented to the American Educational Research Association. San Francisco, CA.

Quintero, Elizabeth P., and Velarde, Maria C. (1991). Non-traditional success stories: Immigrant women and their children. Unpublished manuscript.

Sticht, T. G., and McDonald, B. A. (January, 1989). *Making the nation smarter: The intergenerational transfer of cognitive ability.* [Executive Summary] San Diego, CA: Applied Behavioral and Cognitive Sciences, Inc.

Weinstein-Shr, G. (1992). *Stories to tell our children.* Boston, MA: Heinle & Heinle.

PART II

THE TEACHERS' STORIES

4

BILL SIMPSON

Bill Simpson is a special education teacher who combines his personal life commitment as an adventurer with his work with students. A teacher in whose classroom Bill works said:

> I've never seen a special education teacher work like he does. He works in my classroom, so I see what happens to my sixth-grade students. They usually are very active, and when they sit down to work with Bill they become very focused and quiet. I think they consider it a privilege to work with him. He is such a hero to the students in our district that they are honored to have him for a teacher.

The story Bill told in his interview is a strong example of the power of metaphor fed by early reading affecting both personal life and teaching. From his reading as a child, Bill developed a metaphor of life as adventure. For him it nurtured the sense of "what is out there, what I can reach if I try," which is described by Maxine Greene (1992). Through the language of reading Bill was able to begin to live adventure and to bring dreams into being for himself and his students: "And I always lived in this life of reading and then began to live the adventure even when I wasn't reading. And I still do."

In her work, Maxine Greene (1995) emphasizes the power of metaphor for transformation—both personal and communal. We refer to metaphor in the symbolic sense. Symbolic analogy or metaphor, because of its representational qualities, gives us insight into a person's perception of life (Quintero and Rummel, 1995). It also is an example of the transformation described by Maxine Greene (1992). Symbolic metaphor also vividly names a person's thoughts, intentions, and actions toward life and in this way can challenge the present environment. Bill, growing up in a working-class home and community was able, through reading, to create a vision of life he couldn't know through experience.

Metaphor gives us the power to overcome our personal isolation. Ozick (1989) describes this power: "Through metaphorical concentration doctors can imagine what it is like to be their patients . . . those at the center can imagine what it is to be outside. The strong can imagine the weak. . . . Illumined lives can imagine the dark. We strangers can imagine the familiar hearts of strangers," (283).

It is the life-defining power of early metaphor that creates the recurring pattern in Bill's life and work. To reiterate Lather's (1994) method, our informant, Bill, presents his own faces, motives, and voices through the following interview segments.

Metaphor and Art as Frameworks for Living

I bet I read Huck Finn *and* Tom Sawyer *every year, once a year, for years—from my early teens to my early twenties—because I just could not get enough of that wonderful writing and those wonderful stories.*

Tom Sawyer was a character I just loved because of the sheer adventure and the wonderful life that he led where every day was an adventure. And I always in this life of reading and then began to live the adventure even when I wasn't reading and I still do.

I didn't watch a lot of TV when I was in elementary school. I would read every night and then in the summer all day long. I read alone. I would go off on my own. Sometimes I would go sit in the hills all alone away from home, or down by the river. I spent a lot of time by the Mississippi River. It was that Huck Finn sort of life style. I just loved it.

Now books kind of lead me to places. A book led me to a really fascinating place this summer, to northern Russia. I had been there before, but I went again to go on a kayaking trip. This book I read two years ago called They Took My Father *was a story of Finnish people from the iron range moving back to Russia in the 1930s during the depression. They got into Russia and found out it wasn't the place that it was claimed to be, and then the border was closed and they couldn't leave. So they lived their lives in Russia as U.S. citizens from Minnesota. It just blew my mind that up to 10,000 people had done this. So I found a way to get to that area. It was a wonderful adventure. It was like a Tom Sawyer adventure; everyday was a new episode. So books do that for me; they lead me places.*

Every summer I take a trip to the Arctic. Way up north in Canada to the High Arctic. The special thing about that area is the remoteness. I like cold weather. I like the Inuit people. Mainly, it is the last true wilderness left on earth. I love that you can go a month and never see a sign of a human being. I need that. I have read much of the Arctic literature, all of the explorers.

My favorite adult book is A Sand County Almanac *by Aldo Leopold. It was written in 1948 and became an underground nature classic. I read it in about 1968 and during the back-to-the-land movement of the 1960s; it just kind of blew my mind. Then I read that, like I used to read* Huck Finn *and* Tom Sawyer, *every year, once a year, for many years.*

People always ask me why I don't write my experiences down. But I can't sit still long enough to do it. Writing a book is a lot of work. I always think when I get older or if I get injured I will have to sit down and do it. But now I am so active that I can't find the time to do it.

I keep notes, but I wouldn't call them a journal. They are kind of scattered. What I do is record things with the camera. I have slide shows that I have developed, and I do a lot of public speaking about all of these adventures. Those photos are my journal.

Through reading, Bill used the metaphor of life as adventure to open up wider worlds outside his experience. He has a passion for art and actively engages in one art form, photography, as a part of his life. This art making is clearly a part of his self-nurturance and is something which is part of his teaching as he presents slide shows and brings his students in contact with students from other countries, which again shows the interrelated nature of our theoretical model and our findings.

Nurturance Past and Present (Self and Others)

What I do in the summertime is set a reading goal—the day school is out and when I travel I read. So I combine adventure and reading all summer long. I read about fifty books every summer. I don't know why. It is just something to do. And I always make it. Sometimes more. Then during the year I have to do so much with school. I bet I get twenty-five to thirty periodicals and magazines. Sports related, nature, outdoor. I have a big stack that I read. I use the library a lot, but I also buy special books. Then I have a couple librarians that help me out to find certain books. They are personal friends at this point.

When I was a kid I read some books on how to canoe, and I used to do it. I didn't know that anyone could teach me. So I would sit in a canoe and read my book and learn to canoe. And that would lead to other books. Calvin Rustrum was another early author who I read who lived in the town that I am living in. He died in 1982. But I met him; I think that is why I moved to Marine, because this author whom I had read when I was a kid lived there. Then I read Sigurd Olson and essays on the Boundary Waters. When I was a kid I was obsessed with going to the Boundary Waters Canoe Area.

My adventuring was very gradual. I started working in camps and leading various wilderness adventures. I still do that. It has opened my life, and then it has opened up the lives of hundreds and thousands of people. I have worked with people of all ages, and I like a mix of children and adults. We started a program for people with physical disabilities. When I first started teaching I was combining children with disabilities with children who were able bodied. We just started doing that with junior high students and senior high students, and now it is one of the largest programs in the United States. It is called "Wilderness Inquiry." It was based in Minneapolis, and now it operates all over the country. I actually started it with another teacher, and now the program has a life of its own. And I am sure that I was so hooked on the wilderness experience myself that I had to share it with others. When I first started teaching, I was driven to do this. I said to myself, "I can't just teach. I need to do something more with my life."

I like travel literature. So I read authors within that genre. Now I am reading Latin American authors. I just love them. There is so much romance, so much more than white European writing. I was turned on to that by someone suggesting books to me. Then I have been reading African literature because that is next on my list for travel. Doris Lessing's African Laughter. *A wonderful book. I am going to Africa a year from now with a special program through the school I work at, a program called "Books for Africa." I should talk about that. It's cool. We started a sister city program with Ginja, Uganda, and Stillwater, Minnesota. Then we started a special school project with our school and a school in Uganda. There are three thousand students in this school and no books. A friend of mine started this program, Books for Africa. This month the community and schools in Stillwater are bringing in their favorite new books and also fifty cents for postage. Then we are shipping them to Africa. My goal is to go over there and visit this school. It would be nice to set up some kind of exchange program with students.*

I have to tell you this; my favorite author would have to be Barry Lopez. Are you familiar with him? He wrote a book called Arctic Dreams, *which was really a best seller. It is a wonderful story. We had the opportunity last summer to have him come to our school. So I got to meet him, introduce him, have dinner with him, and then he met with all of our sixth-grade classes and talked about writing. The children loved it too. That was a real highlight to meet your favorite author. He also wrote a children's book called* Crow and Weasel.

If I am not being really active, reading is the thing for me. It is that escapism and romance, being able to get out of yourself.

Bill's love of outdoor adventure began with and continues to be fed by his reading. This spills over into his professional life as he creates outdoor programs for children. For Bill reading is a source of ongoing nurturance connecting both personal and professional life. This began in childhood with Bill reading by the river and in the woods.

Family History

I didn't know anyone who read as much as I did, but everyone in my family read a great deal. My parents read all the time, and I think that their modeling promoted our reading. We were seeing people read and hearing people read. My mother never graduated from high school, but she read all the time.

I remember going to first grade and already knowing how to read. I remember the nun being surprised. She handed me some letters and I read them and then she handed me a book, and I could read that too. I remember the look on her face. It was just so much a part of me that I didn't think anything of it. I remember going to school, with my sister who is two years older than I, and I could already read at that point, so it got me motivated and excited.

There were books all over the house. There were a lot of books that were read to us. I remember the whole family crying over The Little Match Girl. *I remember the original* Box Car Children. *We read it now in school and it seems like such a hokey story. It was like a favorite family story when we were little.*

My mother read mostly novels. Both parents read the newspaper avidly, so to this day I am a newspaper junkie. I began to read the paper at a very young age. We started delivering paper routes when we were about ten, so I had that connection. I was sick a lot when I was a kid, so when I was active, I was really active and when I was sick, I was really sick. Then I would do more challenging reading. I remember reading everything Jack London wrote, and I was still very young.

I read so much when I was little that my favorite book was the last book I had read. I remember a series. It had something to do with pioneer living; it took place in the northeastern states. I think the author's name was Joseph Altshelter. By the time I was in fourth or fifth grade I read every book in the series because of the fantasy and romance and pioneer life. These were really mature, thick books. I would get hooked on a sport, and then I would read every book in that sport. I would get hooked on biographies and read all of the ones I could find, and autobiographies. I read a lot of fiction that had some fantasy and some escapism and adventure.

In those days in the Catholic schools, I suppose because of the training of the nuns, reading and literature were really stressed. The humanities were stressed much more than the sciences and math. Most of the writing was assigned. A lot of following the format of the basal reader with the questions at the end of the chapter. I liked even that because it was reading. I always enjoyed everything that involved reading. I was pretty consumed about it. I was active in sports and a lot of outdoor activities, but somehow I found a lot more time for reading than most kids. I remember going to a junior reading room at the St. Paul Public Library (it is a big, old library) at about fourteen or fifteen years of age and realizing that I had already read every book that was even of semi-interest to me. Then I decided that I'd better start going to the adult part of the library.

I went to Monroe High School. It didn't have a very good reputation, and I was one of the students who was wild, living up to that reputation. But I never gave up reading. When I wasn't fooling around I was reading.

Bill's family history shows a combination of the importance of physical environment and sociocultural context in childhood. It is important to note that while his parents did not make a concerted effort to teach Bill as a child "to read" or a set of cultural values as a recipe for life, there were people in his life who read. These role models who read were crucial. Bill learned to read at a very early age. There was no direct instruction in the Great Books, but newspapers and romance novels were in his environment.

Bill's wide reading and wide global experiences have made him more sensitive to the special needs of his students and more aware of and able to nurture their individual potential. An example of this is his establishment of an organization which arranges wilderness experiences for children with physical disabilities.

Resisting Reader/Teacher

I work with children with physical disabilities, serious health problems and learning disabilities. We are trying to keep them in the classroom, but sometimes I work with them individually or in small groups. I also do some coordinating for the district, so I end up traveling a lot. I also work with the English as a second language program in the district.

I always thought I would like to teach, and when I student taught I was hooked. I just loved it. I started with elementary education and then I went back and got a master's in counseling. Then I went back after that and began to work in special education in a doctorate program. But I quit before I wrote my dissertation. I have tried a little of the collegiate-level teaching, but I feel that I belong with younger learners. I am happier, and I feel that this is where my mission is.

I started at an inner-city school, Webster, in St. Paul. I loved Webster. It was a young, idealistic faculty. It was kind of my mission to be there. All the teachers were friends. It is like we were friends in order to survive there. There was also a wonderful principal at Webster, and eventually I followed her to Jackson School. I loved Webster even though it was hard. I went into counseling because I liked that part of teaching elementary school and then I always wanted to be in special education. I had always liked those kinds of children.

Every day in teaching is challenging. But in earlier days they had schools that were like dumping grounds. They would create special schools and take the worst kids. A lot of them would be minority children because they would get labeled. Then they would take the worst teachers whom none of the principals wanted to work with, and they would put them together. I should write a book about that. It was crazy. I remember getting physically sick and calling in sick. Just from the craziness. I couldn't face going in another day. The kids would act crazy because they wouldn't have any positive role models. Teachers would act crazy, some of them were kind of crazy. So thank God those days are gone. That was when I was sampling the field in special education.

I've taught in all levels in Stillwater. I was the coordinator of curriculum for special education. Now, I am back in the classroom, and I still have some of the administrative work tacked on, but I love it. I have a wonderful school. I work with a great principal. He lets people try what they want to try and is supportive of teachers and students. He doesn't try to dictate. He is a warm person. He believes in teachers having their own strengths and styles, and he lets them bring out the best in themselves. It is like you walk in the school and you know it is special; it's the atmosphere. I didn't just want to go back to teaching, I wanted to work with that principal.

Personally I try to be really aware [of differences among students], and I am always working on it. I am not very critical of other people. Especially when you work in special education, you work with whoever you are teamed with. So you have to be nonjudgmental. You have to be supportive. To me that is how you deliver messages and change minds.

Bill's life and teaching exemplify a pluralistic stance. His love of adventure has led him, first through books and then in actual experience, to an ever-expanding interest in and acceptance of many cultures and differences. He lives in his own life what he wants for his special education students, the awakening described by Barry Lopez (1990) at the end of *Crow and Weasel*:

"I will urge my children to do what I have done," said Weasel. "Whether they are young men or young women, I will urge them to go."

"That is new thinking for you," said Crow.

"Our journey, seeing different ways of life, has made me wonder about many things," said Weasel. They stood in silence together, their breath rising in a fog.

"One day perhaps my son will travel with your son," said Weasel. "They will return and the people will listen to what they have to say. And then their children. It will go on like that, and that way our people will look into the heart of wisdom."

Crow pondered his friend's words . . . "Imagine our daughters," he said. "Traveling." (79)

References

Greene, M. (1992). The passions of pluralism: Multiculturalism and the expanding community. *Educational Researcher,* 22 (1), 13–18.

———. (1995). *Releasing the imagination: Essays on education, the arts and social change.* San Francisco: Jossey-Bass Publishers.

Lather, P. (1994). Gender issues in methodology: Data analysis in the crisis of representation. Paper presented to the American Educational Research Association, New Orleans, LA.

Lopez, Barry. (1990). Crow and weasel. New York: HarperCollins Publishers.

Ozick, C. (1989). *Metaphor and memory.* New York: Knopf.

Quintero, E., and Rummel, M. K. (1995). Voice unaltered: Marginalized young writers speak. In E. B. Swadener, and S. Lubeck (eds.), *Children and families at promise: The social construction of risk.* New York: State University of New York Press.

5

Pamela Russell

> After reading it, I wanted to become a ballerina and she took me into dance class, so that book had a profound effect on me. I pursued dancing and theater arts all the way through college. When I got into teaching, I would teach students to dance and do creative movement part time.
>
> —Pamela Russell

Walking into Pamela's classroom, the library at her school in Brooklyn, New York, one notices the care given to the arrangement of space by this artistic teacher. The arrangements of books, dolls, realia in the form of African art and other "props" gives the sense that the person who enters is being hugged by warmth and being drawn to the center of this dynamic teacher's world. We talked, and Pamela's soft voice explained her life of teaching and her arms occasionally gestured gracefully to a display of children's work or a collection of books. We thought of films we had seen of Martha Graham, moving through space as she danced, carving new dimensions in her art. And we thought how Pamela actively works against perpetuating the status quo (in schools and in society in general) of regarding students of color as *other*. Ferguson (1990) says,

> When we say marginal, we must always ask, marginal to what? But this question is difficult to answer. The place from which power is exercised is often a hidden place. When we try to pin it down, the center always seems to be somewhere else. Yet we know that this phantom center, elusive as it is, exerts a real, undeniable power over the whole social framework of our culture, and over the ways that we think about it. (In West, et al., 1990, 9)

Metaphor and Art as Frameworks for Living

Pamela's artistic sense is an activist characteristic that she uses to enrich her students' experiences.

> *I teach students to dance and do creative movement . . . I appreci-*
> *ate art, I like to do collages and I collect dolls. I really love it, and I try to*
> *bring it into the classroom. A lot of teachers look and say, "Wow, you*
> *really get the kids to bring out their artistic ability in literature through*
> *reading and through writing." It is so much a part of me that I don't*
> *always see it, but it does transfer over to the kids.*

Her students create their own books, and Pamela guides them through
poetry lessons with a sincere enthusiasm that transfers to the students.

> *I find that with young children they often don't see the poetry,*
> *and so it is very difficult to teach it. They love hearing it, they love read-*
> *ing it, but for some reason they are very reluctant to write it, so it takes*
> *a lot of work. To be honest, I don't do a lot of poetry with them in terms*
> *of getting them to write it because they feel so limited. I let them free-*
> *style, but for some reason they feel that there is a certain pattern*
> *that you have to follow so it is difficult. But once they are able to*
> *write something down, they feel good about it, and they love recit-*
> *ing it.*

Pamela is doing exactly what Maya Angelou (1995) recommends in
terms of how artists and writers should respond to the Contract with
America:

> Artists must work to banish this contract, and artists will do it. The
> conservative right has decided that artists are apart from the peo-
> ple. That's ridiculous? I mean, at our best, the writer, painter,
> architect, actor, dancer, folksinger—we *are* the people. We come
> *out* of the people, and remain *in* the people. What we ought to be
> doing is singing in the parks, talking to children, going to gather-
> ings of parents, doing whatever it is we do—dancing, reading
> poetry, performing—all the time, so that people know, "These
> artists are my people—you can't kill them, you can't stop them."
> (Angelou, 1995, 23)

For Pamela, art and education are similar to the way Achebe (1988)
explains:

> I would be quite satisfied if my novels (especially the ones I set in
> the past) did no more than teach my readers that their past—with
> all its imperfections—was not one long night of savagery from
> which the first Europeans acting on God's behalf delivered them.
> Perhaps what I write is applied art as distinct from pure. But who

cares? Art is important, but so is education of the kind I have in mind. And I don't see that the two need to be mutually exclusive. (Achebe, 1988, 45)

Nurturance Past and Present (Self and Others)

As a child, I wrote stories, and I still do as an adult. I write children's stories and adult fiction. A lot of times I bring in my early childhood experiences, and I share them with the students. I am very real and down to earth with them. I had a speech problem growing up. I had a lisp and I went to therapy for it. Sometimes when I see kids come in with handicaps or things that interfere with their reading, I'll share my experiences with them and let them know that it doesn't have to be a hinderance, and I help them to see ways to overcome it. One of the ways for me was practicing reading aloud, and so I read aloud to the children a lot dramatically. They enjoy that, and I encourage them to be dramatic with their reading. They love it!

She discusses a writing group that she belonged to and the context of literary nurturance in New York.

They [the members of the group] are pretty prominent in New York, and they do a lot of readings, and they work with children. Now I believe they are running out of St. Anne's which is a private school. They meet there on the weekends. We've had some successful writers in the program. There's a writer Evette Moore who's written and illustrated children's books. We have a lot of prominent writers that belong to the club that have also been members of the Harlem Writer's Guild in New York.

When asked how she brings out her students' creativity, she explains and talks about the importance of the children feeling safe in her classroom. She says that she does this

Especially with books, I do a lot of book talks. We'll talk about the book, and through modeling I'll try to get them to share their experiences or to get them to talk about how the book effects their lives and to find similarities and differences with the book and their lives and the lives of others that they see. The kids do that, and then they find that they can be open, and I tell them that it's acceptable; whatever you have to say is acceptable. I don't allow cursing, sometimes some kids become a little rambunctious or a little too excited, and they might say, "Can I put the word hell down?" and so I say they can in their private journals, but when you are publishing a piece you have to be considerate of your audience. Or I discuss with them how they think someone else might view it or if they care. I let them know that their voice is important, but to remember their audience and if their piece will be acceptable for that audience, and then we discuss reasons why or why not.

Her students are learning that "writing is a way to capture speech, to hold onto it, to keep it close" (hooks, in West, et. al., 1990 338). Pamela's students are some of the ones Angelou (1995) praises:

Those black children are bravest, without knowing it, representatives of us *all*. The black kids, the poor white kids, Spanish-speaking kids, and Asian kids in the U.S.—in the face of *everything to the contrary,* they still *bop* and *bump* [snaps fingers], shout and go to school somehow. And dare not only to love somebody else, and even to accept love in return, but dare to love *themselves*—that's what is most amazing. *Their* optimism gives me hope. (24)

Pamela is finishing a graduate degree and touches here on the complexities of nurturing herself as a lifelong learner and her commitment to teaching.

Yes, I finish in May, and my degree is in the teaching of reading. My undergraduate degree is in English and communications. I'd like to go back because I sort of see myself going in the direction of the writing and television because I see my artistic side coming out more, and that's what I would like to do; publish some stories that I have. It's hard because I love teaching and I think I'll always love teaching, and I think I'll always be a teacher, but I have some needs inside myself also.

Perhaps she will be one of those creative teachers Maxine Greene (1988) hopes for "to identify the gaps between what is and what is longed for, what (if the sphere of freedom is ever developed) will some day come to be. It's amazing how the two overlap! There are really so many different ways of teaching" (129).

Family History

Pamela's first memory of a book is vivid:

That's easy. I'll never forget it. My first memory was my mother bringing home this beautifully illustrated book. I can't remember the title, but I remember it was about a little ballerina, and I was about four years old. She (my mother) read the story to me, and I would ask her to read it over and over and over again until I learned to read it. That was the first book I was able to read. After reading it, I wanted to become a ballerina, and she took me into dance class, so that book had a profound effect on me. I pursued dancing and theater arts all the way through college. When I got into teaching, I would teach students to dance and do creative movement part time.

That was her favorite book at a young age. When asked about her next favorite, she responded:

I was about six or seven, I remember this book entitled Sam. *It was about a little boy who was the baby of the family. Everyone ignored him at his house; He didn't really have a place, and so at the end everyone gave him a chance to let him help them out. I like that book because I think it was the first book that I saw with a person of color in it. Although it was a little boy, it didn't matter. I loved the pictures, and I loved the story line, and I just really loved that book.*

Then she was asked, "When you read other books before that one did you wonder Why no one looked like you?"

Yes, I did, but when it came to creative things like dancing, it didn't matter. I just loved to read and I loved words. But I remember once in the second grade (I went to parochial school across the street) and looking at the books and saying "Well, why aren't there any books with people who look like me in them?" My second grade teacher at the time was a black woman, and she got a hold of some of those readers like Sam *and* Sam Ran, *and the characters were black, and I remember being excited about them. She only had a handful of them, so we would kind of scramble to get those books. My first name was Pamela, and sometimes they would use the name Pam as one of the characters' names, so I became extremely excited when I would see that happen.*

Even as a child, Pamela used "marginality as a starting point rather than an ending point" (Minh-ha, in West, et. al., 1990, 331) and went beyond it toward other affirmations and negations. She described her family:

My mother is an educator, and at that time she was working with early childhood and day care, and she would read a lot. She was a reader, and she would whiz through books. I saw a lot of books of color for adults, writers like James Baldwin and Richard Wright. So, those were in my home, but I didn't see a lot of children's books with people of color, so I became interested in the adult books and would read them. There was a lot of reading and going to the library in my home.

She remembers the library in Brooklyn.

I would go to the library. I grew up in this area, and I lived here when I was about ten years old, so the library and the museum were very accessible to me. . . . You know, it is so funny because my friends look at me now and say, "We're not surprised you're a teacher," because I would arrange for the children in my neighborhood to go on trips to the library, and I would go there all the time! Anyone who knows me would say, "Pamela was always a reader." I always used my imagination. Books took me places, and I always enjoyed that.

When asked if she started writing when she was a child, she responded:

Oh yes, I started keeping journals because I wasn't a talker. I was more introverted, and so my mother thought it would be good for me to express myself through writing, so she got me a journal and I started writing.

We see her reading and writing at young age, guiding her in what Mikkhail Bakhtin called "dialogism," viewing literary texts as spaces where multiple voices and multiple discourses intersect and interact (Greene, 1988, 129).

Resisting Reader/Teacher

We listen to Ludwig Beethoven, . . . Stevie Wonder or Kathleen Battle, read William Shakespeare, Anton Chekhov, Ralph Ellison, Doris Lessing, . . . Toni Morrison or Gabriel Garcia Matquez,—not in order to undergird bureaucratic assents or enliven cocktail party conversations, but rather to be summoned by the styles they deploy for their profound insight, pleasures and challenges. Yet all evaluation—including a delight in poetry despite his reactionary politics, or a love of Zora Neale Hurston's novels despite her Republican party affiliations—is inseparable from, though not identical or reducible to, social structural analyses, moral and po-

litical judgments and the working of a curious critical consciousness. (West, in West et al., 1990, 31)

I loved Judy Blume. I just devoured everything that she has. Be-
cause I went to a parochial school, I was there from K through 8, and they
were sort of like, "Okay, we have to be careful what we give the kids to
read." But I remember I had one teacher, Mrs. Gallager, who was a very
liberated woman, and she put some of Judy Blume's books in our reading
area. We had a rug where you could lie down, and I would just read those
Judy Blume books. There's another author, Louise Maryweather, and she
has this book, Daddy Was a Number Runner. *Just the title of that book*
enticed me. It is about a young woman of color who is coming of age and
growing up in Harlem. Her experiences were so different, and I was just
so curious. The book had curses in it, so I wanted to read it. It was just a
beautiful story, and it is one that I've gone back to and read as an adult.
As an adult, I worked for a publishing company, and Judy Blume's book
Wifey *came out, and I couldn't wait to get that book, and when I worked*
for the publishing company I found out that she was one of their writers.
They had this room where books reprint and were all stocked, so I went in
and got all of her books. I couldn't wait for her to write another adult
book, but she didn't. She was one of my favorite authors.

Pamela shows what Cornell West advises:

The most desirable option for people of color who promote the
new cultural politics of difference is to be a critical organic
catalyst. By this I mean a person who stays attuned to the best of
what the mainstream has to offer—its paradigms, viewpoints and
methods—yet maintains a grounding in affirming and enabling
subcultures of criticism. Prophetic critics and artists of color
should be exemplars of what it means to be intellectual freedom-
fighters, that is, cultural workers who simultaneously position
themselves within (OR ALONGSIDE) the mainstream while
clearly aligned with groups who vow to keep alive potent traditions of critique and resistance. (West, in West et al., 1990, 33)

When asked about risk taking as a teacher, she responded:

You know, that's really something because I read an article last
semester when I was taking a class that dealt with taking risks. I didn't
really see myself as a teacher who would take risks, but I didn't see myself
as a conformist either. I've had some struggles in terms of the direction

that I like to go and that I find myself going into. So I've decided that, yes I do take a lot of risks. Now I'm just beginning to acknowledge it and say, "I'm taking these risks, and that's it, and this is what I have to do." Anyway, I can get to the children. A lot of teachers are unfortunately stuck. They are saying, "This is the right way to do it and the only way, and we've been doing it like this for years, and all that fancy stuff is nothing new, and we're not excited about it." Then I come in, and I say, "Well, I have to do this, I have to show you, I'm going to be in your face showing you this all the time, introducing it to you, I've done writing workshops here." Some of the teachers are like, "OK, where do I find the time to do this?" or "Is this woman crazy, she thinks I'm actually going to implement this?" I'm sure that is what they are saying, but I keep doing it because I see the benefits.

She discusses the complexities of her conviction about being honest about her opinions.

It's hard, especially expressing that it is my point of view. I have a section of different versions of the Cinderella fairy tale, and so I bring them in a lot. I tell kids that this is my point of view and you have your point of view, and all points of view are different. We all have different views, and that's okay. It helps to develop critical thinkers instead of just passive listeners. I encourage children to express themselves, and sometimes it gets me into trouble. Sometimes I look and I say, "Why did I try to bring out that In this child? Now this child is just too vocal, too verbal!"

Pamela is using her honesty, strength, and skill to encourage her students. As Greene (1988) maintains, "The growing ability to look at even classical works through new critical lenses has enabled numerous readers, of both genders, to apprehend previously unknown renderings of their lived worlds" (129).

Finally, when asked about censorship, Pamela responded:

The writer in me says that everyone has a voice and they have a right to express it. Everyone's voice counts because you might not like what someone has to say, but it may effect someone very deeply that is going through that same experience that may be taboo to someone. I believe everyone has a voice and they have the right to express themselves. In terms of working with children, it's up to parents to decide what they like for their children to read and not to read and what's okay and acceptable in their homes and what they like to expose their children to. But if a child is anything like I was, they're going to read it anyway. I believe in having children select books.

References

Achebe, C. (1988). *Hopes and impediments.* New York: Doubleday.

Angelou, M. (1995, May-June). Interview in *Mother Jones,* 23.

Ferguson, R. (1990). Introduction: Invisible center. In R. Ferguson, M. Gever, T. T. Minh-ha, C. West (Eds.), *Out there: Marginalization and contemporary cultures.* 8–18.

Greene, M. (1988). *The dialectic of freedom.* New York: Teachers College Press.

hooks, b. (1990). Talking back. In R. Ferguson, M. Gever, T. T. Minh-ha, C. West (Eds.), *Out there: Marginalization and contemporary cultures.* 337–340.

Minh-ha, T. (1990). Cotton and iron. In R. Ferguson, M. Gever, T. T. Minh-ha, C. West (Eds.), *Out there: Marginalization and contemporary cultures.* 327–336.

West, C. (1990). The new cultural politics of difference. In R. Ferguson, M. Gever, T. T. Minh-ha, C. West (Eds.), *Out there: Marginalization and contemporary cultures,* 19–38.

6

David Haynes

Using a spatula she smears madame's Neutralizing Facial Flush around Nancy's face. She smears extra on the cheeks where the tears keep washing it away.

"How does it feel?" LaDonna asks.

"It's cold," Nancy says. "So cold."

"We leave it on for just a second. It's only the first step. Go ahead and rinse."

Nancy pats her face with a towel, just the way LaDonna instructs. "What if it doesn't work?" she asks.

"Look," LaDonna says. She frames Nancy in the mirror and stands behind her. She outlines Nancy's jaw with her hands. "Look. Can't you see. You're positively glowing."

"Yes," Nancy says. Her eyes are shining and alive. "Yes. I see. I see."

—Haynes, *Heathens,* 1996, 32

Art and Metaphor as Frameworks for Living

David Haynes' belief in imagination as a transforming act not only guides his writing, but it fosters his belief in his students.

I think that part of what you need to do to be a good teacher is to be able to imagine the lives of your students and to respond compassionately to that and through that compassionate response make a decision that they are worth while and that they are bringing something to the experience and that you as the teacher have an important role in shaping them.

In her work, Maxine Greene emphasizes the power of metaphor for transformation—both personal and communal. Maxine Greene calls it (1992), a sense of "what is out there, what I can reach if I try." It is a way of finding language to bring dreams into being. Metaphor gives us the power to overcome our personal isolation.

David, through his writings, through his stories, through his interactions with the students—all unabashedly drawing on his imagination—transforms situations, places, even people as he goes through his life. One of his short story characters, LaDonna, illustrates what can be done with imagination: "LaDonna knew their problem. These girls lacked dignity and self respect. They had never been allowed to achieve their full potential. They had never unleashed the goddesses within themselves. That's why she was developing Madame LaDonna's Herbal Beauty Care Products" (12). LaDonna came up with a formula for transformation—of a woman's complexion, of a woman's self-worth. The formula was:

Step One: Keep a positive outlook
Step Two: Make a Fresh Start Each Day
Step Three: Make the Most of What You've Got
Step Four: Pay Attention to the Details
Step Five: Never Give Up Hope (Haynes, 1996, 1–31)

David told us,

> *I think that is the other gift of teaching is that you really are around lots and lots of dynamic lives, which if you don't look carefully, they may not seem like they are dynamic. But if you look carefully, and particularly if you listen, you hear that there really are things going on and very often important and interesting things.*

David believes in strengths. He joins Beth Swadener and others who insist upon naming children and families "At Promise" rather than "At Risk" (Swadener and Lubeck, 1995). These visionary teachers live what writer Audre Lorde metaphorically describes: "It is learning how to take our differences and make them strengths. For the master's tools will never dismantle the master's house. They may allow us temporarily to beat him at his own game, but they will never enable us to bring about change." (Audre Lorde, 1984).

David acknowledges that teaching affects his writing and writing affects his teaching.

> *First of all, it is kind of discipline. I think that teaching has affected my writing because first of all there are stories. It is a major part of people's lives, and there aren't people who write very well about it. I'm*

teaching a graduate class right now, and I insist that there are only two really good novels about teaching writing in the last fifteen years that I am aware of, and one is Lesson before Dying *by Ernest Gaines and the other is called* An Honorable Profession *by John M. L'Herurux. So it's material, and I also think that if you work with children every day it informs your world more. Because I've worked with particularly the age groups I have, which is middle school, I tend to not take myself and take everything so seriously. I've learned from them by sometimes having to help them see that everything is not a major catastrophe. There is also a kind of optimism and sense of hope that I've got for my students that sort of flows into my room. I think if a person spent their time in a business, or if a person is in the corporate world, or if a person for example is an emergency medical technician, or if they spent all their time in the mountains by themselves, each of those things will give a different view of the world. So being with children all day gives you a very specific world view. So, beyond material, I mean you really do tend to think of human potential in a new way.*

Nurturance Past and Present (Self and Others)

Given that David believes his art affects his teaching, he is quick to acknowledge that he is nourished as well by the reading that he does regularly:

In fact, I try to make that a special effort to keep up with contemporary fiction. I'm obsessive about buying and having books too. I've stopped being a library person and become my own library. I'm out of space!

He explained that reading

forces you to imagine people more richly, more broadly, and more compassionately because you are always experiencing these lives that are so different from your own. As teachers, that can only help. I think that part of what you need to do to be a good teacher is to be able to imagine the lives of your students and to respond compassionately to that and through that compassionate response make a decision that they are worth while and that they are bringing something to the experience and that you as the teacher have an important role in shaping them. I think that is the primary thing that being a reader has done for me is broaden my world so that I can therefore be a broader person to my students.

Writing is very different. It is very separate. For a long time I kept my writing life and my teaching life very separate. I'm finally trying to start figuring out ways to integrate them. In particularly elementary education there is not much of an opportunity to do that. So summer and vacations have been my writing times and the weekends and evenings too, but then the daytime belongs to school. When my first book was published two years ago, Right by My Side, *I remember it came as a big shock to people who I worked with and to my students because I hadn't ever said anything. Some friends or teachers I had known for a while knew that I would go away to write. When I worked in St. Paul at Longfellow, one of my colleagues was also a fiction writer, and we actually met before we started teaching together at a writing class at the university. She's a very creative and dynamic writing teacher working with her sixth graders. I would do writing and a lot of writing process kinds of things with kids, but my drive as a teacher always went towards humanities, the arts, visual art, and towards social studies. For me writing always felt like a luxury, so I would tell myself that it was a luxury during the school day as well. My colleague didn't operate from that base. Her students would write every day. Her students have always done incredible writing. I know that my writing affects my teaching and my teaching effects my writing, but because they have been so compartmentalized it has been hard to really think about it much.*

Regarding specific nurturance of his students, he advises that some books (like Mildred Taylor's books *Roll of Thunder Hear My Cry*) are just too hard for middle school kids. "I think that is a very practical teacher perspective; they are not written for middle school kids, especially poor readers."

Like Noddings (1991) who advises that "schools should become places in which teachers and students live together, talk to each other, reason together, take delight in each other's company" (169), David recognizes the communal advantages of teaching.

One more thing about teaching that has been important to me is that I am not the kind of person who wants to cloister himself and not have other parts of my life. Writing is certainly a compulsion, and I love it, but one of the things I always tell my students is that there is nothing glamorous or interesting about being locked in a room for six hours sitting in a chair in front of a computer. It is fun, and there are things that happen to you eventually that are exciting, but you have got to have other parts.

Family History

David doesn't remember learning to read.

I have no memory of process. It certainly wasn't difficult, and there was no trauma, and other than the moment that I just talked about where I realized it wasn't going to be tough I have no recollection of anything happening. It's almost as if I always knew.

As far as family memories of reading, David says,

I didn't come from a family of readers except my parents were dedicated daily readers of the morning paper, so I had that model. In terms of books, I think my mother had been a reader when she was younger, but at this point in her life she was not much of a reader.

For me, books were something that came from a library. I had a neighbor who was an avid reader, so I remember starting at a very early age going to the library with her and bringing back stacks and stacks of books to read. I also remember that we had a book club, and I think it was whatever Scholastic was called at the time, and you would clip the coupon and select books. At the time they were very inexpensive, and they were sort of the first flashy paperback editions of good children's books. I had a lot of them. Whenever it was book club time my father would give me two dollars, and I could buy five or six books at least.

I remember one of the books that I bought for myself through book clubs was from the series about Clifford the big red dog. I loved him. I also loved Beverly Cleary's books. I loved Henry Huggens. When I was at the age for those books it was a big thing waiting for the next Beverly Cleary book to come out. I really enjoyed the way that she wrote in sort of a light humorous way. Going back to that same third-grade teacher now; she read a book that really stuck with me. I don't remember the name of it, but I do remember that after she read it I went to the library and found it. It was a book that took place in a boarding school in France. There were about six or seven characters that were in this school and they all had interesting French names. I remember that she didn't know how to pronounce the name of one of the characters, and I didn't either. I remember being very drawn to these interesting names and that whoever had written this book with these six or seven girls in it was very clear that these were distinct characters. It wasn't a real complicated story, and I don't remember much about it, but I do remember that each of them had a personality that was unique. The other book that I remember was from around that same time period, and it was called A Light in the Forest, *which is sort of a classic I think. It was one that I think I had in my own library.*

Heath's (1983) research explores the practice of bedtime story reading and family language use. David doesn't remember his parents ever reading to him specifically as a very young child.

> *I don't remember that they did or that they didn't. I do remember that when I started school in kindergarten, at that point getting read to was a regular [by his teachers]. These were teachers that did it daily and spent a lot of time reading to kids. I have very fond memories of being read to. I have another third-grade memory that really sticks with me. There was this teacher. She loved books, and she loved reading to students, and the last day of school she had packed up all of her things, and we had our daily reading time, and there wasn't much left to do because everything was packed up. She had a Reader's Digest that hadn't been packed away, so she started reading this story about this family whose car broke down in the desert. They were off the road where no one could see them. They were stuck for days and days. The last section she read before the bell rang was, "Color Crayons for Breakfast," and she sort of left us there with them still in the desert. All of these years I have wondered how that family ever got out of that desert.*

Of his elementary years, David has

> *a general memory of just loving books. My first real specific memory of reading that has stuck with me for a long time is a negative one. I think it was in third grade, and I know that I loved reading and had been reading a long time before that. But the teacher was using the Dick and Jane books, and we had worked our way up in the series, and I remember that she was very explicit that we were not supposed to read ahead in this book. So I went ahead and read along farther in the book, and she said, "There will be words that you don't know," but the way that the series was set up was that the new words were at the bottom of the page. So I paged ahead, and I remember distinctly that the new words at the bottom of the page were farmer, donkey, traveler, and soup. I think it was one of those light bulb moments that clued me in to the fact that there were no mysteries, but a lot of discoveries to be made. So that is my first real specific reading memory where I thought, Oh, okay if I could turn ahead in this book and read farmer, donkey, traveler, soup then I could pick anything and read it.*

David grew up in St. Louis, and just as Marshall Finney, the protagonist in his novel, *Right by My Side,* experienced high school in all its complexities. Marshall described the following:

Eisenhower High School is nothing and nowhere. From the road it is another unfortunate pile of suburban bricks it could be the telephone company or sewage treatment plant—and every day is the same there, and nothing of consequence ever goes on. But just tell that to the Pinheads inside. . . . Pinheads: They make a person want to stop every other one of em up in here and ask if they have a license to be as stupid as they act. . . . "Lighten up, Finney," they say: you know how they call everybody by the last name, and I get turned in to Mr. Shannon, the A.P., for being sullen. Sullen means white folks' stale jokes don't strike you as funny." (12–13)

Marshall describes his English class: "The air in Redneck World Literature is charged. Buzz Simpkins broods, his thick neck sunk deep into his shoulders. Connie Jo looks hurt and disappointed, . . . like one of those rich women who come around Washington Park at Christmas and can't figure out why folks don't want their used clothes." (13). Marshall asked the teacher after class about their assignment of reading Yeats.

"That poem . . ." I start, and see: she's already got me off balance. "No one writes English like Yeats," she says. "Reading him you understand how our language should sound." "Any other poets like? Like me, I mean. Black. I figured if anyone would, you might know." I shrug my shoulders to let her off the hook in case she doesn't know. Also, you never let them think it's that important to you. She sighs and makes this little face like she'd heard a rude noise in the room. "As a matter fact, yes, there are wonderful poets of all nationalities," she says, and signals us to walk with her. "But you miss the point, Marshall." (34–35)

When asked about reading in junior high or senior high, David explained

It is hard to say. In my reading life I went through phases. Through the early years until about seventh grade I was a prodigious reader; I read everything. I was one of those readers that it was a good thing that I had a good and patient understanding of my brain because I would go anywhere in the library, and if I found anything that seemed interesting I would read it. I remember at one point having a goal of reading my way around the book mobile. I went through a phase in high school in particular where I didn't read much. Where I don't remember reading much. I don't remember in particular that any of the books in the literature program had a real impression on me. I did like Great Expectations, *but other than that nothing in particular caught my eye.*

He explained further about how his tastes and interests in reading changed and developed.

> *A lot of the books we were reading in school like Brontë and Dickens . . . I had picked those up and read them when I was in my junior high reading phase. At the time I realized I didn't understand them very well. I have sort of an odd thing that I'm really aware of that, when I was younger, the books I was interested in were travel books, geography books. I loved reading about what India was like and read real thorough descriptions of what Indian culture and Indian history was or about countries in Africa. Those were the books that stuck with me when I was younger. Then when I was in high school things that stuck with me most were plays. For instance, I really liked Eugene O' Neill's plays. Then when I was in college even though I was an English major and read a lot, what stuck with me were magazines. I worked in the library so I read* Esquire, Rolling Stone, *and* The New Yorker, *and so I became a predigest reader of what was contemporary journalism at the time. So you go through these phases where your tastes change or shift.*

Since David had explained how his own writing was so closely linked to his reading, we asked if his tastes and routines for writing changed as he grew.

> *It was the same kind of pattern; it was off and on. I don't know if there was a link to it or not. For example, around that sixth- to seventh-grade age I wrote a lot, then shifting ahead to high school I think there wasn't much, and then in college a little bit, and then I stopped and then started again. About six or seven years after college I started writing seriously. Now the interesting thing about it is since that postcollege period, when I really started seriously and almost obsessively following contemporary fiction and writing, I haven't stopped. I am sort of always waiting for the next phase or next trend.*

He explained:

> *The first thing that I remember writing myself is I recall sitting down consciously one night in front of the TV set and writing a story. It wasn't an assignment; there wasn't even anyone who I thought was going to be particularly interested in it. It was just sort of a compulsion I had to sit down and do it. My mother had one of those old manual typewriters that was just a junker and that's what I sat down and wrote it on. That was the first thing I did. My mother has a recollection that*

when I was younger than that I had written a story that was sent in to Weekly Reader and had actually been published. In seventh grade I wrote a poem, and I don't remember if it was an assignment, and it also got published. I never got the story back. I would sure love to see it now! The teacher read it to the class, and the class loved it, so it was like my big debut as a writer. It was really like a compulsion to sit down and write like that. In junior high and senior high there were various teachers I would write for, and in junior high I would always write for my Spanish teacher in sort of bad Spanish. I wrote a soap opera that was really very turgid and I would write these episodes and then turn them in to her. She just loved it. In high school, for example, I didn't have much encouragement. I didn't have much encouragement to write in college either, so it was a lot of internal motivation and internal drive that brought me to writing.

Resisting Reader/Teacher

David teaches in urban St. Paul. His teaching and writing support Maxine Green's belief that we should "think of American culture as a conversation among different voices. . . . The purpose of education is to recognize the voices" (Greene, 1992). David said,

I think teaching in an urban school (for me St. Paul) has given me opportunities to deal with a real cross section of population of the city over the past fifteen years or so. There's another piece that I want to talk about that has to do with stereotypes and clustering and categorizing people together. You really do learn that the general categories are often wrong as well as our specifics are often wrong too. If people carry these images whether it is about single mothers or about people on welfare or people who are poor or low class, they just aren't true! There may be some grain of truth that's there, but really there are other things that we just don't know about, and unless you sat down and had a conversation with somebody you would have no way of knowing. So I've had those experiences with people. I feel like the ultimate gift has been that . . . well I'm a big believer that there is some combination of divine intervention of some kind and an extremely complex mental process that gives us our stories, and I have been fairly prolific over the past couple years, and I think the reason for that is that I'm just constantly being bombarded with stories, and so they just keep coming and melding into something new.

The stories that David hears and tells represent voices that have often been silenced through educational contexts and the hidden curriculum.

David's voices through the characters in his work represent a politics of resistance as described by Giroux (1990): "There is a politics of resistance in which difference is explored through the category of voice. Central here is the need to engage voice as an act of resistance and self-transformation, to recognize that as one comes to voice one establishes the precondition for becoming a subject in history rather than an object" (22).

In terms of risk-taking as a resistant teacher, David explained two categories of risk:

> *I would almost have to divide that up into curriculum risks and risks that were sort of counseling kinds of risks and risks that were working with my colleagues. In terms of working with kids in the classroom I'll tell you one of the risks that really paid off. I was working at Saturn (an experimental magnet school in downtown St. Paul) and going to do a reading class and was chosen to look at drama. I had a wide range of kids. They were fourth to eighth graders with a wide range of interests, and I said, "I'm going to get* Romeo and Juliet, *and we are going to do it together." It was a risk in many ways because there were kids who probably weren't going to be able to read it on their own at all, and there were others who probably weren't going to be that interested in it. It was a wonderful experience, and I, in fact, read a lot of it out loud, and as I started they would want to try. It was like a puzzle to them, and they really got interested and excited about it. They felt like they were really mastering something. I really emphasized to them that it wouldn't be the last time they would be exposed to* Romeo and Juliey *and that it was a really important part of our culture. I did two other plays that term. I did* A Raisin in the Sun *and* Our Town.*
>
> *Interestingly enough they loved all three, and they understood all three at different levels. There were twenty students, and there was this whole range of understanding that they would get out of it. The play that they were closest to was* A Raisin in the Sun *which surprised me. They loved it, and they also really worked hard on the other two. It was an exciting class! I'm glad I took that risk; I'm glad I went down that road. There have been other things like that. You just have to do it sometimes, and you have to be willing to give them up when they don't go with them.*

David went on to explain the multi-aged groups of students at Saturn:

> *Yes, it was basically a project that was designed to take the school from literature such as it was designed in 1987–88 and implement it and say, "We are going to do individualized learning plans for all students;*

we are going to do multi-aged grouping of kids; we are not going to give grades, but come up with alternative assessments. We are going to in-volve parents in the planning and programming, use a lot of technology and computers, do lots of process-based learning." So there was a big chunk of stuff to take on. We were starting from zero, and there were like three or four of us that spoke the language and had some ideas about how to do this. We had no planning time. Basically, I was hired July, and I went away to write that summer and came back when school started. So we were implementing and creating and re-developing all at the same time. It was the most intense four years of my life, and in some ways it was wonderful, and in some ways it was horrible.

David's work, both his teaching and his writing, are avenues for his activism. He (Spring, 1995) speaks openly to the media: "I know my colleagues care about what they do and are highly skilled individuals." He says he was distressed and frustrated by the lack of status for teachers' skills and that competencies were being challenged.

He has been working on the national effort of developing Profes-sional Standards in Teaching. He explained:

It is the National board for Professional Standards in Teaching, and I started working with them in 1990 as a member of the committee that has written the standards for what they call "Early Adolescent Generalists." But basically it is teachers like myself who work in fifth through eighth grade, teaching all subjects—being generalists, trying to integrate across the curriculum. I got involved by being a member of the committee which was a real honor for me, and then about a year and a half ago they asked me to come out to Washington and work with other teachers who were setting standards. I am going to continue to work for them half time as a consultant over the next year or so.

This national activist work has taken him out of the classroom for a while. We asked him about what he has missed and what he is happy to be away from.

What I've really been happy to be away from is all of the things that go on in school districts and schools that don't serve children and aren't set up to serve children; they are set up to serve administrator rules. Surprisingly, a lot of it is not paper work. People think that is one of the things that gets in the way. Well, it really isn't. A lot of it is the way your days are badly structured some days and you have got no control over who comes and goes and you have no say over all those kinds of things. I also don't miss some of the people who are clearly just collecting a paycheck and who aren't particularly interested in it. I miss being with the kids and having that energy in my life. It's a great kind of energy, and you don't get it much anyplace else. One of the real frustrations about being involved in setting standards for professionals is, because I am taking very good teachers from all over the country and having intense and informed conversations about what people do and why, I am always thinking, Boy, I would really love to try that out with kids! The other thing is that you meet teachers and think, I would love to team teach with you for a while. So that is what I miss most about it. One of the things I figured out that one has to do once their writing life takes over them (and in my case that is one of the things that is happening to me) is you have to figure out how you are going to make a new plan. Unfortunately, I don't think schools have the flexibility. I figure there may be some sort of setting that allows me to have connections with young people and to do some teaching, but doesn't rob from my writing.

David's writing will most likely always be intertwined with his quest for teaching contexts which respect students' strengths. He talked of his latest work:

I've got two books coming that I want people becoming teachers to know about. I am doing a series of middle reader books with Milkweed Press. It is going to be a series about multicultural kids. Different boys living in the same neighborhood in St. Paul with different sorts of family structures, different economic things, different races. They all go to the same school, and they get to be friends. We are going to try to make them funny and have some sort of adventure in each book that is not too outlandish. We will have some good values in there, but mostly the sort of things that if you are a sixth or seventh grader who doesn't like to read too much but would pick up something funny or enjoyable. Those will come in fall of 1996 (the first two).

In *Right by My Side,* one of David's novels, Rose writes to her son, perhaps as David would write to all students: "You'll have that power over people, too. That power to hold on come what may. The power to make people believe that, no matter what else comes along, there will never be anyone like you. I will that power to you. Like me, you will always be loved. Use your powers wisely. Enjoy yourself" (Haynes, 1993, 158).

References

Giroux, H. (1991). Giroux, H. A. (1990). The politics of postmodernism. *Journal of Urban and Cultural Studies, 1* (1), 5–38.

Greene, M. (1992). The passions of pluralism: Multiculturalism and the expanding community. *Educational Researcher, 22* (1), 13–18.

Haynes, D. (1996). *Heathens,* Minneapolis, MN: New Rivers Press.

———. (1996). *Live at Five.* Minneapolis, MN: Milkweed Editions.

———. (1993). *Right by my side.* Minneapolis, MN: New Rivers Press.

———. (1995). *Somebody Else's Mama.* Minneapolis, MN: Milkweed Editions.

———. (1996). *West Seventh Wildcats,* a series of four books for middle grade students. Minneapolis, MN: Milkweed Editions.

Heath, S. B. (1983). *Ways with words.* Boston: Cambridge University Press.

Lorde, A. (1984). *Sister outsider: Essays and speeches.* Trumansburg, NY: Crossing Press.

Noddings, N. (1991). Stories in dialogue: Caring and interpersonal reasoning. In C. Wityherell and N. Noddings (Eds.), *Stories lives tell: Narrative and dialogue in education.* New York: Teachers College Press, 157–170.

Swadener, E. B., and Lubeck, S. (Eds.). (1995). *Children and families at promise: The social construction of risk.* New York, NY: State University of New York Press.

7

LISA BOEHLKE

I suppose the whimsical captured me. I also liked stories where someone had a problem or a life challenge to deal with. I read the series of New Americans. My memory tells me as I look back at them that they introduced me to wider worlds.

—Lisa Boehlke

Lisa Boehlke is an English as a Second Language (ESL) teacher in the St. Paul Public Schools. A teacher who works with her says, "She started out being responsible for all the students in one school, but was so effective that she soon ran out of students who needed her help. Then she was given an additional school." Her interviews reveal that her effectiveness is much broader than simply being an expert in ESL methods. Her global perspectives, in a concrete and complex sense, are the twine that binds the academics and affective influences she and her students have on each other.

Research indicates that teachers achieving this global perspective and multidirectional interaction between academics and sociocultural dynamics is difficult. McDermott (1989) states, "The anthropological maxim is clear; kids in every culture on record learn what has to be learned and do what has to be done to live in their culture" (16). Will teachers in the cultural context of the schools do what has to be done in order to live in their culture? As society (and therefore, the school) becomes more multicultural, the demands for pluralistic and multicultural teaching become greater. Our information from Lisa's interviews shows that teachers gain information both about teaching and about learning in particular programs and in other community contexts through being resisting readers and using metaphor to connect the actual and the possible.

Lily Wong Fillmore (1990) comments regarding the importance of the teacher role in society: "The teachers are cultural and linguistic bridges connecting the worlds of the home and the classroom; they facilitate the children's entry to school by building, on what the children have learned in their homes" (5–6). Lisa's development of her imagination through reading since early childhood has helped her cross the bridge into other cultures. Her metaphors for herself and her students point to dynamic patterns in our butterfly metaphor of findings.

Metaphor and Art as Frameworks for Living

I had so many [favorite books]—I was reading all the time. I suppose when I was in first and second grade I was fascinated with books that rhymed, some of the early Dr. Seuss books and the whimsical ones. I remember trying to imagine Mulberry Street. Now [at that time] I was living outside of Princeton, New Jersey. And I couldn't imagine anything unusual happening. There was the little library down the street for kids to go to, right next to the dentist's office. It was just a normal street. Nothing happened on it. So, I suppose the whimsical captured me. I also liked stories where someone had a problem or a life challenge to deal with. I read the series of New Americans. My memory tells me as I look back at them that they introduced me to wider worlds.

There have been many social situations where I would begin to talk to people and they wouldn't know what I was talking about. I expected that even my closest friend could only share but a portion of my interests. That is okay. There are plenty of things for me to read. I have plenty of connections through writing. There are things that I have read, where the authors couldn't know me, and I probably wouldn't recognize the authors on the street. But I feel that I have a relationship with the authors that I read. I feel like they are speaking to me. In my experience with reading certain authors, for example, I have met some professional educational writers, if I like their writing . . . I usually like them and can relate to them as a person.

I have written pieces of things. That is how Mary Kay and I met.

Lisa illustrates what Ayers (1989) calls "voices of engagement, responsibility, investment, involvement, and firsthand knowledge" (6). Lisa's firsthand knowledge is revealed in the interview data as a woven picture of metaphor and factual information gained through reading and living. Her lifelong development of her imagination directly relates to her ability and passion for continued personal and professional growth which is clearly seen as she nurtures her own life and the lives of her students.

Nurturance Past and Present (Self and Others)

There are a lot of reasons why I read. Purely emotional reasons. It feels good. I need the opportunity to read for about one hour periodically. If I can't do this I have a sense of frustration. I feel that there is something I need to do—a gaping hole. Then when I read I don't feel that way anymore. I have got to go and pick up some books at Uncle Edgar's, which is where I buy secondhand mystery paperbacks.

I hate being bored. The kind and variety of information I need is in reading, as much as I like teaching. I am not bored with teaching, but the level that I am teaching doesn't challenge my mind in terms of new information. It challenges my mind in terms of finding that match between interest, skill, and task that you need to find with students to help them progress. I am forty-three years old, and I am half way to my Ph.D., and there are a lot of things that I can do that don't come out when I am working with elementary school children.

Lisa's self-reflection through her reading and writing provides a mechanism for integration of the ethics of critical theory and personal political potential in her life. Her ability to find emotional and intellectual nurturance through reading began very young. The walk to the library, for her, was a bridge to new worlds.

Family History

When I was a small child living in Manchester, Iowa, living in the parsonage, I liked to take books off the book shelf—pull them down and just hold them—open them, and just hold them and kind of look at them. I am told that I was very careful with them.

Another memory was when my father was a young pastor, in his first assignment, or "call," as they say. I remember wandering into his study many times. And I saw papers and books spread all around, and I knew that that was important because sometimes I would hear, "Be quiet, Daddy is working" from my mother or my father himself. I can't remember the earliest time that I was read to. I can remember going on walks, in that same town, to the library. It was one of those stone-front Greek-column buildings that was built with Carnegie money in that small town. It wasn't a big library. The next child in the family was born, and I remember that often my father would walk me over to the library. It seemed like such a long walk in my childhood memory. But as I later found out it was only a two to three block walk. But it was always so wonderful to be able to walk to the library. I was told that one of the first words that I said was **berbery,** *which was my word for going to the library. So they must have been taking me there at a very young age.*

But Dad was the one to go to when you had a question in your reading. I was joking with someone last night, it was like having an encyclopedia on CD ROM, you'd just ask Dad and he knew. "What does this mean? I am reading this story about these knights and they were talking about going off to Jerusalem looking for the holy grail." "Isn't Jerusalem a Bible city, and why would the knights want to go off? I thought they were supposed to stay home and fight." Sometimes I would get a bit of history. Sometimes it would go on too long. But you could always ask him a question about just about everything. It was very rare when he told us to go look it up in the encyclopedia. But many a time in Indonesia (after we moved there when I was nearly eleven) I read the encyclopedia because I had run out of things to read. We would develop our own specialties. My brother became an expert on the Civil War as a nine year old. He would discuss all the battles with Dad; they were very respectful discussions.

I don't remember my mother reading for her own pleasure during my elementary school years. She was a young school teacher who had taught for seven years before she met my father in college.

Reading was always a part of our home even though in the early years there were not the thousands of books present by my early teens. My father's parents owned a small room off the living room of their farmhouse which they called the library. It was filled with National Geographics. After my dad had read all of the books in his library, he would ask to borrow books from neighbors. My father's father had liked to talk with this doctor. Later on, my father discovered that Dr. Houde would loan him as many books as he could read, so my father read all of his books also. My father came to associate books with riches. Even my father today, at nearly seventy, buys more books than my mother, and it is truly phenomenal. Before I had reached five years of age there must have been more than five hundred books in the house.

[Later] My mom read quite a bit. She would read books that had extraordinarily involved plot lines. I remember when I was a teenager she was reading Ulysses *and looking at annotated commentaries for it, also* Lolita. *She just thought that both authors had such good eyes for the idiosyncracies of people. But we didn't share the same taste in reading. I never read either one of those. I have picked them up but. . . . And now I am at the age that my mom would have been reading them, but I am still not interested in them.*

At that time when my mom read, she would pick something that was more of a project than an escape. However, as a teenager I had not figured out my mom's taste in literature. I remember coming back from Singapore with some women's magazines because I figured everyone's mom reads them. When I gave them to her, they went on top of the coffee table, and when I looked again they were still on the coffee table in the same spot. I never noticed her reading them. And she said to me, "I think I am going to give these to my friend, Georgette," she said, "because, you know me, I would rather spend my time making things." She would sketch and paint. "You know me. I don't spend my time reading cookbooks." It wasn't so much the books; it was more that she didn't have the time. She had projects. She did read a lot, however. I think I got my interest in trying to figure out why people do the things they do from her and from reading biographies as a child. I would watch through reading how people would solve problems, the characters that were kids as well as adults. She was a very wise woman in terms of reading people's characters. We would, and still do, have great discussions about why people do the things they do. The discussions tend to be about my friends, too. She would sometimes talk about why some other friends and I had drifted apart.

Most of the time I would read in the living room and sprawl out on a couch or drape myself over a chair. I have casual posture because of it. I would have had a hard time in the military because of my posture. When my parents and friends came over to see them I could usually be found sitting in a soft chair with my arms and legs hanging off. It has always been a chair. I can remember being in Singapore (going to high school at the Singapore American School) living in a place run by the Methodist and Lutheran Board. There were common areas for all the hostel kids and then rooms with the beds in them. Sometimes because there were a lot of kids hanging out in the common areas, I would go to my bedroom and lose myself in a book. I have great memories of my roommates saying to me, "Come on, come on it's time for dinner." "Oh, just wait," I would reply. "One more chapter. I have to finish this chapter." That didn't work very well with my mom. She'd say, "Put it down now!"

I absolutely love mysteries. I still read them. I read them when I am happy, when I am sad, and when I need a good escape. I have so many authors that I refer to as favorites. When I was a teenager I read Mary Stuart, because she has characters speaking bits and pieces of other languages. At that point I had some Indonesian from my Jakarta days and I was taking French in high school.

People read Mary Stuart's work for many reasons. It is significant to our research and to Lisa's work as a teacher that the reason she read Mary Stuart was because she was fascinated with the characters who spoke other languages. Anthropologists and ethnographers are given the advice that by making the familiar strange (Diaz, Moll, and Mehan, 1986) they will in fact be able to see and interpret aspects of a familiar culture that had previously gone unnoticed. This process of *making the familiar strange* was suggested by Gordon (1961) in his synectics training as a way to use metaphor to problem solve. Lisa utilizes this ability to look at the familiar made strange in ESL curricula. Her students make choices in their own reading and write based on their own experiences using the writing process. Both activities she connects to the content of subject matter they are studying in other classes. Her curricular adjustments and adaptations lesson the danger of her ESL students being tracked. Her own memories of being tracked give passion to what she sees as her professional responsibilities of being a resisting reader and teacher.

Resisting Reader/Teacher

I definitely went to a school where I was tracked. I was always in the high reading group, except for first grade. That was when we were living outside of Princeton. We had just changed schools, so it was a different school from where I had gone to kindergarten. My mother was a second-grade teacher down the hall from the kindergarten class that I was in. Over thirty-five years later she said, "The teacher you had in kindergarten was probably the worst teacher that I had ever seen in all of my experience as a teacher." And I don't remember a whole lot except for playing. I didn't know my letters of the alphabet or their sounds when I went into first grade. I remember having difficulty learning to read. And good old, bless her heart, Mrs. Snediker who had white hair, she was probably close to retirement. She was very grandmotherly, and she had a lot of patience and encouragement. I can't remember but one time when Mrs. Snediker got mad at me, and that did not have anything to do with reading. But I was saying "was" for "saw," putting initial and final sounds in the wrong place. Our groups were named "birds." I was in the blue bird group, and I wanted to be in the red bird group. I knew the groups at the time. But I also knew that I didn't read as well as the other kids. At that point I had no idea; I didn't realize until later that I learned things faster and picked up things quicker than other children. But at that point, Mrs. Snediker talked to Mom. I remember my sister was a toddler and my brother was four and all of us were in the living room. I can do a layout of that living room right now. The sun shining in the late fall afternoon and my mom was sitting with me reading. I was snuggled up to her. It was a Tom and Jerry *primer, because we did* Dick and Jane in school. And I remember sitting there with Mom over the entire fall. I remember it going on a long time, but Mom doesn't think that it went on longer than six weeks max. And that was enough to get me over the hump. I always like to tell kids who may be discouraged that it is not a matter of being smart to learn how to read. It is having enough information to start. And I tell them that story, that my kindergarten teacher was terrible, so I didn't even know my letters for first grade.

There weren't very many women in books in the library. Generally the women were in helping professions—nurses, teachers. I remember being so fascinated that Florence Nightingale could go off to faraway places and do something so wonderful with the resources she had, not knowing the language. I was a quiet child, but I also felt that it was right to say what I thought. That was very much encouraged by my family and the community. I remembered as a fifth grader there had been an article in Newsweek. I ended up getting in an argument with a colleague of my father. The article was about the Thresher submarine accident. I was intrigued with this. I remember arguing with him about the number of survivors in this accident. It turned out that I was right about the number of sailors who had died.

Just because I liked to read so much I read all the Nancy Drew and Hardy Boys books that were available. I thought that Nancy Drew and the Hardy Boys were able to use more equipment. I thought that was cool. I can remember the equipment from my house. I thought that was cool, the types of things they could use and get to work for them. I thought that Nancy Drew was insipid. Where was the credibility of this young woman who was forever sixteen. She never had a father who was around and then he would show up once in awhile. She was always bailing out her father, who was supposed to be a lawyer. I had developed a sense at a young age that an educated person should be a good problem solver, and in this situation, this father was not very resourceful in his problem solving. It seemed to me that any father who needed a sixteen year old to keep bailing him out wasn't worth too much as a parent.

My girlfriends and I must have been in sixth and seventh grade, and we would talk about our favorites. We would always discuss books that we had read. And we all decided that Nancy Drew was a very unbelievable character. We always had a book circle in a way. We exchanged books, and we'd argue. The fact that her friend never disagreed with her, and we knew that wasn't true because of our book club. These girls and I were all being raised in families that were straight out of the fifties. Moms and dads were college educated, maybe with graduate degrees. Dad probably had a professional job that required a special talent that made him a resource in a country looking for additional resources of

> *their own. Moms were full-time moms. Quiet girls, you know, we all dreamed of growing up and being mommies and doing good works in the community, whether it was a church women's group or whatever. But we all decided that Nancy Drew was not a believable character And that her friend Bess was totally unbelievable because she didn't disagree and we had disagreed among ourselves. I also was fascinated by those Old Testament stories of the prophet going up against the king. Just because the king had the riches and power, he didn't have more authority. And somehow the message came through that gave me permission to speak up. I am the oldest in my family, that may be why. The other part was that I was so hungry to read. I always felt calm when I read. And as a young child, I was a tom boy. I always climbed trees. I did the friction burn. I could do anything anybody could do. Yet at the same time, I could spend hours just reading.*

Analyses and emphases in education are attempting to be inclusive of issues of race, sexual orientation, class, language, culture, physical characteristics, and other sources of marginalization and oppression (Apple, 1982; Gilligan, 1982;) yet the schools still, through curriculum and hidden curriculum, advocate fundamental beliefs about what is good and important and consequently perpetuate unequal outcomes of schooling, "reproducing the racial, class, and gender inequities in society today" (Swadener and Kessler, 1991, 87). Lisa's curriculum builds on the individual worlds of her students. In a professional article, she states (1990):

> It is difficult to believe that these same children stop writing after a few sentences because they have nothing more to express in their writing. Perhaps we as teachers have communicated that we care more about what we have to say to our students than we care about providing opportunities to help them discover and refine who they are. After all young children try to write or draw on walls, tables, books, and even newspapers long before they enter elementary school They continually find ways to assert "I am." (19)

Lisa's own written words clearly indicate how her personal literacy interacts with her pedagogy, how who she is in closely related to what she does:

> When encouraged to write using a process approach, the LEP [Limited English Proficient] students we taught came to see them-

selves as real authors who create literary pieces similar to the manner in which authors familiar to the children do. It establishes for us that the LEP children we guided had acquired new eyes and ears for imaginative imagery. They had successfully played with language and learned to respond to teachers' work with interest and specific assistance. (Boehlke and Rummel, 1990)

References

Apple, M. (1982). *Education and power.* Boston: Routledge and Kegan Paul.

Ayers, W. A. (1989). *The good preschool teacher.* New York, NY: Columbia Teachers College Press.

Boehlke, L., and Rummel, Mary K. (1990). Geodes like sky blue popsycles: Developing authorship literacy in Limited English Proficient students. *MinneTesol Journal, 8,* 17–26.

Diaz, S., Moll, Luis, C., and Mehan, H. (1986). Sociocultural resources in instruction: A context-specific approach. In *Beyond language: Social and cultural factors in schooling language minority students.* Los Angeles, CA: Evaluation, Dissemination and Assessment Center, California State University.

Gilligan, C. (1982). *In a different voice: Psychological theory and women's development.* Cambridge, MA: Harvard University Press.

Gordon, W. J. J. (1961). *Synectics: The development of creative capacity.* NY: Harper.

McDermott, R. P. (1989). Discussant's comments: Making dropouts. In Trueba, H. T., Spindler, G., and Spindler, L. (Eds.), *What do anthropologists have to say about dropouts?* New York: Falmer Press.

Swadener, E. B., and Kessler, S. (1991). Introduction to the special issue. *Early Education and Development, 2,* (2), 85–94.

Wong Fillmore, L. (1990). Latino families and the schools. In *California perspectives: An anthology.* Los Angeles, CA: The Immigrant Writers Project.

8

Tracy Montero

I think kids like to know about other places and other people. Not everyone goes to Italy and France, so for the kids that don't, it is great for the
kids that do to be able to bring in their slides and pictures and talk about
it. It is also great for inclusion too because the whole thing is like, We are
all alike, we are all different, so it is nice to think about it in a bigger sense.
With social studies and current events we try to do it at least once a week,
and the kids bring in articles of what is happening because things are
changing so quickly, especially now.

—Tracy Montero

Tracy Montero likes to know about other places and other people.
She has become a voyager across borders and across barriers as she
educates herself and provides for the education of her students in her
first-grade classroom in Brooklyn, New York. When she was a student
in college she heard Edward Said talk about exile: "Exile is strangely
compelling to think about but terrible to experience. It is the unhealable
rift forced between a human being and a native place, between the self
and its true home: its essential sadness can never be surmounted" (Said,
1990, 357).

She heard a mission of learning and teaching for herself. She took
his advice as she explored her world and his: "Regard experiences as if
they were about to disappear. What is it that anchors them in reality?
What would you save of them? What would you give? Only someone
who has achieved independence and detachment, someone whose
homeland is 'sweet' but whose circumstances makes it impossible to
recapture that sweetness, can answer those questions" (Said, in West
1990, 366).

Metaphor and Art as Frameworks for Living

This crossing of boundaries has been the defining focus of her life.
Her classroom is conceived of as a home that is inclusive, void of
boundaries. The home of Tracy's classroom contains many forms of art:

We have lots of puppets. We have a puppet theater, and we actually do dance in our classroom and do different kinds of movement activities. We have different kinds of stretches, and at the end of the day we always end with different kinds of meditations which is a nice way to end and get everyone calm and relaxed. We do a lot of drama and a lot of active play and play models outside. We do a lot to help them be creative because I think we like to play so much too.

As a child she began her interest in art.

I was also interested in dance so I read a lot of biographies on different dancers.

In Tracy's classroom, there is a dance of interacting parts connecting art and literacy.

They're making books all the time; especially during writing and even reading, although we try to keep reading the least projects oriented as it can be. They like to copy books and poetry. For example, they are making their own poetry books which might be copying a poem that another child wrote, copying another poem that they love in the class-room, or writing their own poems. They're very excited to make chapter books. They are always making books during writing time. During choice time I would say that half the class always chooses reading and writing and is involved in book making and collaborative kind of writing.

We were reminded of Anzaldúa (1987): "My 'awakened dreams' are about shifts. Thought shifts, reality shifts, gender shifts: one person metamorphoses into another in a world where people fly through the air, heal from mortal wounds. I am playing with my Self, I am playing with the world's soul, I am the dialogue between my Self and *el espiritu del mundo*. I change myself, I change the world" (70).

Nurturance Past and Present (Self and Others)

One way Tracy nurtures her interest and need to know about other people is to travel and live in different contexts.

I was in Jordan for about three and a half months. I was working on my thesis which was on Palestinians in Jordan because Jordan has a huge concentration of Palestinians, especially women who go there to study. I lived in a women's dormitory where they lock the doors at 8:00. So that was the basis of my thesis. It was like an ethnography on my experience living as an American woman in this dormitory.

Like Ruth Behar (1993), the Cuban anthropologist, Tracy not only crossed the boundaries of countries and cultures, but also those of gender. Feminist ethnographers have lately begun to explore the question of whether feminism translates across borders. Scholars want to learn how to listen and respond to the words of women from other cultural, racial, and class backgrounds.

She ties her own learning to that of the children.

I like to know about people in other cultures, and it is not only in the Middle East. I like the kids to know what is going on around them. Like last year we did a whole thing on South Africa because that was such an important thing that was going on. I don't think I was always so good at staying up with current events, and I feel that it is important to know what is going on with the world. I think kids really need a taste of that at every level. Some of the kids get it, and some don't. I think that they need to be surrounded by maps just to let them know the world view; that there is something else out there besides the little place where you live. I think kids like to know about other places and other people.

Tracy seems to emulate Anzaldúa's (1987) belief that "living in a state of psychic unrest, in a Borderland, is what makes poets write and artists create" (73).

With social studies and current events we try to do it at least once a week. And the kids bring in articles of what is happening because things are changing so quickly, especially now. So, I've realized that it is important for kids even in the first grade to have a sense of what is happening out there.

In the classroom Tracy uses lots of resources.

We've got an open library. We're uncomfortable with reading centers, Manny and I, because we feel like, what do you do for the kids who slip through the cracks? But we also use the traditional approach of pulling kids out on a needed basis. So, since there are two of us, with two powers, we are extremely fortunate that we can devote an hour every day. We may do the mini lesson which is focused on a skill or reader response to a book or anything that is related to reading that we feel is important that day. It may be with a partner or questions like, "How did this make you feel?" or "Did you notice the periods?" or "Were you able to read with voices?" or "Wasn't this a great story because . . . ?" or any kind or mini lessons about five to ten minutes in length. After that we have our reading time when kids have the rest of the forty-five minutes or so to be into reading baskets. Those change weekly, they choose them on Friday, and our library is entirely organized by theme, so we have an animal bin, a transportation bin, seasons and holidays and poetry bins. While kids are in those baskets Manny and I will pull kids out; I've got half the class, and he's got the other half. Some days I'll pull out one child who really needs help on one skill for that day, and sometimes I'll pull out two or three. We'll read books and talk about it, and meanwhile the other kids are in their reading baskets also responding in a reading log. It wasn't always an hour long. We started for ten minutes of reading and then we worked ourselves up. They really run it themselves. They've got their reading logs which they respond to, and sometimes they don't and that's okay. We are not very structured in the sense that we tell them exactly what to do or how. It is sort of open-ended so that everyone has the chance to accomplish what he/she wants to do at that reading time. Some of the kids fool around, but a lot of the kids read, and we do have the person power to be able to manage things which is great because I don't think it would happen otherwise.

When asked about the kids that fool around, she responded,

You have to realize that they are six years old, and when you have a bucket of books in front of you and maybe you can't read it is frustrating and hard. What helps is that we do have themes, so that if a child enjoys learning about transportation, for example, the books are there. We also have leeway; if a child gets bored with an area we'll tell them to talk to us and we'll see what we can do. We've got a range of books within each basket so that no child feels that they are all so hard or so difficult. We've got some picture books going up to a third-grade level within each basket. Hopefully, kids aren't bored very often. Also we try to partner kids up with someone with similar interests within their group, and if there's a big problem then I'll say, "Pick a book that you know how to read and read it to me," and once you've kind of established that readerly kind of behavior in the beginning of the time then it carries through and helps them get through craziness.

When asked about reading aloud to the children, she answered,

Oh yes, we honestly try to do it about eight times a day. It is a good transition thing. Each time we have a transition it is like a story or a

poem. We're starting poetry now. We have been reading lots of poems all year, but now we are reading more and more poems.

Tracy's interest in people and places does, of course, include an interest in languages.

We have someone who comes in to work with the children in Spanish, and we also do it on our own through song in our class. We definitely have literature in Spanish. We don't have books in Arabic, and it's also very hard to find books in Chinese.

Another way Tracy nurtures herself is through her writing which was motivated, in part, through her participation in a writing project.

What's great about the writing project is that they force you to write. It's hard as an adult, I think, to just sit down and write. There is like a real fear in just writing stuff down, and I don't know why. We started these journals there, and I've actually kept up with mine as just sort of like an experience kind of thing.

This, too, she transfers to her work with her students.

We've done it with the kids, too. They gave it to us, and it was all wrapped up, and our teacher showed us hers, and it was great. It's a place where I cut out articles and write down things that are important to me. So I do sometimes; I try to keep up and write it down. I wouldn't have given it that much importance in my life if it weren't for last summer [the writing project]. It's interesting because the connections between me and the kids became different too because I can bring in my journal and show them the stuff that I do, and then it becomes, "Whoa, Tracy has a writing journal, look at my journal!" You sort of model stuff.

Family History

My brother and I were read to every single night. It was a ritual with my parents to read to us out of a big huge fairy tale book. I think kids like to know about other places and other people: we are all alike, we are all different. So it is nice to think about it in a bigger sense.

My mother would always read to us, and my father would tuck us in. That is just how it would work each night, and we knew it. We would beg to be read to, and once we finished the book we would start over. It was one of our very favorite books, and it had great illustrations, and the stories were long, and we would hate to stop in the middle, but we would anyway.

All the stories were our favorites. There wasn't one in particular. It was just the way the words would roll off my mom's tongue. I think that got us so happy and the great illustrations sort of put us to sleep. I remember never wanting her to stop reading. Then later when I discovered authors and things, I had to read a book in full, I could never just put it down and stop reading. It had to be the whole book or nothing.

Tracy remembered the story of Jack and Jill as significant in her early reading.

The reason I remember it so well is because we were asked to think about it for the writing project last summer, so I thought about it a lot. It occurred to me that Jack and Jill *was the first book that I was able to read or at least felt able to read. I remember being in my room which had this plush purple carpet and being on the floor, and it was a big mess and my parents' room was directly to the right, and their door was closed. I remember banging on their door after I had finished reading it, and I was just hysterical like it was this massive emergency and everyone had to come out and listen to me read. My father came to see what was going on and I was like, "I can read, I can read!"*

However, in school, she remembers reading in a different way from her excitement of reading at home.

In school we had basal readers, and everyone had a paragraph, and I know I'm not the only person who counted the paragraphs ahead and even one ahead and one below so that you were covered if someone didn't end up reading. You never wanted to stumble when reading in front of the class! I would read very quickly and would always be asked to stop because I was very nervous to read in front of the class. We sat in rows, and there was no library. The only literature we had were those big thick books with the questions at the end of each story. Every two weeks or so we would visit the school library to get the kind of literature that we use now in the classroom.

While this excitement about the newly learned ability to read was great, in Tracy's family the languages of English and Spanish were accepted as a matter of course.

My parents are both bilingual. My father is Cuban, and my mother is Puerto Rican so their first languages are both Spanish. In their time they spoke a lot of Spanish when they were together, and a lot of my family members are Spanish speaking. My grandmother does, and she sort of raised us while my parents were working when we were younger. Preschool was when I really came in contact with English because until then I believe it was only in Spanish that I communicated. I don't even remember learning English at all, it just sort of happened.

There was no bilingual program in the preschool or in the first and second grades she attended.

As a teen Tracy loved

Judy Blume and all the other classics like The Catcher in the Rye *and any of those that are part of the repertoire of the private school. Fine reading was given and then just what I liked to read on my own too.*

Her interest in other people which began with the fairy tales continued.

In high school I was interested in South Africa because of a course I took and a teacher I had who had been in South Africa, so I read a lot of short stories and stuff from South Africa.

This interest in people and places expanded further in college.

There was a group called "Two Peoples, One Land" which was always a center of attention on our campus. It was composed of Jewish students as well as Arab students, and it was when Settlements, which are still being built, were a very hot topic. They had asked Edward Said to come to Wesleyan to speak. He had declined on several occasions, but his nephew had gone to Wesleyan, so we were able to get him in. This was about five years ago. There were strikes and petitions signed that he shouldn't come. A lot of his literature was like basic stuff for a lot of the classes covering Islam or whatever. So he came to our campus, and it was such a big deal: there were vigils, there was a lot of anger: there was just craziness! Two years before that a Bishop had spoken about Palestine at a graduation which was really huge, and articles came out, and there was that craziness. I started taking more and more classes that had to do with the Middle East and became more interested in the history of it, which is so rich and so interesting. When you meet the author of a book you want to read all of his books and everything that he has got to say. So it was fortunate that his literature was basic reading for most of the classes, and I was able to read a lot of his stuff and also met him, Said, and went to his piano recitals and stuff. It was nice to feel like I knew this great person, this important author!

Another powerful influence on Tracy's career is her mother.

> *My mother is a principal at a school that's not far away from here. I think that when you've got a parent that loves their job the way she does it makes a big difference. It used to make us crazy when we were little because she always used to talk about other kids and we were the ones waiting on the corner until 3:30. But, it's really amazing to have someone in your life who is so in awe of kids and is so in love with what she does. It still makes us crazy because it's almost like over the top, but when you have that experience in your life it sort of rubs off on you. My brother tutors kids in the summers; there's a connection there, and you're sort of molded, I mean "apples don't fall far from the tree." I did major in anthropology, but I just love kids, and her experiences have been so great, and I've learned so much from her it was more like, how could I not teach? She's so helpful and wonderful, and whenever I have a problem I have this resource that is in my life.*

Resisting Reader/Teacher

"What I am trying to suggest, therefore, is the still-depressed nature of public discourse [about Palestine] in the U.S., which lags dramatically behind its counterparts in most of Western Europe and, of course, in the Third World" (Said, 1992, xi). Tracy works to open public discourse

> *to the best I can. I really enjoy ethnography, and I enjoy the Middle East because it is an area that I know a lot about.*

And she recognizes the reality of risk taking in the world of teaching.

> *You take risks every day in terms of what kids you reach today and what kids you do not. Do you do reading centers, or do you pull them out on ability basis? Do you let kids kind of roam around and have a good time, or are you more structured? There is so much that happens in any given day, every little thing. I think about if I had a child and how I would want the teacher to interact with the child or how would I want my child's experience to be. That's really always my reference point which is sort of hard because I'm so young and so far from having children. I always think if this were my kid what would I want for them? If a child doesn't understand pointing to words do I work on that today or do I work on sight-word vocabulary? If it is a beautiful day outside do I skip math because I want everyone to notice signs of spring? There's*

always a little bit of give and take, and you're not quite sure where things may fall, so I think you take risks in almost everything.

She takes risks by the ongoing activity of team teaching.

Team teaching is extremely difficult depending on who you're working with. It was a choice. It's hard because you have to be able to work with someone that you respect but there are also some kinds of limits. It's hard to be with a friend, and Manny and I are friends, and it's been difficult to work with a friend; where do you draw the line? He's got changes in his life like a new baby and things, so if you're not at the same mental points in your life it sometimes becomes difficult. It's hard to make time because when you're doing lesson plans or projects there has to be someone else there with you. The time component has really been an issue, that is probably the hardest thing.

However, the advantages to team teaching are obvious to her.

In terms of assessment like when we talk to parents, we've got two points of view. Whenever you have questions about a child you have someone to talk to. You've got two of everything. Even when you have to leave the room quick with a child, someone is there. It is incredible what a difference just another body makes. You've got a bigger pool of ideas from which to draw, and our conversations are just so rich about the kids. I could talk to anyone about my kids, but when I talk to Manny he knows exactly what I'm talking about. It is great in terms of being effective and just getting their ideas as a teacher on how to reach kids.

Also,

What's great about having us both here is that we are equally as important in the classroom; we both have a say. There is no kind of power dynamic.

The type of parent involvement in Tracy and Manny's room is very active. They both resist restraints of time and apathy.

We try to involve parents as much as we can. What Manny and I do which has worked very well is once a month we'll sit down in front of the phone and call every single parent and talk about something great that has been working or maybe something they should work on at home. Kids love to hear our voice over the phone, and it's really an exciting thing, and I don't think enough people take the time to do it. We also have parent/teacher conferences. We always answer notes, always, no matter what! It's great that there are two of us because the second I get a note I'll go and make the phone call. We had a month where it was "bring someone who is important in your life to school." We try to really integrate parents and have them be a part of the classroom. We send them letters telling them what we're working on and ask for suggestions. We send a monthly calendar home. We have writing celebrations and reading celebrations, and we are going to have a social studies celebration. We started the beginning to the year with a breakfast where parents could meet, and we sent out everyone's names and phone numbers.

"To survive the Borderlands you must live *sin fronteras,* be a crossroads" (Anzaldúa, 1987, 195).

References

Anzaldúa, G. (1987). *Borderlands.* San Francisco: Spinsters.

Behar, R. (1993). *Translated woman: Crossing the border with Experanza's story.* Boston: Beacon Press.

Said, E. W. (1992). *The question of Palestine.* New York: Vintage Books, xi.

———. (1990). Reflections on exile. In R. Ferguson, M. Gever, T. T. Minh-ha, C. West (Eds.), *Out there: Marginalization and contemporary cultures.* 357–366.

9

Donn Renee Morson-McKie

At the time I lived in a neighborhood where you couldn't go outside and play with other children because it wasn't safe at all. When I had the chance to actually see other children on TV playing and going outside in the sunshine. . . . Sesame Street was really fantasy land for me. To be able to go to the store and talk to the people there, that was fantasy.

—Donn Renee Morson-McKie

As we considered our interview with Donn, a first-grade teacher in a Brooklyn public school, we kept connecting the child Donn with Cassie, Faith Ringgold's visionary young heroine in *Tar Beach* (1991), and we related the adult teacher-artist Donn to the artist Faith Ringgold who taught for many years in the New York City Public Schools while she was painting and working in soft sculpture.

Ringgold, whose great-grandmother, as a slave in antebellum Florida, made quilts as part of her duties, began using quilts as vehicles for stories about the experience of the black female in America. Cassie, the narrator of *Tar Beach* dreams of being free to go wherever she wants for the rest of her life. Flying is how she will achieve her dream, echoing an important motif in African American folk literature, in which flying to freedom was a metaphor for escaping from slavery. Virginia Hamilton (1985) retold the African American tale, *The People Could Fly*: "There was a great outcryin. The bent backs straightened up. Old and young who were called slaves and could fly joined hands. . . . But they didn't shuffle in a circle. They didn't sing. They rose on the air. They flew in a flock that was black against the heavenly blue. . . . Way above the plantation, way over the slavery land. Say they flew away to *Freedom*" (171). Cassie fulfills Ringgold's vision of a black female doing heroic creative things, the same women she celebrated in her quilt-become-book, *Dinner at Aunt Harriet's House* (1993). *Tar Beach* is the transformation of Ringgold's memories of childhood. Her family often went up on the roof on hot summer nights where she lay on a mattress looking up at the stars. The site of *Tar Beach,* first written on fabric strips around the border of a quilt because she could not get the story published, is the rooftop of an apartment house that Ringgold sees now from windows of her Harlem apartment: "Well, Daddy is going to own that building, 'cause I'm gonna fly over it and give it to him. Then it won't matter that he's not in their old union, or whether he's colored or a half-breed Indian, like they say" (Ringgold, 1991).

The interview with Donn brings together themes relevant to Ringgold's books and other works of art: the magical power of art and imagination and the role of art and imagination in creating a place, a neighborhood. This relates to the rethinking of the narrative of neighborhood and construction of the "poetry of neighborhood" discussed by Crichlow (1995) who described different maps of a neighborhood drawn by parents and children. In *Tar Beach,* Ringgold celebrates Cassie's view of her city, from above. In the story of this teacher we also gain insights into the importance of the media in the lives of young children, for the media gave Donn a neighborhood.

"Sesame Street" has been criticized in the past as a "sell-out," an unhealthy concoction which increased children's dependence on short-term sensory stimulation for learning. In this time of intensified efforts by some Republican legislators to cut all funding for educational programming on public television and radio, Donn's story shows us how important this window is for children both in their reading of the world and in, literally, learning to read.

Television, "Sesame Street" in particular, gave Donn three things: it taught her to read; it gave her a neighborhood; and it stimulated her interest in art, in the visual image that would shape her life. In her story, all of these themes circle as in the wings of the butterfly and make her the teacher that she is.

Metaphor and Art as Frameworks for Living

I remember "Sesame Street," "Electric Company," "Zoom," things like that and getting involved with the singing and acting out of certain things. I was an only child up until I was about twelve years old, so since I didn't have anyone at home I would interact with the TV. My mom encouraged me to watch programs like "Sesame Street," "Electric Company," and "Zoom," and she always tells me that I learned how to read from those programs, and a lot of my skills came from those. She would read to me sometimes, and then one day I just picked up a book, I believe it was a Dr. Suess book, and I started reading it to her, and she was amazed. I got a lot from those programs. I think it was the fact that I could identify, I saw other children.

I loved that blue monster, Grover! I also loved Bert and Ernie because they were pals, and I thought it was so funny that they were living together without a mommy. Big Bird was okay, but I was a little scared of him.

Then I was blessed to have my stepmother enter my life whom I didn't really meet until I was in school, and she encouraged me a lot with reading and things like that, but the school experiences that I remember were not the greatest. Honestly, if someone would have told me in elementary school that I was going to become a teacher I would have told them that they were crazy because I did not like my teachers.

When I finally did graduate from high school and said I was going to go to college I really didn't know what I was going to do.

If I didn't go to Tech I don't know what would have happened. Tech is a technical school where they teach you mechanical drawing and things like that. It's right downtown Brooklyn. They teach you architecture and pattern making, and that part appealed to my artistic side.

The more I think about it the more I feel (and I haven't really discussed this with anyone) like I might want to engage in making books for children because it seems like that is my next goal. I really think I am going to lean towards that.

Donn is an accomplished school artist to whom other teachers turn for help. She gently encourages her students to create.

I try not to show them as much. I've had other teachers come to me and ask me to draw a caricature of something and I'll draw it and then if I have a student take it to such and such a room or they'll see it displayed and say, "Oh, Ms. McKie did that" but I try not to show them because I don't want them to think that their drawings have to be perfect. Sometimes drawing is a chore, especially if you are asked to do it; it is fun if you can do it all on your own. Sometimes I have to step back and say to the children "If you want to illustrate it then go for it" because sometimes we just don't have the urge to pick up our pencil and draw.

Maxine Greene (1995a) describes the roles of imagination: to help create "as if" worlds, to create alternative realities, to synthesize the finite with infinite, particular with universal, and to give the visionary power to transform fear and despair. Within this framework, narrative and storytelling become ways of knowing. Within this narrative framework details are the means of connection. Greene (1995b) describes how details allow the imaginations both of teller and of receiver of the story to particularize, to see and hear things in their concreteness. Details overcome abstractions (29, 36). "The Power of the image is basic to all ideation," she says (1995a), showing how the mind grasps objects— leather ball, silk dress—and they become carriers of meaning. What language uncovers is the meaning of these objects in a life narrative. Diane Brunner (1994, 1995) expands the world of objects by emphasizing the central role of media in construction of the image and the connection between these images and the spiritual in children's lives. She (1994) describes how image making constructs identity through a narrative myth making as "embodied narrative seems to be much more than the articulation of what is understood, more than the framing and understanding of one's experiences, more than play with words . . . this applies to narratives we read, narratives we write, and narratives we vocalize, and, indeed, even those we think but never vocalize" (17–18). Brunner (1995) also suggests that those whom society has marginalized create new myths because patriarchic archetypes such as the conquering hero are not universal.

Donn's is a story of creation of community. She constructs it with artifacts, objects that helped her create a community for herself: Grover, Cookie Monster, Bert, Ernie, and other puppets, the corner store. Toni Morrison (1987) describes the writing of a memoir as a process of gaining access to interior life, "a kind of literary archeology; on the basis of some information and a little guesswork you journey to a site to see what remains were left behind and to reconstruct the world that these remains imply" (104). This metaphor aptly describes Donn's oral storytelling.

Objects become the generative images in our memories. The objects that peopled Donn's neighborhood and her mind worked somewhat the way a Schmidt's beer sign in another city worked for Patricia Hampl (1981). Hampl described herself as a young girl looking down on the neighborhood where she was born and how an image, an object from that neighborhood, instilled the rhythms that would later shape her writing:

> From the St. Clair Hill I looked down on the West Seventh neighborhood, the name of the area taken from its main street. My park bench was situated so that I saw not only the unremarkable houses of the old neighborhood, but the Schmidt Brewery sign, mounted above the nineteenth-century brick factory, that spelled over and over, like an eternal one-word spelling bee, the name S-C-H-M-I-D-T in neon-red chancel-style letters. I looked down on the old neighborhood as if from an airplane, as if on my way to somewhere more important. I was higher, bigger, more life-size

than the toy houses and cars and streets, the miniature twig trees and tiny doll people down there. The only thing approaching my dimension was the brewery itself and its blinking sign. Hypnotized, I watched this sign for hours, for whole seasons. I think I sat there just to watch it. "We know our own rhythms," I read years later in Muriel Rukeyser's book, *The Life of Poetry.* "Our rhythms are more recognizably our selves than any of our forms." Yes. And once again, as so many times before and later, the Schmidt sign blinked behind my eyes. (15)

Nurturance Past and Present (Self and Others)

In another similarity to Cassie in *Tar Beach* who taught her brother to fly above the city, Donn taught her younger brother and his friends. It was concern for him that led her into teaching. In Cassie's words: "I have told him it's very easy, anyone can fly. All you need is somewhere to go that you can't get to any other way. The next thing you know, you're flying among the stars" (Ringgold, 1991). Donn says:

> *I always thought about teaching, especially after my brother was born because I loved children, but that came way after elementary school. My brother was born when I was twelve, and I really loved being with him and his little friends and teaching him abc's and new songs and watching him grow.*
>
> *I hate to admit this, but I really did not decide to become a teacher until I sat in the admissions office and I had to take this entrance exam where you had to put your name and your major. That's when I decided; I put Early Childhood, and I went to King's Burrow Community College, and I met up with some of the most fantastic professors. I met up with Eleanor Barr and Judith Danoff, and they just opened up the world, they really did, and that's what encouraged me to go forward with it. They had all these fantastic ideas, and I said, "This is what I want, I want it to be fun. I want kids not to want to drop out of school," because that was my biggest fear, that my brother or another relative was going to be pressured to leave school, because in the neighborhood that I grew up in that is all I saw. I saw people hanging out on benches with no real goals or anything, and thank God, because of my family I was scared to death by something like that. People like Judith Danoff and Eleanor Barr really opened up the world for me.*
>
> *Then I started teaching in day cares, and it seemed you did the same thing over and over again. I was appointed into the public school system, and I was hired by Mr. Jenkins, and I took workshops with Pam*

Russell. That's another one that really influenced me. Pam did these writing workshops the first year that I was here on children writing their own journals, and it was introducing them to literature and author studies, and I said, "That is what I want to do!" It is so much fun to be able to bring these kinds of experiences to the children. I've worked with other people in different colleges and things like that—to try to learn different things within the classroom and the kids love it!

Artist-teacher Donn builds a nurturing community within her first-grade classroom. Books are an important meeting place within this community.

A lot of things we do, I try to pull from literature. For instance, we made pancakes after reading Eric Carle's Pancakes. *I like them to illustrate and write about their experiences, because I feel there is a solid connection. I have found that if you do that with words the children really hang on to those words. For instance if you write the word* me *down and then have them draw a picture of themselves next to it they will really hold on to that. I have been trying to incorporate that a lot into my teaching. When we talk about seasons we'll make a book about seasons. I think the kids really make a connection with writing and drawing. If we talk about dreams I will have them write about what they want to become. We also do a lot of game playing. We play word games, jeopardy-type games, math relay races on the board. I really try to make it fun, not too many work sheets. We do a lot of planting and hands-on things. I feel that the children really do need their hands on something and not be glued to the chair at all times with a pencil and paper.*

We have what we call "DEAR" time (drop everything and read), and there's is a book entitled DEAR Time, *and it shows that this time happens and the whole school stops what they are doing and reads, and that is what I encourage the children to do.*

Most of what I read now is related to my job. I read a lot of children's books and a lot of literature related to how to teach. That's most of the reading that I do opposed to daily newspapers and things. In the summer time I might pick up a book and try to read it, but honestly, if it's not related to teaching, I really won't pick it up, and it's sad, but it's true.

When asked to discuss her views about censorship Donn responds in the context of the requirements of a nurturing classroom:

Honestly, as I've gone through the years in teaching I haven't censored books, but there have been times when I have left certain types of books out, and I guess that is a type of censorship. I feel that we don't have the right to take books off the shelf, but we have the right to choose which books we encourage in the classroom. There are some books that have children calling other children names that I might actually read to the kids, but I won't use the names that they use like stupid. I might take out certain words, but I think that those books are still good books except for that type of language. There could be that one little part that you disagree with, but the rest of it might be something that you really want to get through to them. Now back to censorship, when they have their time in the front, and they see that book that I read, and they see that word and look at me like, You didn't say that word! I could get away with that in September but not now that they are reading. You know, when we start off the year and we go over the rules and talk about respecting each other's feelings and calling each other by their own names so every moment after that is a teacher's moment.

Family History

A classroom for a young child is a life world; each year brings new forms of power, of possibility, of despair. As educators we are responsible for making school a place in which a child matters-a place away from the edges.

—Polokow, 1993, 162

Donn's reading history returns to a theme common with most of the teachers in this study—the negative, limiting effects of rigid classroom on young children.

Rigid classrooms are not limited to poor children; they cut across the socioeconomic spectrum and across all age and grade levels. Goodlad (1984, 229) has documented the predominance of teacher talk and lack of choice and decision making in elementary and secondary classrooms across the country. This becomes even more damaging when applied to the teaching of poor children.

Polakow (1993) documents research delineating the ways in which poor children receive a class-based education which focuses on drill and rote learning and emphasizes mechanical skills.

In these classrooms children who are different or poor, many of them bright and lively and talkative, are constructed as impaired when they disrupt rigid classroom routines that permit neither time nor space for imagination, for transformation of what they are taught. We return to Donn's description of her preschool experiences with literacy, this time to look at the roles played by her mother and her stepmother. Donn's story deconstructs the popular myths of "mother blaming" against women in our culture. Lubek (1995) discusses cultural subtexts in statements by principals, teachers, and social commentators: *"There are not any parents (meaning mothers) there to show them that there's good stuff on TV; Parents (meaning mothers) are not really concerned about what their kids are doing anymore"* (51). Donn talks about the influences of two mothers in her developing literacy. Her working—student mother is the one who encouraged her to watch educational television and who listened to her first attempts at reading.

> *My mom encouraged me to watch programs like that and she always tells me that I learned how to read from those programs and a lot of my skills came from them. Before I went to school I knew a lot of the necessary skills for reading, but I wasn't reading yet. My mom had to work full time and go to school, so we didn't have a lot of that "quality time," so when she did get home it was cooking, cleaning, getting me ready, and not too much of the reading. She didn't come from a family that did a lot of that reading at home, so I didn't get a lot of what we encourage parents to do now.*
>
> *Then I was blessed to have my stepmother enter my life who I didn't really meet until I was in school, and she encouraged me a lot with reading and things like that.*
>
> *My school memories aren't positive memories. I didn't have a lot of fun in school, and I guess that's why I try to make things as fun as possible. When I was in school you had to sit down with that Jane book, and I hated it, and we sat in a semicircle and each person had to read a sentence, and what I would do is count the number of sentences and children so I would know what sentence was going to be mine, and we would not know what was going on in the rest of the story, but you knew your sentence when it was your turn. I remember things like that, and I don't remember ever really enjoying school, and when it came time to go to college I didn't know where I wanted to go. I was just out of it.*
>
> *I was one of the only children in my junior high school to be chosen to go to Brooklyn Tech according to my scores. I was the only one that passed, and my parents were really proud. I didn't even want to go, but I went anyway, and that was another bad experience. I didn't really want to be there, and they didn't offer the things that I really enjoyed, but now looking back, I got a lot from it. They teach you architecture and pattern making, and that part appealed to my artistic side. The basic things I didn't really like because, once again, it wasn't fun. It was like you had to do it, you had to make a 95 percent, and there was a lot of pressure. When*

I finally did graduate from high school and said I was going to go to college I really didn't know what I was going to do.

Donn credits other women teachers for helping her learn to teach. Like so many of the teachers we interviewed, she is determined that the students in her classroom will have a different school experience than she had. She is committed to changing the rigid classroom, the rigid school.

Resisting Reader/Teacher

Last year we did an authors' study on Ezra Jack Keats who the children thought was African American because of his books. A lot of adults think the same way. The kids were shocked when they found out that he was not an African American person.

They wanted to know why Peter and the other characters were African American. I really had to research it and found that Ezra did grow up in a neighborhood like the one in his books, and he was an illustrator; I learned that he had been an illustrator for other writers, and he found that in these books there weren't any black heroes, so he invented his own black hero and that was Peter, so that is how that all came about. I thought it was fantastic! That is what children need to know. You don't have to be an African American to write about African Americans. They love Ezra, and they love Eric Carle with the insects and the nice toy-like books.

I would say that trying new things in a classroom is always a risk, because you're working with people who have been teaching for so many years, and when they see something new they encourage you. That is what I like about this school, they do encourage you. Sometimes though you can't help but feel, Am I doing the right thing by doing all these things that aren't typical? Even though you're praised for it you still question yourself before you do it, because you don't know if the children are going to respond well to it and you won't know until you try; that's a big risk. I think because I didn't like the way I was taught at all, that makes me more willing to try new ways of teaching.

Donn with her artistic talent and sharing of that talent with children expresses in her life the excitement of creation, creation of works of art and creation of a life. Lucille Clifton (1994) described it this way: "What did I see to be except myself?/ I made it up" (8).

Donn told us about teachers of literacy who have fed her vision. Now she continues the heritage, passing on to children what has been passed to her. She told us of her dreams for a future of creating beautiful images to feed the imaginations of children. She also expressed the sense of ongoing struggle described by many of the teachers in this book as they try to make room in their lives for the demands both of teaching and of other creative work.

> *The more I think about it the more I feel like I might want to engage in making books for children because it seems like that is my next goal. I really think I am going to lean towards that. Like I told you before, I've been teaching here for three years, but on the whole it would be closer to eleven years that I've been teaching. I find that maybe I should not be in the classroom now. Maybe I could touch children in another way or even another grade, because sometimes you just get bored. Maybe still doing this but also doing something else because I would really hate to leave a lot of children. You think about how many children that you did touch and how many children still keep in contact and want you to go to their birthday parties.*

References

Brunner, D. (1994). *Inquiry and reflection.* Albany, N.Y: State University of New York Press.

———. (1995). Worlds of difference: Urban educators speak out on identity and community-school reform. Paper presented at the American Educational Research Association meeting in San Francisco, CA.

Clifton, L. (1994). *The book of light.* Port Townsend, WA: Copper Canyon Press.

Crichlow, W. (1995). Rethinking the narrative of urban neighborhood: Perspectives on the social context and processes of identity formation among African American youth. Paper presented at the American Educational Research Association meeting in San Francisco, CA.

Goodlad, J. (1984). *A place called school.* New York: McGraw-Hill Book Co.

Greene, M. (1995b). *Releasing the imagination: Essays on education, the arts, and social change.* San Francisco, CA: Jossey-Bass Publishers.

———. (1995a). What the arts do with experience. Paper presented at the American Educational Research Association meeting in San Francisco, CA.

Hamilton, V. (1985). *The People Could Fly.* New York: Alfred A. Knopf.

Hampl, P. (1981). *A romantic education.* Boston: Houghton Mifflin.

Lubek, S. (1995). Mothers at risk. In Swadener, B., Lubek, S. (Eds.), *Children and Families "At Promise": The social construction of risk.* Albany: State University of New York Press.

Morrison, T. (1987). The site of memory. In William Zinsser (Ed.), *Inventing the truth: The art and craft of memoir* . Boston: Houghton Mifflin.

Polokow, V. (1993). *Lives on the edge: Single mothers and their children in the other America*. Chicago: University of Chicago Press.

Ringgold, F. (1993). *Dinner at Aunt Connie's house*. New York: Hyperion Books.

———. (1991). *Tar beach*. New York: Scholastic, Inc.

10

Wayne Wazouko

Before we start I would like to add that much of the literacy during my youth was done orally. I remember some of the stories. Most of the stories were passed down from grandfather to grandfather. Mostly animal stories, stories of valor, stories of helping each other. There were also some bad stories that I never understood. These stories were used to keep the kids from going out at night. We would gather around a campfire, and the eldest would talk, a lot of times it was the grandmother. We all sat close to the fire nobody talked, not even babies cried. This is where a lot of the learning about my culture took place.

—Wayne Wazouko

Thomas Peacock (personal communication, April 8, 1995) explains that the Anishinabe (Ojibwe) people tell many stories about Waynabozho, a half spirit, half human. Waynabozho stories are often used to explain life to young children. Why is it dogs are always sniffing? Why do birch trees have black marks? These and many other questions are answered in Waynabozho stories.

Wayne remembers belonging in this circle of culture gathered around the campfire. He was able to see later many juxtapositions between this belonging and his not belonging or feeling welcome. He was able to see later critical aspects of his story left out of what was read and learned at school. Now he is a teacher who has extended his campfire of belonging to include children of many cultures and of both genders in his classroom. The world is a circle, as he sees it, and reminds us of Black Elk's words: "You have noticed that everything an Indian does is in a circle, and that is because the power of the world always works in circles, and everything tries to be round. . . . The wind, in its greatest power, whirls. Birds make their nests in circles, for theirs is the same religion as ours" (Black Elk, in Bigelow, 1991).

Art and Metaphor as Frameworks for Living

We know of land that looks lonely,
but isn't, of beef with hides of velveteen,
of sorrow, an eddy in blood.

—Whiteman, 1984, 1

Like an eddy, this teacher has lived experiences that show vivid contrasts. Like an artist, he uses his gift of vision and expresses himself through his work with children.

I feel that the other students are young and strong, the other students are healthy, yet I'm not. I'm handicapped; they're not. I would rather sit back and do the stuff at my own pace. It is not because I'm shy; I've just never felt in place here.

In his youth, he grappled with contrasts.

I remember a certain detective series that I got into about age fourteen or fifteen. Harold Robbins was a favorite. One of his books was called A Stone for Danny Fisher. *I recall in the book when he passed away that he went through a series of talking to God. He had a choice of living or coming back deformed or blind and handicapped. He chose to die instead of live that way. I can relate to that.*

One thing that the teachers that I have worked with have said about me is that I seem to pick out the ones who need the help the most. I feel good about that, because I went through some of the problems they are going through. If a handicapped kid sees me, they will want to know about [my] leg, because they also have a handicap, we relate right away. It is really a beautiful thing. The Lord has used my handicap for good instead of bad.

Wayne sees the center of his world as his place at the campfire. He does not dwell on the bad; he tells his story through the art of interacting with the students.

For instance that fool crow, picking through the trash near the corral, understands the center of the world as greasy scraps of fat. Just ask him. He doesn't have to say that the earth has turned scarlet through fierce belief, after centuries of heartbreak and laughter—he perches on the blue bowl of the sky, and laughs.(Harjo, 1989)

Nurturance Past and Present (Self and Others)

Wayne has learned what his own needs are for nurturance and reflects this sensitivity in his relationships with his students.

I do really well in college when I can work at my own pace. I feel very uncomfortable being in a classroom setting. I always have. I know that I have some good abilities in some areas; some areas I am pretty weak.

There are a lot of things that, teaching-wise, I know not to do to native American children. If I was in a class of thirty kids and I asked a question. If all the kids throw up their hands with the answer, I would be hesitant to call on the native American kids. A lot of time they will raise their hands just because everyone did; half of the time they might not know the answer. Privately, they might know the answer, but not in front of a group. Also, if I was going to have a native American child read out loud, I would rather have a group of two or three children, if possible, sit with me in a group. Knowing that I was native American, they would open up to me. Because I would be reading with them.

He likes reading even though he said,

I am a slower reader. I am not dumb. I just never had the training. Actually, I guess history books would be my main interest.

Also he explained:

I buy a daily newspaper just to see what the daily events are. I do read the bible every morning. It kind of soothes me for the day.

About reading and literacy in the classroom, he spoke:

In fact, I would probably have one day where we all read silently, including the teacher. And another day I would probably take turns reading with the children. Other times I might have volunteers get up in front of the classroom and read to the class. An interesting idea might be to put a slow reader and a faster reader together and have them read to each other. I think I would probably read the same type of books that they are reading because I missed a lot of it. Although there are probably times I would want to sneak in a newspaper.

American Indian education advisors encourage teachers to seek out elders and those who possess traditional cultural knowledge to come into classrooms to tell stories or to demonstrate cultural expertise (crafts and art) (Peacock, personal communication). It is also stressed that American Indian professionals should be asked to share their expertise, because this sends a powerful message to both American Indian and non-Indian students that this group of adults is important to model.

Wayne likes

the Dr. Suess books. Not only native American culture and folklore, but also black culture. If the story has some sort of a message I think that is very important for children. One of the things about Indian culture is that we are supposed to have respect for elders. That is something that seems to be lacking now days.

About literacy development in the classroom, Wayne says:

It is probably the most important thing of all. I think some of the kids go home, and there is no time or place they can sit down and read. Especially if they are coming out of a semi-bad environment where there might be drinking or drugs, or an overworked mom or dad, or other children. Maybe they are very poor. The children may not even have time to study at home, much less read. That is why I think that classroom time is so important.

In his dream classroom, Wayne would include

literature for every age level, every ethnic group. Good stories for both boys and girls. Things that would encourage them to stay in school, explore science and music and poetry. The books would be of different levels for children of differing abilities. I would also like to have a VCR with a television in the school, where if there is something important going on, like the space shuttle, we could plug right into it. The children would have enough books available to show children how to study . . . to address particular problems they may have.

Indicative of his inclusive nature and visionary ability, Wayne wants to continue to learn.

I would like to continue to expand my areas of interest. There are other cultures I would like to get into. Very much I would like to learn about the Vietnamese children. There is not much literature about these peoples. In the classroom I would like to have a library including every race I can imagine. The more we learn about different cultures, the better we will get along. I think it is very important for children to get this at a young age.

Michael Dorris concurs that "children must be made aware that many people are wrong-headed about not only Native Americans, but about cultural pluralism in general" (Dorris, 1991, 13)

Family History

Wayne's first memory of a book or reading was difficult to call up.

I am having a hard time going back to early childhood, although I do remember something from grade four. I am not sure if it was Cinderella or Black Beauty. My family, as a youth, had horses.

Then events began to show him the contradictions:

In about grade five or six I remember reading a book about Custer, and he was my hero. At grade six I was shipped out to a boarding school in Wakapaula, South Dakota. There I learned a little bit about my culture from other native American kids. Then I quit liking Custer so much. I started reading sports figures like Babe Ruth. Jim Thorpe was my hero. He won the decathlon in, I believe, the 1924 Olympics. Bill Mills, another native American athlete from my era also won the Olympic gold. Any native American who did well in history I tried to read a lot about.

Literature which reflects alternative ways of knowing from voices that have traditionally been silenced in the United States must be available to students. Wayne found the stories about native American sports heroes. He needed access to more stories that reflected his world, his people.

Wayne describes his home literacy environment when he was a child:

Being a native American family, we had eleven children plus two or three cousins or relatives we were taking care of. We didn't really have a lot of books. But I read the Sunday newspaper. Life magazine and Look magazine, I remember reading them a lot.

His parents read

very little. We had too many children, and my dad was a carpenter, who was gone six days a week working. My mother was overwhelmed with all her responsibilities.

In his own reading he says,

> *I remember a certain detective series that I got into about age fourteen or fifteen. Harold Robbins was a favorite. One of his books was called* A Stone for Danny Fisher. *I recall in the book when he passed away that he went through a series of talking to God. He had a choice of living or coming back deformed or blind and handicapped. He chose to die instead of live that way. I can relate to that.*

He goes back to the tragic yet hopeful example of his vision to see paradoxes that occurred in childhood:

> *As a real young person, I really liked the cowboy and Indian magazines. I always found the cowboy to be a hero. Of course, through time I found out that I was an Indian and I was supposed to be on the other side of the fence during their shootouts. I learned to dislike General Custer. Not in a hateful way, more of an understanding.*

In the boarding school literacy experiences were bleak.

> *It was forced reading. We had a certain time where we all sat in rows and were told what to read, when to read it, and how much to read. We actually had to finish the reading within a certain time frame. We had to have a certain amount of chapters read in twenty minutes. I have always been a slow reader, so I really had a lot of problems in the classroom. I, myself, would never teach children to read in that fashion. I understand that all children are different in ability. We all have things we are very strong in and things that we are not very strong in. You can't force a child to read faster than they are capable of doing.*
>
> *The school was so structured that you never really had any fun reading. I was a slow reader. I had to relax and make sure no one was watching me to tease me. In the school setting, I usually just turned pages to make sure the teacher didn't box my ears.*
>
> *It was mostly the three R's. We didn't have music. We didn't have theater. We had a grade one through twelve school. But there were never any plays put on or anything. I think the closest thing to a play that I saw was in church. When I got back into the public school they did have theater, but I had no interest in it because I had never been exposed to it, and I was afraid. I think that for the younger children it is more of a natural thing, but if you wait too long it becomes more of an unnatural thing.*
>
> *We had to do little book reports, I really did bad there. I didn't do so bad in the Indian boarding schools with their grading system. I was*

doing A and B work in the boarding schools, but when I got back into the public schools, I went down to C and D work. That was probably the reason I never went through ninth grade. I got a GED and went to college later. My grade point average in college has been good. I just don't have the study habits I wish I did. I think I missed something as a youth. In the boarding schools, everything was done right in the schools. You didn't take home any assignments because nobody did them anyways.

Resisting Reader/Teacher

As a youth, in boarding school, we had teachers that were so mean I swear they could have been military sergeants. They really didn't know how to relate to us. We were told it was a shameful thing to be an Indian. I remember getting my hair shaved. I remember the people that ran the boarding school would hypnotize us and make us sing "God Bless America." For a part of my life I actually turned against any thought of anything good about America. At about age twenty-eight or thirty I looked in the mirror and decided that I couldn't blame society, and I've accepted myself for who I am. I'm native American, but I'm also a white person. I have French blood and also some German, and I'm proud of that now.

Some of the old stereotyping I would probably throw out of the classroom. I'm sure you have seen the books. Stereotyping blacks, Asians, Indians, even whites—it is all the same. Anything that makes someone less than what they are I really have a problem with.

Regarding the issue of gender, Wayne comments,

I think boys seem to want outdoor things. One good thing is that both of them [boys and girls] seem to have a sense of athletics. They both want to play on a ball team. They both want to swim. When I was little, the girls were not given this opportunity. I think boys tend to stay away from things like cooking and gardening.

When asked about whether he believes sexism is a problem in society, he answered:

I know it is definitely a problem. Among native American people, the women—and I'm not sure if it is for better or worse—are mostly the leaders. I don't like crude jokes, and I hear them a lot from men. If somebody is vulgar I get up and leave. The fact is though, if the man talks like that, he probably acts like that at home. His little boy could sit around him and develop a bad attitude for later on in life.

This concerns him especially when he must act regarding children he loves.

I have had to step in front of a girl student a few times when a boy student was acting like he was going to hit her. I loved him, but he was a pretty mean kid. I don't think a girl should have to go through something like that.

Wayne is able to see critical aspects of life in order to include children of many cultures and of both genders in his world. His circle nourishes him. He tells his stories and does his work. As Paula Gunn Allen (1991) explains: "And in all of those stories she told who I was, who I was supposed to be, whom I came from, and who would follow me. In this way she taught me the meaning of the words she said, that life is a circle and everything has a place within it" (51).

References

Allen, P. G. (1991). *Grandmothers of the light: A medicine woman's source book.* Boston: Beacon Press.

Black Elk. (1991).In B. Bigelow, B. Miner, and B. Peterson (Eds.), *Rethinking Columbus.* Milwaukee: Rethinking Schools, 51.

Dorris, M. (1991). Why I'm not thankful for Thanksgiving. In B. Bigelow, B. Miner, and B. Peterson (Eds.), *Rethinking Columbus.* Milwaukee: Rethinking Schools, 13.

Harjo, J. (1989). *In mad love and war.* Boston, MA: Wesleyan University Press.

Peacock, T. (1995). Personal communication. Duluth, MN.

Whiteman, R. H. (1984). *Starquilt.* Minneapolis, MN: Holy Cow Press.

11

Del Tideman

Del Tideman is a second grade teacher in a northern Minnesota city. A master teacher who influences both teaching colleagues and the preservice teachers with whom she works, Del epitomizes the "teacher as intellectual" described by Giroux (1992):

> If teachers are to take an active role in raising serious questions about what they teach, how they are to teach, and the larger goals for which they are striving, it means they must take a more critical role in defining the nature of their work as well as in shaping the conditions under which they work. In my mind, teachers need to view themselves as intellectuals who combine conception and implementation, thinking and practice. (19)

"I am so fortunate," a preservice teacher who worked in Del's classroom said. "I saw her doing all the things that I read and learned were the best ways to teach."

Del grew up in a middle-class, rural environment and attended small schools. Without wide experience in her life, she grew to be a gifted teacher with unusual sensitivity to differences in children. This sensitivity finds expression in the curriculum which she creates for them. Through her supportive family experiences, her negative early school experiences, her reading, her critical thought and continuing study, she became a "resistant" teacher who has, quietly and with great competence, been able to analyze critically traditional educational discourse and create a discourse like the one described by Giroux (1992). "Within such a discourse teachers can develop an emancipatory pedagogy that relates language and power, takes popular experiences seriously as part of the learning process, combats mystification and helps students to reorder the raw experiences of their lives" (20).

Whole language and process writing are discourses which set the conditions for Del's teaching practice and determine the categories that organize her thinking about that practice. She is one of the visionary teachers who have applied a constructivist view of learning and knowledge with an emphasis on social context to her literacy curriculum. Both whole language and process writing deal with the child's construction of meaning in a socially meaningful context. One manifestation of that view in literacy instruction is in the shift from skills-based to process instruction. Many positive benefits of the use of this instructional philosophy have been reported. Classroom practitioners (Routman, 1994; Atwell, 1987) and academic researchers (Graves, 1983, 1990, 1995; Calkins, 1991, 1995; Hansen, 1987; Goodman, 1990) have led this movement which has changed the beliefs of many educators about the nature of literacy learning. This, in turn, has altered pedadogy. The literature in this area purports that the use of the process approach to literacy enables young writers to be in control of the reading and writing task. The approach relates to children's own passions and purposes and gives power to students as individuals and as members of groups.

Implementation of these theories requires a kind of "quiet heroism" from teachers in the face of resistance from an educational community afraid of change and dependent upon a structured basal approach to teaching reading in the primary grades. This "quiet heroism" is the metaphor that emerges from Del's reading autobiography. By the term *quiet heroism* we mean the change agent who is unintentionally political described by Shannon (1992): "All teachers are political, whether they are conscious of it or not. Their acts contribute to or challenge the status quo in literacy education, in schools and in society" (3).

Metaphor and Art as Frameworks for Living

My favorite book while growing up was about a little helicopter, It was like Hector the Helicopter. It is an old Golden Book. It is as old as the hills. It is about a little helicopter that wanted to be big. It is taped and ripped, and I think my mom still has it. I'd love to get the book for my son, Jake. He would just love it, so would Anica, my daughter.

I liked it because this helicopter cried and had all of these feelings. He couldn't do what all of the big airplanes could do, and in the end he did. It is just a successful story about a hero. I really got into the Hardy Boys. The other ones . . . Nancy Drew. The Hardy boys were originally bought for my brother. But eventually we (my brother, sister, and I) read all of them. The Laura Ingals Wilder books. They are still on my parents' shelves. They are keeping them for grandchildren.

I liked the characters from the Laura Ingals Wilder books and Nancy Drew—the girls that were doing all of these neat things that I didn't do, that I didn't have enough guts to do. Or when reading about Laura Ingals Wilder, I would say, "They didn't have that." It would just intrigue me. But I would love reading about their adventures that we didn't do.

I am still so keyed into authors in my teaching too. You take authors and develop clusters. And you didn't see that before, and it puts a different meaning into these books that you know the people behind them. I am reading A Time to Kill *by John Grisham; I have read* The Firm. *I got into the author. I get into the author kick. Then I read every V. C. Andrews book. Then I read every Mary Higgins Clark Book, which are probably my favorite. They are the mysteries, and one of them took place in Minnesota. I love to hit all the books by a certain author. It is always my goal.*

My students read all the Laura Ingalls Wilder books. We had pioneer unit, and we used some of those. The Incredible Journey, *the Beverly Cleary books—those are very popular books. I guess I set the stage for them and tell them that I have read this book. All you have to do is put that bug in their ear, and every library run they are looking for those books. I mentioned the Ribsy books one day, and every one in the library was gone.* The Incredible Journey, *the same way. It becomes hot stuff after the teacher reads and mentions a book.*

Del, like many of the teachers in this study, shares with students the books she loved. She, a female reader, responded to the strong female characters in the Wilder books. This was the basis of her response to the books. Her students also read books that she loved. In this way, a sort of "canon" in children's literature is promoted. Del, as will be seen later in the interview, is constantly learning about new books available and new approaches to teaching. Because of this she also brings in new books for children, books written from social contexts different from her own and different from that represented in the Wilder books. Some people, particularly American Indian people, hate Wilder's *Little House on the Prairie* series because of its negative portrayal of Indians. The limitations of perspective in these books and others are addressed through questioning and discussion that helps even young children to read critically and through the sharing of many books that involve many perspectives. The multitext, response-driven pedagogy used by Del and the other teachers in this study provides the opportunity for children to look at life through eyes different from their own.

Whole language theory emphasizes the connectedness among different functions of literacy skills, for we learn to read by writing and write by reading. Some researchers describe the reading-writing connection as reciprocal, reading as a writing strategy and writing as a reading strategy (Appleby and Langer, 1986). The research also emphasizes the importance of the teacher as literate model.

This very strong belief that good reading and writing teachers must read and write is the cornerstone of the development in children of an "authorship literacy" in which the reader and writer claim ownership for and vigorously participate in the processes of literacy. Del understands the importance of this modeling. She shares her writing with her students.

> *I keep a journal, and I want to write a children's book. I have written one, but I haven't printed it yet. But I wrote one entitled* Moon Peeker. *And it was about the moon peeking in my daughter's window when she was young and very frightened. The book is about the shadows that would come in from the shadows of the moon. It is a poetry type book. I have never published it yet. Sometimes I read to the students what I write. For example, I read a story and poem that I wrote in a teaching writing class about my twin sister. Then they wrote about people important to them.*
>
> *I read books from the "Book Nook." I feel that is a good time to see what I am giving the students to read, and so I know what I am giving parents. I read the kids books. Once in awhile I will read from my own books when I am looking for a lesson. It is the biggest part of the curriculum. Everything revolves around it. The entire day the students are working on this area.*

Del's personal literacy is wholly connected with her teaching. She has a passion for reading and writing, and this becomes the ethos of her classroom. The reading and writing which she does for self-nurturance become a driving force in her professional life. They also shape her relationships with others, her colleagues and her twin sister who is also a teacher.

Nurturance Past and Present (Self and Others)

> *I am one who likes to keep current on educational things. So my goal is to be tuned into the hot-off-the-press educational books with strategies, teacher magazines, and also books for the kids. I get a lot of my information from the book store. I love to sit on the floor in Waldenbooks and read them. They hate when I come in there. That is where I got* The Animal That Drank Up Sound *which is a gorgeous book that no one in*

this school had ever heard of until I brought it. I read to stay current for me professionally and for the kids, because kids don't see these materials if they aren't brought in by teachers.

"Reader's Choice" time is a getaway. It is a free time where your brain can just float and think. It is a great motivator for writing. A relaxer. If the kids are really keyed up at two o'clock in the afternoon, we will just stop everything and go into Reader's Choice. It helps to just slow the pace down.

I have dream students. They are very motivated, independent students, who are self-motivated, who can get excited about anything you do. I would like to be able to go out and buy books on a whim and not have to worry about how much you are spending. To have a library, a fantastic school library, which is very difficult to have. Our school is pretty good. I would like to have incredible resources, fantastic videos, the hot-off-the-press books, videos about the authors and illustrators, to have an unlimited amount of money to buy whatever you need. It would be wonderful to have a permanent book nook and to have permanent books in it. I would like to have a bigger place for centers as centers are a trend and to have motivating areas and activities for students. Currently I just improvise space.

My sources of support are professionals. No one knows if you are not a teacher what goes on in the classroom. Most of my support is my sister who is also a teacher. The people here are a big support too, but you don't always have the time to talk to them. But you have to talk to another teacher. Usually when you get together with another teacher you can gab and gab all night and drive your husbands nuts.

We (my twin sister and I) talk about books a lot. I find a book that I like and tell her about it, and then she is out the next day buying it. If she finds a book that she likes, I am out doing the same thing. Also about neat activities to do, whole language activities, curriculum ideas.

Family History

Even though Del had a difficult time with reading in elementary school, it was a central part of her family life and a source of nurturance for her from the time she was very young. Her early school experiences in reading were very negative, yet she is a self-described "book worm."

My grandma lived with us, and she would read to us because my mom and dad worked. So she would read to us. I don't even remember specific books. But Grandma read every day, because I had a younger four-year-old brother, and he needed something to occupy his time, so she read to us as we sat on her lap. We fit on grandma's lap very nicely. She was kind of a bigger woman, so we fit very comfy.

I don't remember a lot of books being read in school. I remember a lot of basal books being read. I do remember the fairy tales, Cinderella and the Mother Goose rhymes, and some poetry. The basal readers were read day after day.

I do remember the Dick and Jane books, so word by word. It was difficult for me. I was put into another class because it was so difficult for me. And it was word for word. It made no sense to me. All the kids around were reading like gang busters, but I couldn't keep up with them. And it was all out of Horizon Books. Every year we got a new color. It was fun to get a new color.

I was below average, definitely below average. They were going through the basal, I don't even remember if they called it "basal." But they just kept going, and going and I wasn't ready. I was still back in the beginning. I wasn't ready to read one story a day or whatever it was. I am sure I wasn't the only one. But I got lost, and I wasn't noticed until I got punished and sent to the other room.

I came from a very small school, one second grade and one third grade. There were eighteen kids in a class. So I remember going off with a special teacher sometimes alone and sometimes with a group. We'd go over flash cards and letter sounds and words. It wasn't very fun.

We had tons of books around the house. Mom and Dad would read at night, so we would read with them and try to be like them. We'd sit on the couch. They would be reading the newspaper. Dad would read the newspaper, and Mom would always be reading a novel of some type. When we were very young we would look at the pictures. When we got older we'd be in our room reading. We became readers. It was quiet after supper. We weren't big TV buffs either, which was nice.

I remember reading To Kill a Mockingbird, in junior high. I loved that book. We had to do that for school. The Incredible Journey—I enjoyed reading them in our English class, and then we read them elsewhere. That is the first time I remember a teacher that pushed reading. In junior high. That is the first time that I remember a teacher saying, "It is neat to read."

I look back at it now because the memories are so vague of elementary school. I remember junior high. I remember going to the book store, picking books up, and buying books. Reading was tough for me in elementary school, but if I would have done that maybe it wouldn't have been so tough.

Del's family history reinforces the importance of modeling which we have seen in other interviews. Like Lisa Boehlke, the positive influence of home modeling overcame negative school experiences. Both positive and negative school experiences have had a great influence on Del's teaching and may explain why this woman developed the beliefs about literacy that have enabled her to resist a skill-based discourse or approach to teaching and to create curriculum that empowers children.

Resisting Reader/Teacher

I think a big impact of my school experience, now that I think about it, is that I let kids read what they want to read. I don't stick to these yucky basals. They love Stephen Kellogg books; they love Frank Ashe; they know authors' names. They can go to B. Dalton and say I want Swimmy by Leo Lionni. They can name a book and an author. And I could have never done that when I was in elementary school. They know authors and illustrators. They pick books from an author or illustrator whim. It is so different. Their reading is ten times better. They are reading so much more advanced than a second-grade reader. It is an every day thing. Just find a little nook and let's read. And I read. So it is not just the teacher patrolling them like a policeman.

I understand how important school is. I was read to at home. My parents were very supportive. If I would have been more so at school maybe it wouldn't have been so tough. There is an incredible tie between the two. The kids can make it by being read to at home, but their abilities can be even stronger if it is tied to school also, if the teacher is in tune to their likes and dislikes.

I try to satisfy the interests of all my students by doing Reader's Choice, where they every day are in the Book Nook and they have their chance for thirty to forty-five minutes of the day to choose their book. Some kids go for the informational books; others for poetry. They just go for all genres.

I use basal texts a couple days a week. I don't ever use the skill part of the texts. I just read the stories and talk about them and explore ideas. I try to get multiple copies of trade books, such as Tomie de Paola's.

Values influence all our choices as teachers. This is exactly what Friere (1985) means when he says that all teaching is political, even, as in the case of Del, when the teacher is not involved in direct political activism.

> *My values influence what I read aloud in the classroom. I was just talking with someone about environmental things. We were talking about the book* Brother Eagle, Sister Sky. *It is a gorgeous book with the native American idea to it. Not everyone would read that book if they didn't have an environmental or a cultural interest in it. I think that a lot of books are not read because of lack of information or interest. Definitely values have an impact.*

The previous comment may seem exclusive because of her choice of words. In fact, Dell is a very inclusive teacher. The way she says what she says and the words she uses definitely reflect northern Minnesota culture and language use. We hope that this glimpse into Dell's classroom shows that we should look beyond those initial impressions which often arise from culturally influenced linguistic choices.

> *At first when I read* The Stupids *I didn't like the books. Because they were stupid. But as we listened today for "Book Nook" the kids roared. Sometimes I look at thing from too much of an adult point of view. And I forget that their little minds love this stupid kind of stuff. Sometimes I don't like the Dr. Suess books. (That may be terrible for me to say about the famous Dr. Suess.) But they are an insult to the children's intelligence. They are great for preschool, but I am not too keen on them for a first- and second-grade room.*

Critical theorists (Shannon, 1990, Shor, 1987) have criticized whole language advocates because they do not promote action outside the classroom and help students connect their language and literacy to useful transformative currents in their personal lives. These interviews indicate that the most effective literacy teachers are those who do just as these theorists suggest within the social contexts of their own lives. Along with her resistance to skills-based curriculum, Del is aware of and reacts against gender stereotyping.

> *In Pine City there was an almost entirely female staff. Except for one man, and I never saw him. The principal was a man. And at Pattison there is also a man principal. When I first came here there was one man teacher also. But now there are quite a few. I have, a few times, caught some hints of things as far as the men saying that they are everything. I don't know if we are more driven or what, but there were comments made to that respect like "Lighten up." I didn't worry about it; it didn't bug me at all. Otherwise it is a cool staff.*
>
> *I see a difference in my students this year because of one particular girl in my room. Her mother is a very strong woman who is very aware of*

that type of thing. I commend her for it; it comes off on her daughter. If I do anything even unintentionally, if I talk about a fireman, she is on me. Women can be firepersons. She has made me be very careful. I do not have a boy/girl line. I have equal lines. I do flub up, so to speak, but I do correct myself in front of the kids.

I hope that my daughter will be able to achieve what she wants to. I hope it won't be reversed where my son, Jake, will be discriminated against. Before, boys and girls played separately on the play ground. Now they don't Even when I went to school the girls who played with the boys were tom boys and the boys who played with girls were sissies. That is not true anymore. Or just the girls were smart or just the boys. The activities are very mixed now. This class is very close. Even when we pick teams, which we don't do often, the boys are not all on one team and the girls on another. Things have changed tremendously. Just the way boys are acting. For example, if a boy cried he would be laughed at, but now if a boy cries he is comforted by everyone.

I have not come across anything that boys have refused to read. I think that it is all how you approach it. If it is a new book and I say, "Oh, I just love this book," I can get everybody interested in it. It could be pink and about dolls, and they would read it.

When we had a water theme, there was this book called Fishing for Boys. *I took the book and threw it out, and the kids knew what I was talking about and how unfair the title was. I see girls reading about boys more than boys reading about girls. It might be because of their parents and the books that their parents help to choose. In the classroom I push books that are for boys or girls, and they all want to read it. If I read it, it is hot.*

Del is an example of a teacher who in a quietly heroic way listens to her students, questions traditional schooling, searches for solutions to problems, and creates what will affirm and challenge her students. In doing this she affects many in the educational community. The literacy endeavor involves both individual transformations and transformations in context of various groups of people: parents, her students, other teachers. In a quietly competent manner, she has integrated her learning from childhood experiences and her personal passion for language with the writings of theorists and researchers in order to create a true literacy community among the people she touches: "All who are privileged and burdened to live just now do have some responsibility for creating a world that is safer and saner and more just than the one we have. What better way to do it than with words, holy words" (Sewell, 1991, 16).

References

Appleby, A., and Langer, J. (1986). *The writing report card*. Princeton, NJ: ETS.

Atwell, N. (1987). *In the middle*. Portsmouth, NH: Heinemann.

Calkins, L. (1995). *The art of teaching writing*. Portsmouth, NH: Heinemann.

———. (1991). *Living between the lines*. Portsmouth, NH: Heinemann.

Friere, P. (1985). *The politics of education*. South Hadley, MA: Bergin & Gravey.

Giroux, H. (1992). Critical literacy and student experience: Donald Graves approach to literacy. In P. Shannon (Ed.), *Becoming political*. Portsmouth, NH: Heinemann.

Giroux, H. A., and McLaren, P. (1986). Teacher education and the politics of engagement: The case for democratic schooling. *Harvard Educational Review, 56* (3).

Goodman, K., Goodman, Y., and Bird, L. B. (Eds.). (1990). *The whole language catalog*. Santa Rosa, CA: American School Publishers.

Graves, D. (1990). *Discover your own literacy*. Portsmouth, NH: Heinemann.

———. (1995). *A fresh look at writing*. Portsmouth, NH: Heinemann.

———. (1983). *Writing: Teachers and children at work*. Portsmouth, NH: Heinemann.

Hansen, J. (1987). *When writers read*. Portsmouth, NH: Heinemann.

Routman, R. (1994). *Invitations*. Portsmouth, NH: Heinemann.

Sewell, M. (Ed). (1991). *Cries of the spirit*. Boston: Beacon Press.

Shannon, P. (1992). Introduction: Why become political? In P. Shannon (Ed.), *Becoming political*. Portsmouth, NH: Heinemann.

———. (1990). Whole language and critical literacy. In K. Goodman, Y. Goodman, and L. B. Bird (Eds.), *The whole language catalog*. Santa Rosa, CA: American School Publishers, 53.

Shor, I. (1987). *Freire for the classroom: A source book for liberatory teaching*. Portsmouth, NH: Heinemann.

12

VICKI BRATHWAITE

My grandmother used to tell stories;
she was from the West Indies, and
she used to tell a lot of folk tales
that her mother had told her
when she was growing up. We would
lie in bed together every afternoon,
and she would tell those stories to me.
Scary stories and ghost stories that taught
a lesson about how to behave . . .
I would ask her to tell them to me
again and again. Then my mother
introduced me to books, and I still
have some of the books that she bought for me.
She would read aloud to me, and I had favorites
that I would bring to her again and again.

—Vicki Brathwaite

We wrote the beginning of Vicki's description of her reading history in the poetic form that it suggested to us. Vicki's is a rich story with the density and rhythm of poetry. Throughout her interview she describes her literacy experiences as circular: her grandmother's stories lead to her work with children; they sit in circles to read and write; stories appear and reappear; reading leads to writing leads to reading; she belongs to circle groups of professionals who share their literate experiences. The human circle of literacy is a central metaphor for her.

Stories go in circles. They don't go in straight lines. So it helps if you listen in circles because there are stories inside stories and stories between stories and finding your way through them is as easy and hard as finding your way home. And part of the finding is the getting lost. If you're lost, you really start to look around and listen. (Metzger, 1991, 104)

Metaphor and Art as Frameworks for Living

When I was an undergraduate in college I majored in elementary education, but I sort of realized that I needed to specialize. I knew I had this love for books, and I liked working with children, so I figured why not specialize in reading. I became involved with a circle of people who were always exchanging titles, and we always had books in our hands and were talking about ways of sharing literature with children. We wanted to break the mold of the basal reader; we couldn't stand it. It seemed that books were being published at such a fast pace with so many different ideas and so many varied concepts that I wanted to write, I wanted to read, and I just couldn't get enough.

I'm interested in the arts, theater, dance, all of that, so if those things are in books I expose them to my students, and again, I'm a big advocate for getting the real firsthand experience. One of the things I always tell the kids when we start to write is if I could be a teacher like Mrs. Frizzle who has a magic school bus I would just love it! When I used to be a classroom teacher of just one group of children I said that my teacher wish was that I could have a bus. We would all have matching sweatshirts and baseball caps, and we would get on a bus at least once or twice a week. A school is the whole community, and we have such a great resource here in New York. What better way to learn than to go and explore these places. Every morning we would get on the bus, our lunches already made, and there would be no problem; all would be taken care of. We would go to China Town, Radio City, Rockefeller Center, go watch a taping of a show, go to a play or opera, really bring the community into the school.

All of this mix of experience and dreaming grows out of a matrix of story. The words of Lucy Calkins (1994) with whom she has studied at Columbia describe aptly Vicki's approach to literacy with her students:

It will not always be the dancing flame of a candle or a shared chorus that creates the space for a story. Sometimes a tape-recorded song will move among clusters of children whispering, "Story time." Whatever the ritual, the community will gather, the circle will grow silent, and in that silence we will sometimes say, "Today, in the silence after the story, in the silence of the story, let's write." (254)

I do journal writing. I always say I want to write a children's book, but I haven't. I make lists of topics and lists of ideas and settings and characters. I buy blank journals for a possible book.

Another generative theme in Vicki's interview is the power of story in human lives and learning. Her ever-expanding experience with literacy seems to have its roots in listening. She hears the voice of the author in much the same way that she heard her grandmother's voice. Vicki seems especially sensitive to the cycles of literacy: there are those who have gone before and have prepared the way for present life; in turn, present life will give way to new. Thus it has been, and thus it will be forevermore. It is for us to take the best of what we have been given and carry it forward into the future for our children and our children's children. Thus Vicki's narrative continues into more circles of nurturance.

Nurturance/Past and Present (Self and Others)

I became involved with a circle of people that were always exchanging titles, and we always had books in our hands and were talking about ways of sharing literature with children. This group of people, we were always sharing, "Look at this; this is a counting book; this one is rhymes; this one is based on a Puerto Rican's experiences; this one is a young adult book; this would go well with even early childhood kids; my students would understand this young adult book!" We just started mixing everything! I was lucky enough at that time to have a so called gifted class so, because the core curriculum was to read the Open Court reader, we finished that book. I read all the stories, and I just rushed the kids through it, and I would ask all the questions. Then I said, "Now we are going to read our supplementary readers," and we got into the Chronicles of Narnia *by C. S. Lewis. We read the five or six chronicles one right after another. It was great! I would read a couple chapters ahead of them, and I tried to embellish their reading. This was a third-grade class, but these kids were on a sixth-grade level. In the chronicles they talked about Turkish delight. We went down to the Arabic market (we have a large Arabic community here), and we got Turkish delight. We tried to embellish everything that they spoke about, and we tried to bring it to their experience. We also did a lot of independent reading where the children would read what they wanted to read and do different projects about it.*

That is basically how I got started in literacy and then having a six year old was truly my chance to see if all this stuff really works. We have two bookshelves, and they are all filled with paperbacks. He has got thousands of books at home and, interestingly enough, he was a reluctant reader because Mommy read so much and he didn't have the confidence to do it, but now he is beginning to get more confident. I was beginning to worry, but my girlfriend said, "Vicki, you tell parents not to worry all the time. You are doing the right thing with the exposure and all the books."

That core group of teachers that started here about seven years ago heard about Lucy Calkin's Institute at Columbia University. At that time we were studying the writing process, and we all went to the Summer Institute. Lucy wanted to explore the reading/writing connection. At first she had just taken off on writing, and then she wanted to see what kinds of connections readers made with writing and writers made with reading. A number of teachers went, and they started to critique and write their thoughts about young adult literature, and from that we started a teachers' book club. We would read children's books. That was nice, but we were doing that anyway, so we wanted to do something different, so we said, "Why don't we start reading books that are interesting to us?" and so we would meet once a month after work and discuss our novels that we had chosen. These were really great debates and discussions. We would all stand and speak for the book that we had suggested, and then somehow we would decide on what we would read. Sometimes we would make a list which I didn't like to do because I didn't like to know what I was going to read for the whole next ten months because new books were always coming.

Some of the people who were in that original group have since gone on to other jobs, so it wasn't easy for us to meet here in school. So we decided that we would have a book group, and we formalized it; we called it "Brown Women," and we meet once a month at each other's homes. That has continued for about eight years now. At first we started reading a list of black fiction; we do read some nonfiction. Then we started reading multi-ethnic women such as Amy Tan. Really everything! We just bring out critiques from the Times *or from* Essence Magazine *or what we have heard, everything! We keep notebooks, write journals, sit around the table, and say what we are going to read next and after that. There are about fourteen members, and it is not only a time to talk about books, but it is like a support group talking about life and being social. I think all of us agree that* Beloved *by Toni Morrison is our favorite. Another favorite is* A Lesson before Dying *by Earnest Gaines. It is a social kind of thing. We look forward to it. We were just dealing with the issue of if we want to open it up to new members. We get our books from a bookstore, and people ask if we have room for new members. We are sort of cohesive, and we know each other's experiences. We have worked together, and of course a newcomer brings a different perspective to the group, but it is kind of something that is ours now.*

The past three years we had a children's bookstore which I initiated in our school. It is low cost because we don't have a local book store in our neighborhood to provide low-cost access for parents and the community to books for children. That was blooming at one time. We had it open three or four times a week and at lunch time. The books were from fifty cents to a dollar and up. The children could eat and come to the store and then you would see more and more children reading over lunch and at recess. We had some problems in logistics in our school, so we had to close it for a while, but I just opened it up again in my room. The grand opening was last Friday. I just get a high watching the children browsing over books and talking about them with each other and reading the covers. It is wonderful to see that! In those ways we try to provide literature for the children. I am sure every teacher takes their classes to the library, but the parents need to do their part. Teachers can't do everything. Parents are the first teachers, and we try and let parents know that.

In Vicki's description of children, their families, and their teachers reading, one sees a literacy community forming. As Keen (1988) says: "Stories open us up to the stories of others, as common and singular as our own. They are the best way we have found to "overcome loneliness, develop compassion and create community" (46–47).

Vicki is always searching for books that will help her students of diverse backgrounds feel pride in their own identity and heritage and learn about diversity and the complexity of American society.

Right now my favorite children's book is Hue Boy, *by Karen Lynn Williams and Kathryn Stock. I have so many favorites!* Galimoto *is a big favorite. For older readers, I, Juan de Pareja. All of Patricia Palacco's books, but* Chicken Sunday *is my favorite this week. I like a lot of nonfiction too. We subscribe to* Zoo Books *magazine at home, and I devour every issue. There is another book called* Drop Everything and Read, *and that is another favorite.*

My students like reading about people in other cultures, different countries, and their populations and landmarks. Animals are always a favorite; dinosaurs are a hit, and whales too. Insects are real big. Another favorite book is The Pinata Maker. *It is a Mexican nonfiction book. It is a photo essay of a master pinata maker, and it is in English and Spanish. The children love that book. They like books from their experiences.*

Children who are bilingual love books that are written in both languages and speak of their experiences from their native country. Asian children love to identify with Omi Wong *and other Asian books. Children love to identify with books and solve problems through characters in books. Children just love to be read to, and I think adults do too. You have no behavior problems when you really speak from your heart about, "I'm reading this to you for a purpose, and I want you to find out what this character does and says," and you ask if, from their real experience, they can relate to it. It sort of invites them into the book regardless of how you are going to share it with them. You have to catch children's attention. I mean, if you have a TV next to you, and you want to read to them, what are you going to do? You have be real and correct.*

I think that there should be certain experiences that all children should have. . . . One thing that comes to mind is in the public school system in New York. Most of the early childhood teachers are female, particularly in our school. We don't have many black male role models outside of the principal. We do have a handful of male black teachers but it is not enough. In terms of teaching, you just can't be everything to everybody. There may be certain things that little boys need that they are not getting. I'm very conscious of that with books that I select.

Through discussion of books, Vicki helps young readers question, become critical:

I wish there were more books published about boys and their experiences. A lot of my favorite books are female characters, and I think about the boys in the group. They may think it is a really great story, but it could be about a boy too, so I talk about that or ask what they would do, or I'll say how it would be great if there were another book about a boy too. That is why Hue Boy *and* Galimoto *are the two books I like so much, they are about little black boys. I find that when you do luck upon a book that is some interest to boys you can't get enough of them! This one book that comes to mind, I had about ten copies but am now down to one. It is called* Willie the Wimp *. It is about a male gorilla who is always getting picked on because he is so gentle and wouldn't hurt a fly. He reads a comic book, and there is an add about how to get strong and all about a special diet, and he does it and gets all muscular. The boys really love it!*

We did a literature circle a couple of years ago with fourth and fifth graders with Walter Dean Myers' work.

Family History

One can almost hear the voice of Vicki's grandmother throughout her interview, soft and mesmerizing, like the voice of the Haitian grandmother of Sophie, Danticat Edwidge's young heroine in *Breath. Eyes. Memory* (1994):

"Listen. Listen before it passes. Paro'l gin pie' ze'l. The words can give wings to your feet. There is so much to say, but time has failed you," she said. "There is a place where women are buried in clothes the color of flames, where we drop coffee on the ground for those who went ahead, where the daughter is never fully a woman until her mother has passed on before her. There is always a place where, if you listen closely in the night, you will hear your mother telling a story and at the end of the tale, she will ask you this question: 'Ou libe're'?' Are you free, my daughter?" (233–34)

My grandmother used to tell stories; she was from the West Indies, and she used to tell a lot of folk tales that her mother had told her when she was growing up. We would lie in bed together every afternoon, and she would tell those stories to me. The stories from the West Indies were kind of scary stories, not stories with specific characters, scary stories and ghost stories that taught a lesson about how to behave or morals. I would ask her to tell them to me again and again. Then my mother introduced me to books, and I still have some of the books that my mother bought for me. She would read aloud to me, and I had favorites that I would bring to her again and again, so my mother was the first one who introduced me to books. My parents always ordered magazines, so I saw my father come home every evening, sit in his chair, and read Time *magazines. I also remember riding in the car every day from my grandparents' home, and my dad would stop at the newsstand, and I would wait in the car and watch him pick up this newspaper.*

Vicki, like so many other teachers whom we interviewed, remembers Dick and Jane. She also describes as do so many other female teachers, the process of imaginative identification with the female character, even when the object of identification is so far removed from experience. Her comments also indicate the beginning of resistance, again much like other women interviewees.

I remember Dick and Jane and those readers. I identified with Jane, being a female. Her life was dramatically different from mine, but I always imagined what her life was like. It was basically that repetition scene, "mother cooks," that type of thing. That's what I learned to read on. The beautiful part of reading again came from home because school was always so structured. Everyone read the same thing at the same time, and we had word lists to study; it really wasn't exciting. Basically it came from home.

There was one favorite book called The Lonely Doll *which is a book my mother introduced to me from the library. I had a library card when I was four years old. I remember practicing to write my name small so I could get a library card. My mother would help me practice by giving me sheets of lined paper.* The Lonely Doll *was one of the books I always wanted to check out at the library. That character was an only child who lived alone. I identified with her.*

We didn't have a local bookstore in our neighborhood in Brooklyn at the time. We went to bookstores in the village. We would have a great time. My mother would buy me books. She would say "We don't have a lot, but you can get something," so I would come out with a cookbook maybe or another book. I remember when I got a little older my mother bought me Our Bodies Our Selves *by the Boston Women's Health Collective. WOW, that book spoke to all of my needs. Anything I wanted to know; I just felt like she was identifying that I was a growing young woman and she knew that I had to have this kind of information. I turned my friend onto that book also.*

Vicki's reading as a young adult led her on the long path to becoming a master teacher.

The first longer novel I read was in junior high right here in this district during the seventies, and many of the teachers we had were the "hippie" type. The book that this teacher introduced us to was Man Child in the Promised Land *by Claude Brown. I read that book from cover to cover. It was just the best thing I had ever found between the covers of a book. I just didn't know literature like that was written down. He discussed it with us and it spoke to the here and now of inner-city life growing up and gangs and teens having their first experiences with everything, and that was really something I could identify with. It was appropriate for me. After that I wanted more, and I really loved this teacher, and I asked him what else he could refer us to, and he said another similar book was* Down These Mean Streets *by Perry Thomas. After that I think my mom took me to Barnes and Noble in Manhattan, and that was the first book store that I really started going into, and she taught me how to just go in and read. She said, "Vicki, we don't have a lot*

of money, but just go in and let's just browse," so then I would look for
special interest sections and I started reading everything I could.

Vicki's enthusiasm for books and the sharing of stories has roots in the storytelling of her grandmother and the thoughtful literacy of her mother. These women were her best teachers. Their teaching was an art somewhat like the gifting art that Alice Walker (1983) writes about as she describes the creative, generative literacy she received from her mother:

> And so it is, certainly, with my own mother. Unlike "Ma" Rainey's songs, which retained their creator's name even while blasting forth from Bessie Smith's mouth, no song or poem will bear my mother's name. Yet so many of the stories that I write, that we all write, are my mother's stories. Only recently did I fully realize this: that through years of listening to my mother's stories of her life, I have absorbed not only the stories themselves, but something of the manner in which she spoke, something of the urgency that involves the knowledge that her stories—like her life—must be recorded. (240)

Resistant Reader/Teacher

Breaking through the Open Court reader to do the fun stuff was my biggest risk.

One year I really wanted to break the mold. I wanted to try some things I hadn't tried in school. I was tired of the traditional classroom, so I moved everything out into the hallway on the first day. The principal walked down the hall while I was doing this. I hadn't even thought to ask him. I figured it was my room and I could do what I wanted to it. I ended up asking him, and he allowed me to do so. At the time I had a low achievement class, and I found that it was fine for some of the kids, but on the other hand, they needed that structure of a desk. The next year they would be moving to another classroom that wouldn't complement what I had done. For test taking, art projects, those kinds of activities, the desk is good for them. I found that children really need a whole list of spaces. They need a space when they can lie down; they need a space for struc-tured activities; they need a door that opens up to the outside. That is another one of my teacher wishes is to have a door that opens up to a big lawn.

I had read Jonathan Kozol and Sylvia Ashton Warner and other books like that. I wanted to do something different for the kids. I know I was always comfortable crawled up on the floor reading or writing. At that time we were trying to aim towards group activities. I found out a nice way was for the kids to sit on the floor. I wanted to explore learning styles, and I think that lends itself to moving around the room and having an open space. I liked having a circle rather than rows and a square. I was able to see everyone; I wasn't necessarily the head. Everyone felt important in that set-up. In traditional classrooms it seems that those who sit at the front get most of the teacher's attention. Those are the children that the teacher can take and know they won't drive him/her crazy, and the ones you don't want near you, set them in the back. That sort of creates an image.

The program that I teach now, Chapter One Reading, is a federally funded program where we teach children who don't score well on the DRP [Degrees of Reading Power] test. They are eligible for individualized service, so it is a pull-out program. We take those kids out of grades three, four, and five, and we give them individual attention in reading. We try to break the mold and get away from traditional basals and expose them to what their interests are.

A part of that program is to have meetings with parents three or four times a year to give them support and suggestions as to how they can work to maximize their success with their children at home in reading. Unfortunately as many parents do not come to these workshops as should. The information in the workshops talks about having books at home, being a role model for your children, letting them see you read. Even if they [parents] are uncomfortable with their own reading skills they can buy books on tape or have their children read aloud to them or a sibling. We also share information about adult literacy; they can go to the library and learn how to read; we share PBS broadcasts; there are programs that come on such as "Famous Amos" that teach reading. We talk about buying books, the value of books, setting aside an appropriate time and place for reading without TV and radio or other distractions. We talk about having a desk so that children have an assigned area to study in. We tell them to buy books from the school book magazine sent home once a month. We make sure they have a library card, share how to get a library card. Not only do we talk about reading and writing, but we try to tell parents to visit community resources because the more experience the children have with language and life, the more they bring back into a reading situation; it makes reading more accessible to them. We try to boost their confidence up so they can continue along with their children at home.

We also have a program here called the "Saturday Family Reading Program" where it is sort of like a read-in. We have parents come on

Saturdays with their children, and we make it fun. We do interactive books. We may read The Hungry Caterpillar, *and then we may have the parents make a book with their child. We talk about reading or how to read books and the telling of oral stories if they are not comfortable with writing. We talk about making lists, brainstorming, and really letting kids see the value of reading not only in elementary school but in life and how in order to be successful and to function as a reader you have to be literate.*

Unfortunately, I don't feel that I see the kids blossoming at a rate which would make me joyful because, unfortunately, I don't get to see the kids as much as I would like to. I have eleven different classes, and that is over 180 different students. I see them in a large group. I used to have three; it used to be myself and two other assistants. One assistant has since gone, and they haven't replaced her. So, where it used to be a small group of six it is now a group of ten or twelve. You have children who haven't had good book experiences. It is just a challenge to provide books. Unfortunately, there hasn't been a lot of money spent on the program, so a lot of the books are ones that I have bought with my own money, that are part of my son's library, and I bring them to work, so I don't like to lend them. It's like you make the connection, "Look at this book, it is really great, but you can only look at it for a little while and then you have to leave it."

Vicki never gives up in her efforts to reach children and their families. If she does not have enough money or a program does not work, she tries something else. She believes we all have a right to the ecstatic experience that literature can bring and to the self-transcendence it requires.

This year we have gotten more money, so I have gotten a more expansive library and the children are allowed to take home the books finally. That is a big help! You can't tell somebody to do something very practical like make a bed if you don't give them something to practice with. So if I tell these parents you have to read and I don't send home books, it doesn't make any sense. Now the kids are taking home books, and they are talking about them and having conversations between themselves about the books. My hands have been tied around my back for a while, and I try to make the best of it. I try to have them write their own stories, but it is not the same as having all those beautiful books. You know that would be the perfect marriage, to hook the child with the right book. Like I say, if it happens to me, it can happen at an early age too. I am optimistic that things will get better in the future.

Vicki seeks connection points between dimensions of her own personal history and the personal histories of those she teaches; together she and her students tell and choose; they look toward untapped possibility. She is a necessary link in the long history of teachers described beautifully by Jane Uruquart (1993) in her novel *Away:*

> He showed her the teachers poised on the edge of the moment—a brown-robed brother guiding the hand of an acolyte through the deliberate strokes of calligraphy, a gypsy woman demonstrating the exact turn of a bare ankle to a young girl eager to begin dancing, a sailor showing a cabin boy how to twist a length of rope into the patterns of various knots, a woman setting threads on a loom while her daughter's head was illuminated by the window that lit the task. And everywhere around was the quiet that accompanies the act of passing skill from one mind and hand to another. Last he showed her Brian gently breaking open the marks of the alphabet to reveal meaning and the light of understanding on her own face. (127)

References

Calkins, L. M. (1994). *The art of teaching writing.* Portsmouth, NH: Heinemann Publishing.

Edwidge, Danticat. (1994). *Breath, eyes, memory.* New York: Vintage Books.

Keen, S. (1988). The stories we live by. *Psychology today,* 22 (12).

Metzger, D. (1991). Circles of stories. In C. Witherell and N. Noddings (Eds), *Stories lives tell.* New York: Teachers College Press.

Uruquart, J. (1993). *Away.* New York: Viking.

Walker, Alice. (1983). *In search of our mothers' gardens.* New York: Harcourt, Brace & Co.

13

KATHRYN MONGON

Metaphor and Art as Frameworks for Living

I think it became an outlet for me, and it got that voice that was in my head on to a page, and then I think it became more real for me when it was in written words.

When Kathryn speaks, the image of the journal presents itself—a young girl bent over the journal writing with the kind of empowerment a whole line of women through the years have found in the journal as a tool of survival. In it she could practice a kind of imaginative work, the "defamiliarization" described by Caroline Forche (1991, 184). Gilligan (1982) documented the importance of journal writing to the self-concepts of young girls as they move from preadolescence to adolescence. The importance of the journal to Kathryn's development of a sense of self is evident.

As a child, writing became really very important to me; maybe even more so than books. My ability to be able to express in a journal what was going on in my life. I kept volumes and volumes of journals from the time I was a preadolescent on up, about my life. I think that my ability to be able to write down what was going on with me and how I felt about it was more important than any of the books I could have chosen to escape into. I think that writing is a very important aspect of literacy.

Writing was a real outlet for me as a child going through some really difficult things in my family and not feeling like there were a whole lot of people I could talk to about that. My friends' lives were very different; they had real stable family lives. Back then divorce wasn't as common as it is today, which is not to say that kids don't suffer the same kinds of pain today as they did then, but I think I felt more alone with it and more abnormal, like our family was so different because we were going through that. There was also domestic violence involved in that situation, and that was more than twenty-five years ago, so there wasn't the kind of awareness like today. You didn't see billboards on the highway that said, "Hands are not for hitting" or "Love shouldn't hurt." That awareness just wasn't there. There wasn't that. . . . I don't know if it could be called an openness, but it was definitely not OK. I had the message that it was not okay to talk about. I couldn't even tell my best friend even though I was very close to her and also very close to her family. I couldn't tell them the kind of pain I was going through and just how crazy and horrible my home life was, so I wrote about it, and I wrote volumes.

When I was a child of probably about ten or eleven, I started to write, and I continued to write throughout high school in journals. Sometimes I would write letters; letters that I would never send. I think it became an outlet for me, and it got that voice that was in my head on to a page, and then I think it became more real for me when it was in written word.

Later as an adult there was a time in my life where I could go back through and look at that writing, and then there came a time when I actually burned all those journals. It was just too painful, and I felt like I needed to let go of it; it was sort of a ritual experience of trying to, not so much put it aside because I don't think I ever put it aside because it is a part of me and it is very much a part of the work I do with kids today, but I needed to feel separate. I needed to feel that I was my own person and that I was an adult now and that I was not being held back by it and that I could create for myself a happiness in spite of it.

I still journal from time to time but not on a regular basis. I seem to write when I am in pain. It has just always helped me sort out things. I went through a period in my life where I suffered from really severe depression as a result of, I think, a lot of abuse in my childhood. I was in a psychiatric hospital for a number of months, and writing at that time was part of what saved my life. I remember that I struggled with picking up the pen and beginning to write because I think I knew that, for some reason, the flow of the thoughts in my head to paper would start this process, and I wasn't sure I wanted to start it. Yet it was absolutely necessary to my survival at that time. I kind of fought doing it for a number of weeks. I don't think I was ready to do it, and I also wasn't even physically capable of doing it, but once I did start it was truly the beginning of an incredible healing process for me. I don't think I would have gotten through that time if I wouldn't have been able to write out what was in my head, and I don't think I would have been able to write it if it had not been for my past experience of doing it as a child.

Little weight has been given to women's journal writing as an art form. It has never been considered until such recent works as the journals of African American women edited by Bell-Scott (1994) and the new work by Bunkers (1996). "Personal writing is/has always been a dangerous activity," Bell-Scott tells us, "because it allows us the freedom to define everything on our own terms. For those seeking to defy culturally imposed negative identities, personal writing has offered avenues for resistance and re-creation" (17).

Kathryn wrote and still writes of her pain and longings, her experiences of oppression. She often makes the connection between her personal, inner experiences and her understanding of the systemic injustice which institutionalizes and perpetuates that oppression. What Sewell (1991) writes of women poets describes the work of women journal writers for whom journal writing is a way to the heart, opening the door to the spirit.

Where can we begin? Perhaps with the silences, the monumental silences: the multitude of feelings and understandings that we have discounted as not real because there has arisen no word, no phrase nor pattern of thinking to legitimate our experience. To remain in these silences is to be alone. There is no way to connect flesh with flesh, no way to perceive, to preserve, to know. So we fumble with words, playing with them, caressing them, trying to tease out meaning. We work as if our lives were at stake. As if life were at stake . And we would be right in supposing so. (1)

Kathryn's experience of the power of writing when she was young clearly has influenced her teaching.

I think writing should be used in just about every subject area. I know lots of teachers do journaling with kids in school. People all do this differently, but I believe that when people write they need to have a sense of an audience that they are writing for, even if that's just the teacher. If you want people to write and you want them to talk about things that are important to them and how they feel about those things, they have to have a sense of who that information is going to be shared with. I think that is important in all kinds of writing. I don't really know that much about writing; I just know that when I respond to them they write more, and the more that I respond the more they write back. Even kids for whom it is just so painful to write, even if they only get down a sentence with four words in it, if you can respond and encourage more to come out, I think it does.

Some teachers have kids journal and they never read their journals or respond to them, and once in a while they will say, "Does anybody want to share their journal?" The students that feel the most secure about themselves will, and the rest won't. The ones who won't share need to have someone hear what they are writing, and I think teachers can provide that for them.

The whole process of taking thoughts from your head and putting them on paper can help kids in so many different areas. I don't mean just personally but academically. I have used journaling in math class, "Write about what you think when you do this problem, what goes through your head, tell me how to work this out." That really can help children who struggle with math to see what their thought process is. Just saying it is different than writing it down.

Kathryn's words as she describes her use of dialogue journals with students echo the words of Mosle (1995) as she speaks of the power of having ongoing conversations with students in their journals.

In education classes I was constantly taught to be sensitive to those differences between my students' backgrounds and my own. But by emphasizing the differences, I think, we sometimes forget that other peoples' children are like our own. As I read my students' journals I came to appreciate our unexpected similarities. My students . . . were recognizably children. They, like me, had a secret life that they were yearning to share. (61)

Kathryn senses the generative power of journal writing the way Bell-Scott (1994) did when she wrote the following in her introduction to *Life Notes:* "I hope that *Life Notes* will instill the faith I found on December 10, 1986, when after a night of fighting influenza induced by emotional and physical fatigue, I cuddled myself, pulled out my journal, and wrote; 'Reality *can be* (re)created by one who writes.'" (25)

Nurturance Past and Present (Self and Others)

Writing has been most important in Kathryn's developing literacy. But reading, writing's twin activity, has been very important both in her self-nurturance and in the nurturance of others.

Stories about women, especially about women who are adventurers, that portray women in strong roles have always been important to me, and I've really enjoyed them. I have read lots and lots of true life adventure stories about women, about women who biked across Turkey, or who rode a camel across the Kalahari Desert (a book called Tracks*). I especially devour adventure stories that have taken women to different countries.*

There's always a pile of books by the bedside. Right now one is about a woman doing a white water rafting trip down the Amazon River. I don't remember the exact title. I have Cry of the Kalahari *because I'm going to be taking a trip to Africa and South Africa this summer, so that is kind of a re-read.*

I've read just about everything that May Sarton and Marge Piercy have written. I guess they would be my two favorites because I've read almost all that they have written. As far as children's authors, I like Robert Munch; he's a Canadian author. His stories are so full of fantasy and imagination, and they are really fun to read to kids. They are often times funny, but he has written some serious ones too.

I read for information, to learn and educate myself. It is relaxing, an escape from how chaotic, complex, and complicated life can be. I even read to fall asleep at night. I read for lots of reasons!

When asked about the role of literacy development in the classroom she said:

It is probably the most important thing that we as teachers can do in the classroom. I think that I've recently learned more than ever how important it is because I'm working with a thirteen-year-old boy who is totally illiterate. He's not even reading at what most people would consider at this point a kindergarten level. There are a lot of other reasons why his education has been difficult, but he still has spent a good part of his school-age years in school, so I am amazed that he still is not reading at a level that is considered at all functionally literate by today's standards. If we don't teach anything else, we at least need to be able to have kids walk out of our schools and classrooms and be literate in today's world.

Kathryn, like many women writers, speaks fiercely and prophetically of her own pain and anger and seems acutely sensitive to the pain of other oppressed groups, especially children. This is clear in her description of her dream classroom as

a classroom that would have a variety of ages of students in it. It would have lots and lots of space and no desks, but lots of work space and floor space, big tables, big double doors that open up into the outside and are open. Kids would be able to make more decisions on what is important for them to learn. Everyone could agree that learning is important and that there are great things in the world to be learned and then from there go about deciding how they want to go about learning what is out there. I think we should give children more choices and more power as to what they want to learn, because I do think they want to learn; it is just natural for them, kind of an innate thing, and we need to foster it instead of squelching it. There should be lots of books in the classroom and the freedom to go find information that is not in the classroom.

Computers are really important in classrooms today. It is especially important to have computers available to kids who are low income, kids who are minorities, kids who may not have that exposure to computers. I work with kids whose parents don't have telephones in their homes, and to think that they'll have a computer is just absurd, so having open access to computers is very important.

Having the entire classroom be more open as a community place for people is also important, for parents or caregivers to have that be an environment that they can come into. Also, every classroom would have a bus or a mini van to pile their students into and take them anywhere.

I think kids can learn a lot from each other. The idea of all the same age children being at the same developmental point all in one classroom seems sort of crazy. We all agree that within that group of twenty-seven children there are twenty-seven different learning styles (or at least fourteen or fifteen). If you also mix in different ages, then you create even more of an exciting learning environment for kids and much more opportunity for them to learn. It kind of fits with my idea of a classroom being a community. Communities don't consist of people who are all the same age or are at the same stage, but our classrooms do; that gets pretty weird.

I think it's so important to understand and get to know children for who they are and what's important to them and know what their life is like. It's so important to have time where you can connect one on one with each child, where you take fifteen minutes and sit down and talk with this student about what life is like this week and what they're thinking about and just really get to know them.

I like the idea of having kids for more than one year. I think the same teacher should have the same group for maybe a couple of years or maybe even longer. I think that promotes the idea of getting to know them and establishing a relationship with them. I think we also need to give kids as much freedom as we can as far as how they are going to learn and what they are going to learn and why it's important for them to learn that.

Kathryn sees her relationships with children as contributing to her own self-nurturance and growth:

> *Kids have taught me so much about life. Oftentimes they teach me about priorities, about what's important and what's not. I think they've taught me how to listen better, especially to listen to what they have to say. They have certainly taught me patience and perseverance. I think they give me permission to be silly and playful as an adult. They inspire me to be creative. Most of what I think of as my creative energy is motivated through the children that I work with; they are certainly the push behind that! With this boy that I'm working with now, I'm learning so much about this whole literacy topic and the benefits of being exposed. This student has struggled so much with crisis in his life, and has also struggled with a mental impairment that hasn't allowed him to learn in the same ways that the rest of us learn. I can just see the things that are not open to him because he can't read and write.*

Division, distrust, physical and economic violence—human life is not the way she would wish it to be. There is in Kathryn's words a sense that hope is real and change is possible. How does change come? Through the sensitive and loving concern of persons each for the other, and a willingness to do the hard work of organizing and planning in order to change. She is a witness by voice and deed and does not stand aloof from the problems of students and their families. She takes the responsibility to make a difference in the lives of individual students. Kathryn's own experiences of a childhood trauma help her understand the needs of her students.

> *Teachers have an incredibly difficult job to do today, and I hope that people going into teaching are prepared for that, and if they are not, then they need to do something different. Teachers are secondary only to parents in kids' lives, and sometimes they are the primary adult because of the huge amount of time children spend in school.*
>
> *I know as a child, when I was in school and going through what I was going through, there were a lot of teachers that labeled me as being uncooperative or daydreaming and not paying attention and not on task and all those other little statements that they check off on your report card, but there was nobody that asked me why. I was a poor student, and I think that was because there was so much going on in my life that I couldn't focus. I would come to school exhausted and tired and have my head on my desk, and oftentimes it was because my parents had been fighting all night long and I had been worried that my father was going*

to kill my mother. I had to get up and be at school at eight in the morning and try and learn whatever it was you learn in fourth grade, and that just wasn't happening for me; yet no one tried to figure out why. So I think that teachers need to be in tune to why kids aren't doing well and, if they don't bring their homework in, don't just keep them in from recess to do their homework, but talk to them about why. You know like, "What's it like at home when you try to do your homework, or is it just not even a possibility?"

I also think kids look at teachers as being really important as sort of keepers of the knowledge of the world, and in some ways teachers need to dispel that for them. We need to say, "No, I don't know everything here. There are some things that I know because I have lived longer than you, and I am willing to share that with you, but together there's lots that we can find out." Because I deal with children that are at risk and in crisis and children that are dealing with domestic violence, I see how much trust they give their teachers and that school becomes an incredibly safe place for them. We need to understand that and work with those students from that place of, "Oh wow, you mean this classroom where these children are every day is safer than their home!" For many kids it very much is!

Family History

As Kathryn described her difficult childhood experiences, she showed the vital role that reading played for her as an escape and how this led to her enthusiasm for helping children develop reading and writing as survival strategies.

My favorite book growing up was a weird book, Cora Barton's biography. I read it when I was in third grade, and I read it about five times. I don't know why, but I really like it. She just seemed like a real neat person to me.

I don't have any memory of my parents reading to me. I'm sure there were a few books around but not a lot of books. I think the newspaper was around. Most of my access to books was through school.

I brought books home from the school library and read them. As I got older and could go to the library on my own, I would go to the town library. Reading became really important to me the older I got. It turned into an escape for me. My home life was so hectic, and there was not much good stuff going on there, so reading was important as a way to escape from it.

In school we did book reports, but nothing like what kids do now with reading and writing, certainly not the kinds of writing that they do in terms of journaling. First graders and even kindergartners are now doing journaling. We did penmanship, and that was our writing.

I think most of the children's literature that I like and use in teaching are books that I have been exposed to as an adult. Because I missed out on children's books as a child, I go nuts with them now.

Resisting Reader (Writer)/Teacher

Linda Hogan (1991) described the connection between writing and survival—her own and that of others:

Writing begins for me with survival, with life and with freeing life, saving life, speaking life. It is work that speaks what can't be easily said. It originates from a compelling desire to live and be alive. For me, it is sometimes the need to speak for other forms of life, to take the side of human life, even our sometimes frivolous living, and our grief-filled living, our joyous living, our violent living, busy living, our peaceful living. (80)

Kathryn speaks out on many issues that affect the lives of children in schools including domestic abuse, sexism, racism, and homophobia. Most important is her willingness to share herself with her students.

Every day there are risks that you take when you go against the status quo in speaking out about sexism, racism, and homophobia. You face risks from the other teachers and administrators, and if students go and tell their parents, then you may upset parents too. You have to play a balancing act with that all the time, and it is really exhausting. A lot depends on what kind of support you feel from your administration in terms of risk taking.

Those are kind of blatant things that you might take risks on, but there are little things that are risks every day such as interacting with a student about an intuition you might have about what does or does not motivate that student. You know, saying it out loud and maybe taking that risk that they are going to look at you and say, "No, that's not true at all." Taking a risk happens when you even attempt to have a relationship with a student that is meaningful, different from what they are used to having in school.

When asked about her work as a children's advocate in a shelter for homeless families Kathryn described her willingness to share herself with her students. Her words show us a nurturing risk taking:

> *The risk of letting kids know that you don't know it all and letting kids know that you are human and you don't go in the coat closet at night and come out in the morning, that you have a life and that you had a past life—there is a balance there. You can't burden kids with horrible stories about yourself; I don't think that is appropriate at all. I had to find a balanced way of letting kids that were hurting and kids who are dealing with hard things in their lives know that they weren't alone, that I also had been there and I knew how lonely and hard it could be, and that I wanted to try and help them not to be alone with it. I guess that is a risk, and as a teacher it is hard. I think there is always sort of a balance that you have to maintain.*

Kathryn sees teaching and learning as dialogic processes, a perspective stressed by Freire (1987) in which the learner is challenged to engage in critical analysis and the teacher is challenged to enter the learner's world.

She criticized children's literature that is stereotypic:

> *I don't like books that put out stereotypes or are sexist. It's interesting; I was in a first-grade room on Friday, and there was a student teacher in there reading a St. Patrick's Day story about a leprechaun, and it was an older book, not too old, like 1980 (I checked the copyright date), and it had a description of this leprechaun screaming like a banshee, and I think that is an Indian derogatory term so I asked her, "Well what do you think about that word?" and she didn't really think about the word. I don't know if she just didn't know what it meant or what. I think it is important to be careful and to preread books, especially before you read them to kids, and either self-censor those words or decide on a different story. So . . . I don't like that kind of stuff.*
>
> *I am pretty much against censorship. It is important to teach kids to select books that are meaningful to them. More than having someone else decide for them what they should and shouldn't read, it's more important to teach children how to do that for themselves in terms of selecting books and good literature. Also, teaching kids that with freedom of speech there can be books written about anything but that what's written about may not reflect what is important to them.*

Kathryn is critical of sexist and racist practices in schools:

> *Schools are just a reflection of what is happening in society, and so discrimination is there; it's everywhere! There are really overt examples of jobs that boys get to do in even the first-grade classroom that girls*

don't get to do. Even in high school when you have A.V. equipment and the teacher will automatically ask Tom to take it back to the A.V. room instead of asking Sally to take it back. I work mostly with elementary students, so I'm thinking of the little jobs they are assigned: line leaders, chalkboard erasers, messengers, etc. Hopefully, those are not assigned according to gender, but I think that sometimes they are. How we as teachers interact with students within that learning environment plays a part in it, the kinds of questions we ask boys and girls, or how we respond to questions they ask us.

The more damaging sexist practices are the things that are subtle in terms of curriculum that we choose, or sometimes we don't choose. We don't always have the choice as to what we teach, but I think we have the choice as to how we teach it. We have the personal responsibility as teachers to bring out those things that are sexist and talk about them. It's the same with racism in lots of areas, especially in history. We are responsible for talking about it. The example of that little leprechaun screaming like the wild Banshee, that could have been a time where if I was reading that story to the class I would stop and say, "Oh, that word banshee, what does that mean?" and have the kids talk about the meaning of that word and ask them if that is a good word to describe a native American person.

I think a lot of teachers are just very ignorant about it. More has to be done to get teachers aware, and hopefully then they will feel responsible for talking about it with their students. You can talk about it with first graders as well as seniors in high school.

There are changes definitely happening. I think there are still teachers out there that really resist that change. It's hard when there isn't an effort among all the people in the school to fight sexism or fight racism. So, if you have a first-grade class and all through first grade you make an effort to point out things that are sexist and to talk about it, and you try as hard as you can not to perpetuate that sexism in your classroom, but then they go on to the second grade and get a teacher who thinks you're a little bit crazy, so the students get a whole different kind of experience. There needs to be more of an effort to create that kind of change in all schools.

Kathryn describes with the words of an artist her metaphor for the nurturing classroom and her commitment to child advocacy. Like other teachers in this study, she is a critical educator for whom literacy leads to action. Language is central to change, and Kathryn uses it to speak for children. It is the strength that she developed in childhood—the girl with the journal who now speaks powerfully and without fear about her perceptions and dreams:

> *I left the full-time job of children's advocate at the shelter six months ago, although I still do consulting work with them. Since I've left there I realize that I will never stop being a child advocate. It is not about a forty-hour-a-week job; I will always advocate for children in any work I do; it is in me now. I will advocate for all children, for their safety and for their voices to be heard. The kids that bring those experiences of being different to the classroom, whether they are different because of their cultural background or because their family looks different than other families or because they've had experiences that other kids haven't had, are all part of the diversity picture. Those children mingled in with all twenty-five other students in your room make up that fabric that is beautiful. Those children are the pieces of the weaving that you are doing throughout the school year, and they create beauty. Each of them has to be heard and considered as important as all the other kids in the room. It is a very hard job, and there are teachers that do great things with that, and there are teachers that need lots of work. But it is happening, and it is certainly happening more in classrooms today than it did when I was in school.*

It was a personal literacy that saved Kathryn as a child and a young woman, and it is literacy that she sees as necessary to empower her students:

> *For me it is just continuing to look for ways that I can provide students with literacy that is meaningful to them. By that I mean, with all the diversity within classrooms, making sure that we take into consideration what is out there in print that is going to capture some student in the class. I guess that is really my goal, to always be striving for that. In order for me to do that, I need to continue to get to know my students, not just what I see when I look at them in terms of skin color or what sex they are, but also who they are and what is important to them, and then from there to make sure that what's accessible to them in school is somehow connected to them.*

References

Bell-Scott, P. (Ed). (1994). *Life notes: Personal writings by contemporary black women.* New York: Norton.

Bunkers, S. *In search of Susanna: An auto/biography.* Iowa City: University of Iowa Press, 1996.

Forche, C. (1991). The Province of Radical Solitude. In J. Sternburg (Ed), *The writer on her work*. New York: Norton.

Freire, P., and Macedo, D. (1987). *Literacy: Reading the word and the world*. New York: Bergin and Garvey.

Gilligan, C. (1982). *In a different voice*. Cambridge, MA: Harvard University Press.

Hogan, L. (1991). Hearing voices. In J. Sternburg (Ed), *The writer on her work*. New York: Norton.

Mosle, S. (1995). Writing down secrets. *The New Yorker,* Sept. 18, 52–61.

Sewell, A. (1991). *Cries of the spirit*. Boston, MA: Beacon Press.

14

Mary Tacheny

I think it is always good to clarify to children what is reality and what is fantasy, and I think there are times to use both. But actually, I think fantasy lends itself more towards instilling real creative ability in students. It is a form of higher level thinking which is what we want to move all our students to.

—Mary Tacheny

In a letter thanking sponsors for a trip to a Children's Theater presentation of *Amazing Grace,* one of Mary Tacheny's first graders said "I think they teach us to pretend like Grace did in the play." This child is benefitting from the influence of her teacher's three main goals for her students:

1. Your opportunities are not limited by your gender.
2. Your opportunities are not limited by your race.
3. To reach your dreams, you must put forth effort.

Discussion and research abound in early education about the fine line between fantasy and reality in the young child's mind. How much fantasy is too much? How much is too little, not allowing the child to experience a creative approach to thinking? Does delving into fantasy help the child's social development? Does fantasy come into the equation of constructivism? These are often the questions asked.

Mary Tacheny considers, and is appreciative of, fantasy on a different, more complex plane. Mary learns, through fantasy, how she can nurture the learning and the souls of her students. She learns how to nurture herself, and even, through fantasy, how to understand alternative ways of knowing.

As C. S. Lewis describes the Shadow-lands as "different, as different as a real thing is from a shadow or as waking life is from a dream" (160–61), Mary sees fantasy as a very complex support in her students' and her own frameworks for living.

We propose that while C. S. Lewis is one of Mary's favorite authors, it is Lewis' use of and respect for fantasy and worlds outside the visible, tangible world of Western contemporary thought from which Mary gets her nourishment of ideas and attitudes. While Lewis is often discussed in terms of the symbols used in his stories reflecting a narrow Christian view of the world, some readers do appreciate the work for its blending of the natural and the spiritual worlds, the logical and the fantastic. Mary Tacheny would also agree with Said Nasir who is a scholar of Islamic art, philosophy, and science. For example, he speaks from a different historical and philosophical position from that of Lewis, yet he criticized Western science because of its inability to integrate the logical and the fantastic, the hard facts with spirit and nature: "I attacked Western Science is its claim to be the only science of the natural world which is valid. It is no use to try to solve the ecological crisis on the basis of a science which is based upon the exclusion of the sacred from nature." (Nasir, 1990, in an interview with Bill Moyers). He continued by saying that "the emphasis in education from kindergarten on, that nature is no longer the enchanted world that a child almost automatically experiences" is wrong. He pointed out that "other civilizations, including western civilizations, try to preserve" this fantasy and respect for spiritual contexts through poetry, art, and science.

Metaphor and Art as Frameworks for Living

First of all, fantasy is a lot more abstract. If you can get children to move from their own selves and place themselves in different characters, you can get so much more out of them. They actually come alive when they can take on the character of someone else. I use a lot of fantasy in writing. They can write to imaginary characters or they can make imaginary characters. We do fantasy and creative dramatics where they can act out some of the characters. Sometimes I think fantasy is a very nice break from the reality of their world. They have to have something to look forward to. I think fantasy also develops children's sense of humor. I think another reason I use fantasy is to help children transfer themselves to a different place. They can move from the present and be something that they want to be, but then maybe they don't think they are right now. It is so affirming for them.

For instance, I teach a high percentage of young Southeast Asian students, and some of them are very quiet; a lot of the girls are very quiet.

Some of that has to do with traditional roles. Today we read this story about Jane and her new mittens, and I had different people reading the various parts. It was very interesting. One girl, Yer, is always so quiet, but when she was the voice of Jane, because Jane was kind of this bois-terous person, all of a sudden I heard this voice I had never heard. She was talking so loud and clear, she took on a different role. All the kids noticed and commented on how they could really hear Yer. Yer was just beaming, she was so proud of herself. I think it is always good to clarify to children what is reality and what is fantasy, and I think there are times to use both. But actually, I think fantasy lends itself more towards instilling real creative ability in students. It is a form of higher level thinking which is what we want to move all our students to.

Lather (1993) believes that we as educators would do well to "worry less about 'the real' and more about effects of representation." We see the issue of representation relating to Brady's (1995) discussion of identity. She discusses student identity in terms of pedagogy which allows students to reconstruct cultural differences and social identities which allow them to create new forms of knowledge free of sexism, bigotry, and domination. We also see the issue of representation as it relates to teacher expectations of students, in particular in literature related to the need for teachers to maintain high expectations for lan-guage minority students (Reyes, 1993). Mary takes this idea of repre-sentation to be closely tied to the use of fantasy.

With C. S. Lewis, part of that is the transcendence. He talks about reflection. It is very much of an inward journey. I think a lot of teaching comes from having the students look inward and reflect on an evaluation question like, How do you feel about this piece of writing? Have them look inward with the portfolio assessment. The children can see their own progression. You need a lot of lofty ideas and inspiration. I suppose that's what C. S. Lewis is to me, an inspiration. He's sort of farther along the journey than I am, but some of his is fantasy and some of it is experience.

This transcendence, this journey, is guided by reading and by many aspects of creative drama. Mary, like Deavere Smith (1995), believes "a voice" formed from the "juxtaposition of other voices," (77) is instruc-tive in the journey. When we make meaning and take meaning from narrative, the goal is to grasp both specificity and discontinuity (Lather, 1994). We are advised to make use of drama, artistry, and literary practices (Patai, 1988; Richardson, 1993) and to present knowledge in a fragmented way versus an "exhaustive" way.

> *I do a lot of dramatic play in my classroom. I like to incorporate dreaming and fantasy interaction with characters. This helps the students to really get inside the book and experience it. I like to do vocal, speaking activities instead of silent reading all the time.*

By blurring fact and fiction distinctions, by developing characters with names, faces, motives, and voices and to leave the reader or the student to interpret the events (Lather, 1994), Mary and her students learn from many of the alternative forms of knowledge represented inside and outside her classroom.

Nurturance Past and Present (Self and Others)

Mary nurtures her students with a depth of respect and intensity that is unique.

> *I like to read books with a message. I hate stupid books. I try to connect the stories to a meaning or value. I often try to have students discuss by using their personal experiences.*

There is much similarity between the manner in which Mary nurtures herself and the manner in which she nurtures her students. The effects seem to be generative. She reads and reflects for herself and with the children. She suggests readings for them and reads to them. The excitement continues throughout their time together, as C. S. Lewis says, "What it is is just itself—it's magic" (*Shadowlands*, 1993).

> *I read a lot of spiritual books that have had an influence on my life. A lot of C. S. Lewis books also. . . . . I read to connect myself to a world beyond. I also read to keep up on current issues. I read professional books to keep up with new theories. I read for pleasure. It is an active engagement of your mind instead of watching TV. I like to share my love of reading with my students.*

As she describes reading to connect herself to worlds beyond, she "reads" her children—through her teaching and her nurturance—and is connected to worlds beyond.

> *Over the years I think I've learned a great deal from children. I've learned about the human condition that many children's lives take. Chil-*

dren are not just these sweet little things that come to school and learn. They come with a lot of brokenness and a lot of tragedy. Sometimes these children's eyes are like they are looking at you through the eyes of an adult because of their experiences.

I think I've learned a sense of resiliency in seeing some children that are at risk and how they rise above situations. It kind of reaffirms your faith in. . . . I don't know what it reaffirms your faith in. It really touches you and makes you want to work harder, go all the way for these children. They are the voices that challenge. So often in teacher education you talk about needs that are academic, physical, emotional, spiritual, and too often I think teachers get wrapped up in the academic. What I've learned from children is you truly do need to balance all of those areas to be able to bring your teaching to a successful point. Kids can learn from different types of experiences, and they can't have something that is just one sided. They need a variety of instructional strategies.

I believe a lot of education comes from influential learning, from discussions, from talking about values. For instance, what do they value from a book instead of what color the can was that Judy dropped on the floor. So, I guess I've learned a variety of things from kids. One thing that is really interesting—I learn all the hip stuff. I learn all the cool new words. I learn definitions of words I've never even heard of. You know like, "Well, what does that mean?" and the kids answer, "Oh, Ms. Tacheny!" and they go on and on. I think I've learned a lot from children about life. I've probably, maybe learned more than I've taught. You learn a lot of different things about kids! The thing is, most children are so open. They don't know what they are saying. They talk about the tragedies of life. I had a little boy today who came up to me and said, "Ms. Tacheny my Auntie's boyfriend bought a bud last night." I said, "Oh, did he buy a Budweiser beer?" he said, "No, he bought a bud, the kind you smoke." I seriously had never even heard of dope or anything being referred to as a bud. I said to him, "I'm sorry to hear that, Alex. Would you ever want to buy a bud?" Alex replied, "No!"

You have to acknowledge what children say and to try to help them deal with their conditions that they are presently in and help them move beyond it. I guess the number one thing I've learned is that you can't change where the kids are coming from. You can only help shape their future, and darn it if that isn't the hardest thing because you want to change it and you can't. The wisdom is to know the difference. It is rare to be able to influence a family to change on behalf of their child, so I choose to believe that what I learn from children and what I try to communicate to them is for them not to be victims. They can rise above their circumstances.

Unfortunately, some educators in the past seemed to be unsuccessful in including alternative ways of knowing in their classes. For example, Maxine Hong-Kingston (1989) tells a story about cultural knowledge passed on through families that was not attended to by an elementary teacher: "When my second grade class did a play, the whole class went to the auditorium except the Chinese girls. The teacher, lovely and Hawaiian, should have understood about us, but instead left us behind in the classroom. . . . I remember telling the Hawaiian teacher, 'We Chinese can't sing 'land where our fathers died.'' She argued with me about politics, while I meant because of curses" (Hong-Kingston, 1988, 167).

As Edelsky (1990) says, "Learning is best achieved through direct engagement and experience. . . . learners' purposes and intentions are what drives learning" (24–25). When past and present experience and engagement about that experience occur in a context, the learning is multidirectional—for children and for teachers.

> *One thing I have noticed about children with different backgrounds and diversity is that there isn't a lot of judging. I have seen a lot of empathy grow in children. They rally around each other when someone is low or has had a bad day, and the kids are kind of like, convey the message Don't mess with my people, we're all in this together. They are good buddies. I had one boy talk about this story from Cambodia. He was talking about how his mother saw one of her children killed and there was nothing she could do and she had to keep running with the baby or she might die too. These divergent life experiences are not something the kids would have seen even on TV. The different ways that the kids respond! Diversity is something I almost wish that every school had. Even when you are talking about counting. Children come at it from so many different ways. If they are counting in another language they naturally start sharing their language. If you happen to be reading a book with a cultural background and a child has connections, they show a lot of ethnic pride. I think diversity lends itself to, hopefully, someday, erasing prejudice. We should all realize that we have a lot of things in common and that we all have past histories. What we bring to the present and where we want to be in the future are parts of who we are, but I think we are parts of each other's stories too.*

Wong Fillmore (1991) contends that "teachers and parents must work together to try to mitigate the harm that can be done to children when they discover that differences are not welcome in the social world represented by the school. Parents need to be warned of the consequences of not insisting that their children speak to them in the language of the home" (345).

I do interest inventories to find out the different interests of my individual students. I also have a book box in my room, and I'm adding to it all the time. I'll highlight new books before putting them in the box to spark interest. I make sure there is a variety of books in the box, from different cultures, interests, and genres. When the students are reading, I'll grab a book and read myself to model good reading habits.

When students are finished working on a task, I'll sometimes call them over to read in small groups. I like to have oral reading time every day. I will read either a chapter from a chapter book, or I'll read something interesting that I came across, usually having to do with different cultural holidays, or stories with a message. I always make sure to read books that reflect the cultures of all my students.

Right now our school district is working to support prelearning readiness so that children are prepared when coming to school. I would like to have portfolios for reading and writing. I would like to do something to foster adult literacy. Sometimes kids have problems with literacy because their parents do.

Family History

Like many of the outstanding teachers we interviewed, Mary's parents didn't do much bedtime story reading.

My parents didn't read to me much. I had brothers and sisters, but they really didn't have the time to read to me.

Yet there were books and printed materials around and in her life.

I always had access to books, because I lived two blocks away from the public library. I remember that I wasn't allowed to cross the street by myself. I was lucky that the library was on the same side of the street as my house.

I read mostly in my bedroom. It was hard to find somewhere quiet to read because of my big family. I didn't watch a lot of TV. I'd rather be reading.

I remember pre-primers in first grade—the Dick and Jane books. Mrs. Sather was my teacher. I didn't try to read fast or show off. I remember that some of my friends would try to read really fast when reading orally. I would know all the words, but just had to read them slowly. This stands out because reading was a really big thing in first grade. I was a pretty good reader, so this was a positive step for me.

Reading came pretty easy to me, plus I loved to read. I would ask for books for my birthday. I won the St. Paul summer library reading contest one year for reading the most books.

Not only were books a part of Mary's early life, but she identifies a pattern of curiosity and respect for worlds outside her own realm of knowledge and experience.

[I read] a book called Snow Treasure. *It was very intriguing. It's about these children who helped save all the gold from Norway during a war. It was based on a true story. The book was read to me by a teacher, and then I still liked it so much that I decided to read it on my own. I still read it every few years. I don't remember authors very well. I do remember that I liked books about the Amish, pioneer days, and mysteries.*

I remember reading a lot of novel books. I can't think of a book that really sticks out in my mind, but I remember that I loved reading books about Jewish people and the World War II era.

Resisting Reader/Teacher

I think Mary Kay knows, there are times when I really am, on a basic level, a shy person, but I have learned to stand up for so many things. Really, I've found my voice. I cannot stand injustice, and I won't tolerate it when it has to do with my students. It's a virtue and it's also a vice, because I have to learn that there are things that you can't change. But you do learn advocacy, and I think it's a good thing. I believe it has helped me not be so shy, and people now can't believe I am shy. I'll get up in front of a group of three hundred people and tell them if I don't agree with something based on integrity and experience, but I don't know if I could stand up in front of three people.

Mary exemplifies the self-confidence of taking risks in order to "teach against the grain" (Cochran-Smith, 1991).

I think one area that has really helped strengthen me in taking risks in curriculum has been embracing an integrated approach, and inter- disciplinary strategies. For example, Mary Kay's help with COMPAS [A Literacy Writing Project in the St. Paul Schools] writing really was a turning point for me. You can incorporate a lot of learning into the writing process and writing strategies just by following the brainstorming, prewriting activities, what your follow-up is. You don't have to be "married to a manual"; you don't have to take the curriculum and follow every scope and sequence activity. I can do things to put together the objectives that are more appropriate to the needs of the students in my classroom and not let the manual dictate that. It's well worth the risk to go beyond that and to extend curriculum by embracing an integrated approach. I might be teaching reading, and then I'll branch off into a math lesson that came from that reading context. That is what I mean by influential learning.

Children remember those things and come back to them, so that is a risk. I'm probably not a traditional teacher. I like to do a lot of creative dramatics. I like to give children experiences of leadership within a framework, where you teach them leadership skills, then give them opportunities for leadership. I think my children are just as important as an author. My students write to state senators; they have written to a judge, for example. It is overwhelming the responses they get. I have had a state senator come and meet my class based on their letters. We've been invited down to the Ramsey County Court House by a judge. Whether they are first graders or third graders, they really respond when children write genuinely from their hearts.

To give children a voice is a risk, because a lot of teachers want control. I think particularly with students at risk, you have to help let them know that it is okay to talk about things, or it is okay for them to question, because who wants robot kids? If we want to program their answers, forget it. There's no thinking or evidence of that critical thinking process that is the buzz word in trying to instill in them. Along with that you have a climate that offers children the opportunity to question, and you have to set up an atmosphere where it's okay to make mistakes. I really applaud kids that are willing to take a risk in not knowing what the outcome will be.

Mary Tacheny's classroom is a positive, real example of a safe and respectful context where the students are able to grow, question, support each other, and take risks. Mary's combination of respect for the learners and knowledge of writing process techniques provides the kind of classroom that some critics (Lensmire, 1995) aim for, and when they are unable to accomplish it, imply that the blame should be owned by the children or the philosophy underlying the method, or the methodology itself.

These dynamics of Mary's classroom extend beyond her classroom walls.

As far as reading and risks, I even think of assessments as risks, to take a risk and do a lot of portfolio assessment things and not your typical grading. Because I'm dealing with children that don't always have phones, I don't have a way to talk to the family if I'm worried about my children's reading ability.

Yet, for example, my children take home books every day, and every day they have a chance to go to the library and read that book to an adult. We have community tutors or even aides in our building and a librarian. So they get that experience of reading one to one with someone.

And I'll go to the homes in the housing projects and various neighborhoods if I'm worried about a child. I think maybe that is a stupid risk. I'll knock on the doors. I want to get parents connected. I want them to know what is happening in my classroom. It is a risk when you invite parents into your room, because they don't necessarily come with educated eyes. They might have a vantage or view point, and you're trying to do the best you can for all of your students. I will definitely partner with any parent that's wanting to come into my classroom, and it is an open invitation. I feel I have to be accountable to the parents and to the community at large and I have no problem with people questioning me, because I better know what my techniques are and what my purposes are for doing them. So, I think those are all risks.

I could go home to my nice quiet neighborhood and just tuck myself in, but I can't now because of what I know about my children's lives and different things about school. Then you have the added emphasis to fight. Fight not only for the rights of your particular program but for equal rights for all children. It takes so much energy. Like right now with the governor and budget cutting in education. I feel I've got to fight now even for college. He has reduced the college budget by 21 percent. If all anyone ever did was think about what was happening to themselves, collectively nothing would happen. I think we have to have these global eyes. These eyes that the children have so that we can make a difference in their lives. As one person standing alone, we are not going to accomplish much, but as we gather together like these little packs of kids that stand up for each other we can. I mean, they are going to make the difference, and they are going to be the voice of the future. So, why would we want to squelch their voice now? They've got ideas!

A college professor said something once that impacted me greatly:

> *If not now, when?*
> *If not here, where?*
> *If not me, who?*

References

Brady, J. (1995). *Schooling young children: A feminist pedagogy for liberatory learning.* New York: State University of New York Press.

Cochran-Smith, M. (1991). Learning to teach against the grain. *Harvard Education Review, 61* (3), 279–310.

Edelsky, C. (1990). Whose agenda is this anyway? A response to McKenna, Robinson, and Miller. *Educational Researcher, 7–11.*

Hong-Kingston, M. (1989). *Woman Warrior.* New York: Knopf.

Lather, P. (1993). Fertile obsession: Validity after poststructuralism. *Sociological Quarterly, 34* (4), 673–693.

———. (1994). Gender issues in methodology: Data analysis in the crisis of representation. Paper presented at American Educational Research Association Conference, New Orleans, LA.

———. (1991). *Getting Smart: Feminist research and pedagogy within the postmodern.* New York: Routledge

Lensmire, T. J. (1995). Learning gender. [Review of the book *Shards of glass: Children reading and writing beyond gendered identities.*] In *Educational Researcher, 24* (5), 31–32.

Lewis, C. S. (1956). *The last battle.* New York: Collier.

Nasir, A. (1990). In an interview with Bill Moyers in *Spirit and nature.* Coopers Station, New York: Mystic Fire Video.

Patai, D. (1988). Constructing a self: A Brazilian life story. *Feminist Studies, 14* (1), 143–166.

Reyes, M. de la Luz. (1993). Challenging venerable assumptions: Literacy instruction for linguistically different students. *Harvard Educational Review, 62* (4), 427–446.

Richardson, L. (1993). Poetic representation, ethnographic presentation and transgressive validity: The case of the skipped line. *Sociological Quarterly, 34* (4), 695–710.

Smith, D. (1995, January). Interview in *UTNE Reader,* Minneapolis, MN: LENS Publishing Co., p. 77.

Wong Fillmore, L. (1990). Latino families and the schools. *California perspectives: An anthology.* Los Angeles, CA: The Immigrant Writers Project.

Wong Fillmore, L. (1991). *When learning a second language means losing the first. Early Childhood Research Quarterly, 6* (3), 323–347.

15

RAÚL QUINTANILLA

At that point I wanted to change things. But you need more than one person to change a book. That professor said this is the book and this is it, and I said this is not it. I will bring you a book from across the border, and it will be the opposite of what this book says. So, I think they are better now. It was the sixties and seventies.

—Raúl Quintanilla

All his life, with a passionate loyalty to and love for his Mexican roots, Raúl Quintanilla has worked for change. He was born in Minnesota, the son of migrant farm workers who had immigrated from Mexico. He has lived and worked in various contexts with people who represent diverse groups on many complex levels. Now he is an English as a Second Language teacher for the St. Paul Public Schools in Minnesota. His activism demands that his convictions about people, learning, democracy, and discrimination reach far beyond the classroom walls. His background, his reading, and his current work take him throughout the state and region as an advocate for various Latino groups, their potential, their differences, and their similarities.

Some research discusses the correlation between formal education (a high school diploma) for mothers and school success for their children (Sticht and McDonald, 1989; Teale, 1992). Other research has begun to question and contradict that information, its assumptions, and its limiting ramifications. Weinstein-Shr (1992) cites research which discusses family strengths. The research indicates that when families participate in a variety of literacy activities, including home language literacy and activities in which children read to parents (Tizard, Schofield, and Hewison, 1992; Viola, Gray, & Murphy 1986), the literacy development of the children is enhanced. Raúl's personal story illustrates family strengths supporting him as a reader and resisting reader/teacher.

Metaphor and Art as Frameworks for Living

Reminiscent of the title of his favorite book, *A Light in the Forest,* Raúl followed lights leading to meaning through his reading and activism.

> *My favorite book was* A Light in the Forest. *I don't remember the author. I think it was about an Indian. That is one of the first bigger books that I read. I really was much into encyclopedias. I had a teacher in seventh grade, because we were really poor and everything, she gave me a set of encyclopedias. The old ones. Real small. I just wanted to know everything. It reminds me of the Hmong students now. Like I taught seventh and eighth grade last year. If they have nothing to do, they will get a dictionary and they will just read the words. I don't know if they are comprehending, but they just like looking and looking. The visual aids.*
>
> *I did a lot of reading. I always did and I still do to learn about other countries. I majored in geography too. I wanted to learn about different people and would look at the map and say, "I wonder what they do in school," or "I wonder what they do when they get home from school. What do they do, do they have a TV?" . . . I read a lot of historical books. I read a lot about the presidential administration. I read about politics— the Republican party and Democratic party and the Gras Unida party. I wanted to know where it came from; I wanted to know the background. I would get the books at the library.*
>
> *The library became my friend. I knew that anything I wanted to find out was there. I would walk four to five miles to get a library card. You didn't see many Mexican Americans. And the library was on the north side of town where all of the white kids lived. So I had to go over there. Somebody helped me, pushed me, or I just liked it. But I still believe in the library. Anything you want to find is there.*
>
> *If I were going to the mountains I would read a book about the Sierra Madre. Something about the place where I was going to. If I was going to Mexico I would read about Mexico.*

Nurturance Past and Present (Self and Others)

Raúl at an early age began reading, asking questions, and noticing his family ties as a type of self-nurturance.

> *We were so many [in the family, and] there wasn't a big house. So there wasn't a lot of space. I would read outside. I wasn't the only one. There were two little ones that I read with. We would play school. I*

would read inside even though my brothers and sisters would look at me and wonder, What is he doing? Well, reading. Or if I had a project to work on for school I would practice a speech or a presentation with them, but they couldn't understand. They would laugh, because they didn't understand.

As a child in school Raúl realized:

We didn't have any heroes to identify with. We didn't have General MacArthur. We didn't have Roosevelt, We didn't have . . . we couldn't identify with them because we were Mexican Americans. People that they would consider heroes like David Bowie and Davy Crocket were white people. To Texas history or American history they are heroes. But if you look at northern Mexican history they are not heroes. They are the crooks who kicked people out of areas. In fact, the school I went to was Sam Houston Elementary, and they would praise him. We didn't know him, so we tried to learn. We didn't really have anything or anyone to identify with, except for the Cinco de Mayo. We had one person. General Zaragoza. The reason that we identified with him is because he was born in an area of south Texas, which is now Goldeanne, and he was the one that won the final battle.

He went on to explain a common problem for young Mexican Americans in terms of identity:

The Mexicans didn't want us because we were Chicanos, and Americans didn't want us because they think we're Mexican. So we made this guy our hero. Then John F. Kennedy. He was a hero.

When I got into high school there was a Chicano movement, so I got into that. I got into migrant Mexican American Chicano litera-ture. . . . I did a lot of that type of literature reading. . . . All of my favorite authors were from southern California: Valdez, Sipuedes, Guerra, más y más. I got very involved. When teachers asked us to write a report I would use our type of literature. I would say, "Why can't I use Mexican American books?" Everybody else did the opposite. But it was good because the teachers started to learn or understand about diversity.

As an adult, he continues to nurture himself through literature and the arts.

I haven't been to the theater in fifteen years. I don't watch TV either. I watch the educational shows. The news sometimes. It is kind of depressing to watch the news, with all of the shootings. I do like to watch the Spanish channel because their shows are very positive. They include a lot of children, and everybody is happy. I mostly watch the National Geographic *or education shows. I subscribe to* Educator Magazine *and two or three magazines about Mexican Americans, and two or three are educational.* American Education *and* Psychology Today. *I will read anything.*

Regarding teaching Hmong and Latino students, Raúl advises,

Number one when working with the students: use a lot of positive reinforcement. Instead of using negative statements, turn them into positive statements. That is one of the things that we went through that the Hmong also went through. You have to respect their language. You have to learn about them. I didn't know anything about the Hmong students. But I have read about them and their culture. I learned about the style that they use for teaching. In my country, too, they had to recite everything from memory. They still have corporal punishment. It is way different here. I would say that from my training, to be able to help these children, use a lot of positive reinforcement. Not because they are right or know a word. Just because they are sitting; just because they came. About speaking their language [The positive aspects of that]. Some teachers say no, no don't speak in your language; practice your English. I have learned a lot.

He shakes his head, and we discuss recent research and our own experiences that support home language use in the learning of a second language.

As West (1990) maintains, "Yet we will struggle and stay, as those brothers and sisters on the block say, 'out there'—with intellectual rigor, existential dignity, moral vision, political courage and soulful style" (36).

Family History

How do teachers and schools become aware of the students' desires, visions, realities, and repertoires? Greene (1986) notes, "I think of how little many teachers know about their students' diverse lives and thinking processes, how little they can know because of the paucity of dialogue in the classroom space" (80). It is important that the family's voice be part of the dialogue so that we "hear different voices tell their stories about how they experience education or schooling" (Bloch, 1991, 106).

Raúl explains,

> *My parents lived in Mexico, and then they crossed to the United States. I was born right on this side of the border. I have eight brothers and eight sisters. In the summer I would work every day from 5:00 A.M. 'till sundown. We didn't work during the school year except for weekends.*

He goes on to describe the days in the fields,

> *Everything was very positive. Your father is there; your mother is there; and your brothers and sisters are there too. You are all working together, and your father is saying good things all day, every day for a long time. I didn't know at that time, but it was a close family unit. They talk about supporting a family now with two incomes. With the migrant families we were doing that long ago.*

Raúl noted that by third grade, he was blatantly aware that

> *Dick, Tom, Jane, Paul, Tim, and Sally, the old reading books in school. . . . I couldn't understand the one where Mommy dropped Daddy off at the airport, with a suitcase. And Daddy always had a tie. We would go home and say, "My father never wears a tie," and we didn't know anything about airports. But that is what the book was teaching us. The food, too. You know, if there was a breakfast, it was eggs, milk, and toast and orange juice. But with our breakfast it was a cup of coffee and a piece of Mexican sweet bread. We could make no relation between the school and the home setting.*
>
> *My parents never read to us, but I saw them reading. They read novels and magazines. They read magazines like Superman—these were Spanish, the comic type, very simple. That is how I learned to read. Nobody taught me to read. I was curious because I went across the border. My cousins in Mexico, across the border, were learning to read in Spanish. They had all these magazines lying around. I can still remember reading, La Bruja, etc. and many others. Spanish seemed really easy to me. I learned to read and not to write. There is a difference, because we were right on the border. We were sometimes criticized because they would say, "You can't speak English correctly, and you can't speak Spanish correctly." So you are not bilingual. You are not monolingual. You are alingual. You are not either one.*
>
> *Like still in the eighth grade, I'd turn the radio on, and I'd be listening to a song, and I still couldn't understand what they were*

saying; it was too fast. Because when we went home from school you know, we didn't speak English at home. Because the parents didn't speak any English, and it would be disrespectful. The other thing was that we were all Mexican American, and you spoke English, and your brothers would say, "Hey, he thinks he is a big shot, because he knows English." It was kind of a shame thing to do. That doesn't help you when you are learning the language. I didn't have trouble with reading and comprehension, because I had very good teachers. I think. I learned the library quickly. I need some computer training now because everything is on computers. A lot of teachers need training on this.

Resisting Reader/Teacher

Sleeter and Grant (1991) point out that "ideally, education should help all students acquire knowledge that empowers. This implies that knowledge should include a perspective of history from the students' point of view and be selected and constructed in relationship to the students' desires, visions, descriptions of reality, and repertoires of action" (50). Raúl, when asked what book influenced his life, answered:

Teaching as a Subversive Activity. It opened my eyes to the messages and methods of teaching. It was a strong book. I don't remember the author. We felt that they were only teaching us one side of the story. So, the book said, when the professor talks about his side, question. Question the book that you are reading. Again this is more factual. . . . I was going to major in Texas history, but I got in an argument with a professor because he had a Texas history book according to "Texas" history. There was nothing else included. So I dropped that class and didn't major in Texas history. At that point I wanted to change things. But you need more than one person to change a book. That professor said this is the book and this is it, and I said this is not it. I will bring you a book from across the border, and it will be the opposite of what this book says. So, I think they are better now. It was the sixties and seventies.

Henry Giroux (1988) and other advocates of critical pedagogy (Freire and Macedo, 1987; Shor, 1987) advocate the fruition of "teacher as intellectual." Giroux (1988) states, "I want to argue that one way to rethink and restructure the nature of teacher work, is to view teachers as transformative intellectuals" (25). He maintains that this quest of the intellectual is helpful for three reasons. First, it defines teachers' work as an intellectual endeavor as opposed to a mere technical one. Second, it brings to light the conditions necessary for teachers to combine ideological and practical issues. Third, it legitimizes teachers' roles in combining political, economic, and social interests through daily pedagogy.

Raúl is an activist in the classroom:

> *I work with Kindergarten through sixth graders. We have our own literature books from Addison Welsly, ESL books. What I do is a lot of oral language. We feel that the books are not adequate. We have to jump around and figure out what to do for different levels of students. Many, many different levels. They have stories in there like the "Little Red Hen," "The Three Little Pigs," so we have the stories that everybody else has, only they are at an appropriate level. I also read to them a lot. Books like* Rosie's Walk. *ESL students need a lot of visuals, especially in the first grade. A lot of poems, writing. We read a lot to them. We do a lot to get them interested in us, because if they are not interested in you they will not be interested in what you have to say or do. So you have to show interest.*

Regarding satisfying the interests of the students,

> *It's not easy. In the summer I had a class of two Africans, four Hispanics, seven Hmong, and about seven Vietnamese. I had never had that type of class. I had to go home and think a lot. And they were all at different levels. You have to do a lot of individualized instruction. You have to do a lot of walking around, and you better have something for them. You have to be aware of their level. If you lose them, they get a negative thing about ESL. When you have a group like that you do a lot of individual work. It is a lot of work. A lot of teachers don't do that. You might teach them oral language. When you get to writing everything falls apart. We work on the writing process in the school district. Our students can master speaking and writing. Our students can master writing first because of the process of writing.*

When asked about outside activist activities, Raúl explained,

> *The Minnesota Migrant Council is in the Minnesota Department of Education, Migrant Section. I am the state chair, president. I was appointed by another former migrant worker. I was appointed and then elected. I wanted to get involved, and they said, "Here's what it would take. You would be going to meetings all over the state." So I went to the first meeting, and all of these parents from St. James, Willmar, St. Paul, and Moorhead were there. I was new at the meeting, but they elected me right away. I said to them, "You don't have to elect me just because I am a*

teacher. I would rather have you represent yourself, a parent representing your family." But they felt because I was a teacher I would have more influence on principals.

So what we do is work with parents in different migrant communities. We make sure that the migrants are being served in the schools. We make sure there is an ESL teacher or a Chapter 1 teacher available if needed. There are a lot of problems involving principals. There is a little town in western Minnesota where sugar beets are farmed. Okay, the migrants work for six months during the season. Let's say in this small community three families decide to stay. Then the principal doesn't have a bilingual teacher, so he gets one and says, "You are going to take care of these children." Then the weather gets cold, and he has hired this teacher, and the Latinos decide to go back. What does the principal do with this teacher? So it is hard on both sides. What we try to do is again we meet with the parents, and for example, in St. James the representative says that the Chicanos that have settled have nothing to do after school. When teenagers have nothing to do they start getting in trouble. So what are we going to do? There is money in the state, get some sort of program for these types of children.

Another problem in these areas is that all of the teachers are white. These teachers have seen the migrants come and go. They tease them. These teachers are not sensitive to the cultural needs of the migrant workers. So we can propose to the state; all we can do is propose. We are proposing many inservices and credits for the teachers. But we can only propose. But we need consultants from this area to go to the smaller towns and work with them on cultural diversity. Maybe, too, have a mini Festival of Nations in the summer that would not only include the migrants. To include the Germans and Swedish people. It is not easy. The migrants are in Willmar, and I am here. We only meet three times a year. So I don't know how effective this committee is anyway.

And still he questions,

I will tell you the truth, how I feel about it. I feel that we were just put there by the education committee for them to say, "Well, we have a committee." Then everything is okay. They send the forms, and we have the meetings. But how much can you get done in three meetings a year? Then they are there, and you are here. There needs to be a regular full-time position to do a job that would be sufficient.

It is a volunteer position. Someone has to be there. I am saying all these things that we want to do, but I will be gone next year and they will start all over again. Who will do it? Again we meet three times a year y nada. Last year we went to the National Convention in Colorado. We got so many ideas for migrant students at the high school level. I am working with Penn State and the University of Minnesota and other agencies that we have connections with. We want to provide some training for some counselors in Willmar and areas such as that because we see the statistics for migrant students' drop out rates or graduating and not continuing on. We want to find out where it is coming from. Is it the student, is he being misguided, maybe not? Who has time to check all of that? To interview all of the students? And Penn State is over there, and I am over there. We will try as much as possible. College assistant migrant program. There are only five in the states: Texas, Pennsylvania, California, Michigan, and then . . . I started in the program. They should start one here at the University of Minnesota. Who is going to do it? Is it going to be the Chicanos? I talk to them and say, "What are you going to do about it?" They have a lot [of ideas], but are they willing to start something? It is a program where the first year they are guided by peer counselors and then they become peer counselors, to help the migrant Chicano population of the college. I don't know who can do it. I am so busy working at two schools.

Raúl values bilingual and multilingual children's language processes and sociolinguistic skills and the resulting interpretations of their worlds. He validates the intellectual, cognitive, and social processes the children take part in. He supports the sociocultural relationship between family, community, and child and especially applauds and learns from the contributions of caring, active parents and teachers. He also knows that alternative ways of knowing that are represented by minority parents and children are not currently accepted in most school curricula. This is a loss to the children who bring this knowledge with them to schools *and* to the children brought up with traditional, mainstream cultural knowledge. This is a loss to parents who want to pass on cultural traditions and ways of knowing and find themselves fighting not only the school information, but also the issue of their children believing that the forms of knowledge of the home are as important as mainstream cultural knowledge. Furthermore, this is a loss to teachers, who could be opening new worlds of exploration to children and providing a link between the culture of the school and the culture of the home.

Yet, Raúl remembers and goes on, in the sun.

I recall having come back from the migrant fields, traveling from Indiana down to Texas. Traveling for two days in the back of a truck with eleven kids. It is fresh in my memory. I can still see the sun . . .

References

Bloch, M. N. (1991). Critical science and the history of child development's influence on early education research.*Early Education and Development, 2* (2), 95–108.

Freire, P., and Macedo, D. (1987). *Literacy: Reading the word and the world.* South Hadley, MA: Bergin & Garvey.

Giroux, H. A. (1988). *Teachers as intellectuals: Toward a critical pedagogy of learning.* MA: Bergin & Garvey Publishers, Inc.

Goleman, D., Kaufman, P., and Ray, M. (1992). *The creative spirit.* New York: Dutton.

Greene M. (1986). Reflections and Passion in teaching. Journal of Curriculum and Supervision, 2 (1), 68–81.

Shor, I. (1987). *Freire for the classroom: A sourcebook for liberatory teaching.* Portsmouth, NH: Heinemann.

Sleeter, C., and Grant, C. (1991). Mapping terrains of power: Student Cultural knowledge versus classroom knowledge. In C. Sleeter and C. Grant (Eds.), *Empowerment through multicultural education,* New York: State University of New York Press, 49–68.

Sticht, T. G., and McDonald B. A. (January, 1989). *Making the nation smarter: The intergenerational transfer of cognitive ability.* [Executive Summary] San Diego, CA: Applied Behavioral and Cognitive Sciences, Inc.

Teale, W. H. (1992). Reading to young children: Its significance for literacy development. In H. Goelman, A. Oberg, and F. Smith (Eds.), *Awakening to literacy.* Portsmouth, NH: Heinemann.

Tizard, J., Schofield, W., and Hewison, J. (1992). Symposium: Reading collaboration between teachers and parents in assisting children's reading. *British Journal of Educational Psychology, 52.*

Viola, M., Gray, and Murphy, B. (1986). Report on the Navaho Parent and Child Reading Program at the Chinle Primary School. Chinle School District,, AZ.

Weinstein-Shr, G. (1992). Learning lives in the post-island world. *Anthropology and Education Quarterly 23* (2), 160–165.

West, C. (1990). The new cultural politics of difference. In R. Ferguson, M. Gever, T. T. Minh-ha, and C. West (Eds.), *Out there: Marginalization and contemporary cultures.* Cambridge, MA: The MIT Press.

16

JUDITH BORER

I remember a National Geographic special on television in 1976 in which experts talked about the future. They were all men at the seminar. Only one woman taking notes, and she wasn't quoted. I still count today. When a presenter gets up at a school assembly, I count how many boys and how many girls she calls on.

—Judith Borer

I last saw Judith at a poetry reading which I was giving at a bookstore in St. Paul. I noticed her as I read the poem "as in a French painting."

> as in a French painting
> a mirror darkens or clarifies
> gives off an unbiased reflection
>   not so a painting
>
> a museum afternoon of looking
> at women created by men
> dancer by Degas courtesan by Renoir
> Raphael's madonna illusive accessible
>
> women eat for these men
> are not angry Matisse
> paints wife and mistress
> at tea in the garden
>
> women breakfast
> with curled hair and red lips
> and are clean for these men
>
> what of the woman in Bonnard's painting
> washing in the bathtub upstairs
> near the window her long hair golden in sun

she bends, washes with suds
please keep the cloth slightly on—

what of the fourteenth century
madonna in the rebuilt cloister

who turns from the window
who ponders the secrets of the universe
god asks for her womb his hands
            surround her neck

is she a man's soul as he paints
her in that dream moment?

and how would women
whose best work is lost
have made her? Rummel (1994, 31)

   As I finished reading, Judith began to cry. I believe that she responded to the words about the lost works of women artists, because her story is the story of a woman born into silence, struggling, almost from the beginning, to be heard. Hers is a story of silence imposed, kept, broken. Hers is the silenced voice described by women writers in diverse contexts. Tillie Olsen (1978) described women's "hidden silences; work aborted, deferred and denied" (8). At the end of her life, Anna Akhmatova, one of the great Russian poets, who was banned from publication by Stalin's government from 1923 to 1940 and whose work was censored long after that, described the silence imposed on her as a palpable thing: "The silence of arctic ice" (1994, 468).
   In 1941 she wrote to her friend, the poet Tsvetayeva, both of their husbands killed, their children prisoners, describing the millions of women like them and "of a snowstorm erasing all traces of us" (1994, 237).
   Yet silence, because it is so palpable, can be broken. "The reed, revived, might start to sing" (Akhmatova, 1994, 237). Judith's interview chronicles this coming to voice. It is clear that from the very beginning this emergence was and is connected with the act of reading. It is also clear that this struggle defines Judith's sensitivity as a teacher of young children.
   The writers whose words Judith read created many of the watershed experiences that helped her break out of repressed life into action in the wider world. These writers, in her adult life most of them women, have been her spiritual mentors, her guides, their words often becoming catalysts that shaped the constellations of moments that create

weight over time. Eliot Eisener (1994) described the act of writing (also reading) as an occasion through which ideas get born. The writer starts with vision and ends with words. The reader starts with words and ends with vision. It is a conversation between what you tell the paper and what the paper tells you. Things you didn't know come across. Metaphoric forms are created that enable both the writer and the reader to go beyond the literal to the ineffable. Eisener tells us that passion and vision are fundamental in literacy education, because our capacity to envision a society worth having is fundamentally rooted in the imagination.

Metaphor and Art as Frameworks for Living

At the center of Judith's reading, life, and teaching is a coming into voice—both literal and metaphorical. This coming into voice is a breaking out. In the first part of her interview Judith tells of a literal glass case from which she took books to read. The silence imposed upon Judith by her family, schooling, religion, and culture had to be broken.

> *We had a library with books in a glass case. The nuns would lock the case, and we could only read the books in school. This friend of mine and I took the books out during the school day, then brought them home.*

From the beginning there is a questioning, a breaking of rules. This breaking of rules is tied to her love of reading, her desire to know more. The following passage from the poem "Letter to a Former Mother Superior" may reflect Judith's thoughts:

> dear mother and sisters
> I must confess
> last week I broke silence
> fifteen hundred times
> and I still break it
> smash it like a coffee cup
> the brown eye of silence
> stares from the floor. (Rummel, 1989)

Judith's life history is one of active resistance connected with reading beginning in childhood. Throughout her story there is a progression of strong female characters from literature and strong women who create them. Like them, she tallies up occasions of oppression that she sees and about which she speaks. Judith's reading, as a young adult woman, of philosophical novels such as *Zen and the Art of Motorcycle Maintenance* taught her skills of spiritual resistance. Like one of her favorite literary characters, Celie in *The Color Purple,* Judith grew out of oppression into resistance with a strength nourished by other women, and her concern now is to continue this cycle in the nurturance of young girls.

> *I still get this image that I am sticking out too much when I speak up for something or question. I think it's like that for girls—how to be heard, to speak out in the classroom, and not feel that they are sticking out or be afraid to stick out.*

Art is also central to her life in the love of literature—especially poetry—and of music. Her empowering sensitive response to the written word evokes a strong female spirituality that results in a rejection of injustice and a continuing breaking of imposed silences.

> *I remember reading when I was in sixth grade. We had a library with books in a glass case. The nuns would lock the case, and we could only read the books in school. This friend of mine and I took the books out during the school day, then brought them home. I got caught because I wrote her a note that said, "Are you bringing a library book home tonight?" I spelled the word* library *wrong, so the teacher called each student from the class up to her desk to write the word* library. *Everybody knew that I had done it by the time I got called up, because I was the last one to get called.*
>
> *Now I mostly read books by women authors: Toni Morrison, Margaret Atwood, Alice Walker who wrote* The Color Purple. *I also like Adrienne Rich and Marge Piercy and other women poets.*
>
> *With children's books I find mostly that if I like a book, they [the students] will too. I start off the year with William Steig books. I adore his books. I get a personal kick out of them. I have this ritual where I go through the book and say, "This is Mrs. Borer's favorite author." The students chant, "This is* Sylvester and the Magic Pebble, *Mrs. Borer's favorite author!" or "This is Bill Peat, Mrs. Borer's second favorite author!"*

Anna Flanagan (1994) tells us how Kenyan poet Micere Mugo "came to appreciate the political nature of creative writing and poetry as she saw how it enabled her and others to reclaim themselves and give voice to the liberation struggles of the people. . . . Within colonial systems, people are named and defined by those in power." The art of writing is closely related to Judith's reading and teaching as well as the development of her own voice. She reads and responds to the works of feminist poets and fiction writers. It was these writers who helped her in early adulthood to move from the covert resistance she described in the above passages to the overt resistance of the feminist.

Nurturance Past and Present (Self and Others)

I read for information, enjoyment, escape. Sometimes I read for something to do. I want something exciting in my life, so I pick out a book. If I have to be waiting anywhere, I want a book with me.

The Art of Motorcycle Maintenance *was important for me. It is a philosophical book. It was big in the seventies. It's about this man's journey into his psyche through motorcycles. It's about his journey physically on the road and his journey not to go crazy.*

I also read a lot of books on civil rights like The Autobiography of Nat Turner. *I always had a bent toward liberalism, toward caring for others. I worked in the civil rights movement. When I was in the convent, after high school, I read a lot of religious books, theology books having to do with spirituality and inner growth. I also like books about women. One I just read is called* Charms for an Easy Life. *It's about three generations of women.* A Thousand Acres *by Jane Smiley is another book dealing with women's issues. I'm really drawn to books like that.*

Judith uses books in school to nurture students' acceptance of each other.

I think I am very interpersonally gifted, so all the books I read have to do with friendship, life, getting along, things like that. I'm always talking to my students about things like that.

I sometimes worry if I talk about divorce or homosexuality. I'm not afraid to talk to the kids about it; I just sometimes worry about parents' reaction, but I haven't ever had a parent complain about it yet. I don't think books in school should be censored. I think censorship comes out of fear. Most of the time people are afraid of what they [the students] are going to learn or how they will handle it. Parents are sometimes afraid that information that they feel is harmful can't be kept out of their children's learning.

There was a discussion here about censorship, because this year we bought a book about gay dads. The librarian was really worried. She asked what she should do with the book. We said, "Put it on the shelf!"

She said, "But what if someone contests this?" So, we pulled out our challenge policy. This is a school policy established in case someone challenges a book. I don't like the Babysitter books; or the American Doll series. But if the kids want to read them, they are going to. At least they are reading. Sometimes kids who are not the greatest readers like to read these books; so I still have them around, because they are interested in them.

It has helped me to be in education all these years. I am always thinking and always getting new ideas. It has kept me tuned in.

Women have gone within themselves to find their own sources of spiritual truth. Where else were they to go for meaning, for identity? The books they read, the churches they attended when young assumed that the male perspective is also the human perspective. In the arts, women were pictured as madonna, virgin, or whore. Tales written for children such as Andersen's *The Little Mermaid* were stories of female silence. The little mermaid had her physical ability to speak cut from her mouth. She surrendered her feminine voice in order to have a chance for success in the patriarchal world of air, sun, and legs. Brown and Gilligan's 1992 study addresses the ways in which women's voices have been trivialized and dismissed. They recorded how girls progressively give up voice in order to be in relationships. Judith's struggle to find reading that helped her in this going within is the story of all women. This female spirituality does not thrive in a vacuum. Wholeness in our own lives is inevitably tied to the well being of others, particularly the ones who have been set aside as "other" because of their color, class, sexual orientation, or frailty of mind or body.

Family History

We got the papers at home. When we were old enough, we could read the comics. That was fun to do, especially on Sundays when they were big. My mom read, and my dad read; they read the paper every day. I do remember that. I know my mom was a reader. I remember her reading magazines, Magazines and church stuff. I had older siblings that read. My sister was always getting yelled at because she was hiding in a book instead of helping with the dishes or cleaning. But I don't remember my older siblings reading to me either. I learned to read in first grade. I remember sitting around on little reading chairs. Basal readers were used. I simply remember reading. I don't remember it being a struggle. I think I was kind of proud of myself that I could read. I picture myself in these little chairs reading.

*My second memory is cleaning out my desk and handing every-
body these worksheets to do, because I hadn't done them. The teacher
caught me and was really mad. I thought I was being clever.*

*I've been told I always asked questions, but I didn't consciously
start questioning until college. I was absorbed by reading. It was my way
of widening the world. I came from such a narrow world in my family,
Catholic schools, and then the convent. College was my first taste of
discussion. It tasted so good! I loved philosophy; I couldn't believe that
they thought like that. I walked about the campus talking about those
theories. When I was a nun in the convent [for seven years after high
school], I was always angry and questioning. Imagine, we were supposed
to keep silence, spend most of our time not talking, and never question.*

*Later, leaving the Catholic church was a big step for me. One day I
just didn't go. I knew I was not getting my needs met as a woman in the
church.*

Judith describes her adult growth into feminism as tied to reading:

*My husband at that time made fun of women, so I was constantly
thinking about femininity, who I was as a woman. This led me to therapy, and I had a feminist therapist. At the same time, I read Marilyn
French's* The Women's Room. *It was a turning point.*

*My feminism took another turn when I could get angry with men
in my family. It happened when I was going to Adler Institute for a
degree in counseling, raising a daughter, and while in therapy. In all of
these places people said things about men that no one had vocalized for
me. My family adored men and gave them no responsibility for themselves. It was unheard of in my family to get mad at men when men
weren't ready to hear what I had to say. I didn't know how powerful some
of the things I said were. Now I know that they are not ever ready to hear
some of those things.*

*One of my favorite poems is "The woman in the ordinary" by
Marge Piercy [1972]. It starts, "in her bottled up is a woman peppery as
curry." It reminds me of myself.*

Resisting Reader/Teacher

*I interned at Chrysalis, a woman's shelter, because I was divorced
then, and they had groups for women who were thinking about getting a
divorce and I knew I could help them. At the same time I was raising a
daughter, and I was so aware of things in society that would hurt her.*

I started reading the magazine New Woman. *I thought it was a
glorified version of* Seventeen. *Then* Ms *came out.*

I started to analyze everything—movies, TV shows, books—from a feminist viewpoint. I analyzed everything I saw and read. I began to count how many women would appear on a show as experts. I still count today. When a presenter gets up at a school assembly, I count how many boys and how many girls she calls on.

Judith's experience mirrors the research Barbierie (1995) and the Sadkers (1994) have conducted. Using a systematic observation instrument in classrooms for two decades, Myra and David Sadker discovered that even the most well meaning teachers tend to focus on male students, because they demand attention. They found too many girls missing in classroom interactions and sitting on the sidelines. Judith constantly works to change this dynamic in her classroom.

I don't like the way boys are so loud in the classroom. They dominate, shouting out answers, and I have trouble ignoring them, and bright girls are quietly sitting there. I had a very bright girl this year. Her parents were concerned that she was too bossy. The bossy label is a way of keeping girls down.

I am aware that I say "boys and girls" a lot. I'm trying to break that habit, because there's no reason to break up the class by gender. I think that's a gender issue. This year in my classroom I had more girls than boys, but the boys were quite loud, so I was always saying, "BOYS!" That gives the wrong impression that boys are naughty, boys need to be yelled at. That's not okay. I've also noticed in assemblies that when we have outside speakers, boys are usually called on more than girls. It is usually the boy who jumps out of his seat to get attention who gets called on rather than the girl who politely raises her hand. The boys in my class this year were quite boisterous, but I had some girls who spoke out as much as the boys did. I was happy that I had some of these girls and that I had to remind both girls and boys to raise their hands.

Parents are changing too. Parents don't want their girls to be really compliant. There are still some. The sanctions for girls are still very much there. I also think that little girl aggressions are not the same as boys' aggressions. Boys often will kick and shove, and that's "boys will be boys." Girls get into fights and want to work it out; they want to talk about it; they want to talk behind backs. That's not "girls will be girls"; it's taken very negatively. I think it is just a way of them expressing their aggression.

My principal told me that she always counts on me to bring up issues that are problems at faculty meetings. I'm still afraid of that part. I feel (as I learned from my family) that you have to say it loud to be heard,

*because they would never listen to me. I still get this image that I am
sticking out too much when I speak up for something or question. I think
it's like that for girls—how to be heard, to speak out in the classroom, and
not feel that they are sticking out or be afraid to stick out.*

*Sexism is all over the place. They always say that women have
come such a long way. But when I read about certain things I don't know
if we really have. A lot of awareness has been raised, like the Anita Hill
case. I think she aroused the knowledge and awareness of sexual harassment and how deadly it can be. There are also laws and things that have
happened since then that have helped. But if you "tattle," your place in
the work place will not be the same. Maybe in a situation like this
[teaching] where we're all pretty openminded about talking about it and
we have workshops about sexual harassment, it's better. Maybe things
wouldn't be the same if the harassment was reported. Maybe action
would be taken quickly and things would be just. But I don't know about
out there in the big world. I think women are so hurt by the economic
inequities in their lives. Women end up being more poor when divorce
happens.*

Judith's risk taking goes beyond speaking out. It is integral to her
teaching.

*As a teacher you take risks all the time. Trying to remain open to
new ideas in education is a risk.*

*I team taught with a woman for eighteen years, and after you get to
know a person, you don't take as many risks, because you are comfortable; you already have your curriculum and so on. This friend retired last
year, and this was my first year with a new partner. This man is thirteen
years younger than I am, and it's very hard. I think the whole year was
one big risk for me. He did things differently. I was afraid parents weren't
going to like me. Were they going to like the man better than the woman?
It was a constant struggle not to just close the door and say, "The hell
with you! I have been teaching here for twenty years, and I can do it my
way!" It was probably the hardest year in my life for a while in terms of
teaching and not being scared of his ideas. He had some wonderful ideas
and some not so wonderful ideas. We used many of them, and they
turned out great. He used some of my ideas, and they worked. But I think
that's the biggest risk; staying open to ideas and people and not being
isolated in your classroom.*

Many women representing diverse cultural and class experiences
document the painful processes of assimilation and socialization in the

United States often in the context of voice. Diane Glancy (1988) writes of her trouble with the spoken word, an often "macaronic breach of two languages," English and Cherokee: "a bifurcation of thought not only from within/but also pressed inward from the out" (38). Rita Dove (1995) tells of the shock of recognition and relief she discovered when, in graduate school, she came across Toni Morrison's *The Bluest Eye:* "As soon as I started reading it . . . you still can't tell if the author's black or white. But I just knew. I remember standing there and leafing furiously through the first few pages of the book because I was trying to figure out where she came from. I thought, 'This is my country she's talking about'" (56). Maxine Hong-Kingston (1989), in *The Woman Warrior,* writes that "when my second grade class did a play, the whole class went to the auditorium except the Chinese girls . . . our voices were too soft or nonexistent" (167). She compares this to the education she experienced in the evening Chinese school: "There we chanted together, voices rising and falling, loud and soft, some boys shouting, everybody reading together, reciting together and not alone with one voice" (167). This classroom in the Chinese school sounds like the one Judith envisions.

There is a relationship between what we teach in school and the unequal outcomes of schooling based on social class, race, language, or dialect and gender. (Swadener and Kessler, 1991). School contexts are constantly reproducing mainstream society's biases regarding race, ethnicity, class, and gender. Yet schools can also be a place for change. The passion and vision described by Eisener (1994), those fruits of an imagination fed by reading literature, are the results of Judith's breaking out of the "glass case" and into her own voice. Now she passes this vision on to her students. It is very important, as Maxine Greene (1995) tells us, "to look at a classroom in terms of what might be but is not yet."

References

Akhmatova, A. (1940). Belated reply. (1941). Quoted in R. Reeder (1994), *Anna Akhmatova: Poet and Prophet.* New York: St. Martin's Press.

———. (1940). Inscription on a book. Quoted in R. Reeder (1994), *Anna Akhmatova: Poet and Prophet.* New York: St. Martin's Press.

———. (1921). The seventh elegy. Quoted in R. Reeder (1994), *Anna Akhmatova: Poet and Prophet.* New York: St. Martin's Press.

Andersen, H. (1981). *The Complete Hans Christian Andersen Fairy Tales.* New York: Avenel Books.

Barbierie, M. (1995). *Songs from the heart.* Portsmouth, NH: Heinemann.

Brown, L., and Gilligan, C. (1992). *Meeting at the crossroads: Women's psychology and girls' development*. Cambridge, MA: Harvard University Press.

Eisener, E. (1994). Artistic thought in scientific research. Keynote address presented to the National Council of Teachers of English in Orlando.

Flanagan, A. (1994). Kenyan Poet Sees Poetry as a Political Statement. *The Council Chronicle*. June, 7. Champaign-Urbana: National Council of Teachers of English.

Glancy, D. (1988). *Offering*. Duluth, MN: Holy Cow Press.

Greene, M. (1995). What the arts do with experience. Paper presented at the American Educational Research Association meeting in San Francisco, CA.

Hong-Kingston, M. (1989). *Woman warrior*. New York: Knopf.

Kirkpatrick, P. (1995) The throne of blues: An interview with Rita Dove. *The Hungry Mind Review*. (35). St. Paul, MN.

Olsen, T. (1978). *Silences*. New York: Dell-Delacorte.

Piercy, M. (1982). Unlearning not to speak. *Circles on the Water*. New York: Alfred A. Knopf, Inc.

———. (1972). Woman in the ordinary. *Circles on the water*. New York: Alfred A. Knopf, Inc.

Rummel, M. K. (1994). As in a French painting. *Mythos Journal* (1,3).

———. (1989). *This body she's entered*. Minneapolis: New Rivers Press.

Sadker, M., and Sadker D. (1994). *Failing at fairness: How America's schools cheat girls*. New York: Scribner's Sons.

Swadener, E. B., and Kessler, S. (1991). Introduction to the special issue. *Early Education and Development, 2* (2), 85–94.

Part III

Reflections

Introduction to Reflections

In this book, teachers wear the mantle of expert. We used the ideas of trusted mentors in the field of education as guides for a framework as we reflected on the findings around the four themes of metaphor, nurturance, family history, and resistance. Yet we still emphasize the actual words, thoughts, and experiences of the teachers in this study as the focus of the reflections.

We open this section with a poem about the wisdom of every day experience as expressed through the language of the ordinary.

A Story She Wraps around Herself

The boot marks of the unfortunate
are to be seen on the grey stones
of the beach. Peig Sayers

Here on Clougerhead waves crash
on granite cliffs, steaming shafts
of rock shatter the Atlantic.

Three miles out the deserted green hills
of the Blasket Islands mourn the lost
civilization of the tongue.

I imagine your black skirt
slicing through the wind out there
your rosary dangling from your
large red hands.

It was this sea that gave
you stories
for your neighbors
and later for the scholars
who came to hear your words
songs foreign to their ears.

You carried your dead son

from the cliff bottom.
With unshaking hands
you rearranged his skull
for burial. Once—you allowed yourself to cry
then clapped the end of mourning
and found the words to pray.

And you made the men pray
those who came to listen.
Made them kneel on the cold flagstone.
They had to say the rosary with you,
the angelus, blessings for the sick
and you kept them at it as long as you could.

You talked with your hands
as well as your tongue
a clap of the palms for urgency
a flash of thumb over your shoulders
your hand over your mouth
to show a secret.

It's hard to grow old you said
but I'll be talking after my death.
A woman's tongue is a thing
that doesn't rust. (Rummel, 1993)

17

METAPHOR AND ART AS FRAMEWORKS FOR LIVING

Metaphors structure our thinking, our understanding of events, and consequently our behavior (Lakoff and Johnson 1980). This is as true of education as of anything else. This book is a celebration of the symbolic lives of classroom teachers. The importance of generative metaphors can be approached from many perspectives. Stanley Kunitz (1985, 111) said that poets have a few metaphors arising from early experience and they keep returning to these in their writing. These metaphors are the heart of personal myth making. An example of this is in the work of E. B. White who in his journal, written when he was twelve, described in great detail a spider that he watched in the corner of the barn. Twenty years later in a poem to his new wife, "Letter to Katherine from the King Edward Hotel," he developed an extended metaphor for a spider's web as a connection with his love. Twenty years after that he wrote *Charlotte's Web* (1952).

As we listened to the interviews of the teachers in this study, we discovered metaphor at work in the same way. As each teacher talked about early reading and present teaching, we heard verbal imagery repeated which clustered around particular metaphors and seemed related to early reading experiences. We are not claiming a causal relationship between early reading and these generative metaphors. Many experiences could give rise to them. Early literacy experiences, in oral language, reading, and media gave these teachers images and stories that helped to expand and to give flesh to their metaphors.

In a study (Rummel and Quintero, 1994) of metaphors for literacy developed by preservice teachers over time we found three types of metaphor: process, for example a sports-centered metaphor; visual, for example a sunrise or a river; and a combination process and visual metaphor, such as growing a garden. The generative life metaphors of the teachers interviewed in this study seem to be of this third type. It may be that reading and other literacy experiences provide the details for the visual expansion for metaphors that involve a sense of process or development.

Bill described the way in which reading fed the early development of his idea of life as an adventure.

> *I bet I read Huck Finn and Tom Sawyer every year, once a year, for years, from my early teens to my early twenties, because I just could not get enough of that wonderful writing and those wonderful stories. Tom Sawyer was a character I just loved, because of that sheer adventure and the wonderful life that he led where every day was an adventure. And I always lived in this life of reading and then began to live the adventure even when I wasn't reading. And I still do.*

These early metaphors continue to be generative for the teachers in this study. They reappear in new contexts making them metaphors of journey. Bill continues:

> *Now books kind of lead me to places. A book led me to a really fascinating place this summer, northern Russia. I had been there before, but I went again on a kayaking trip. This book I read two years ago called They Took My Father was a story of Finnish people from the Iron Range moving back to Russia in the nineteen thirties during the depression. They got into Russia and found out it wasn't the place that it was claimed to be, and then the border was closed and they couldn't leave. So they lived their lives in Russia as U.S. citizens from Minnesota. It just blew my mind that up to ten thousand people had done this. So I found a way to get to that area. It was a wonderful adventure.*

The metaphors continue to generate thought and action in their work as teachers. As a child, Raúl saw the sun, a light leading to meaning. He now follows his metaphor of light leading to meaning through his reading and teaching.

> *I had a teacher in seventh grade, because we were really poor and everything, she gave me a set of encyclopedias. The old ones. Real small. I just wanted to know everything. It reminds me of the Hmong students now. Like I taught seventh and eighth grade last year. If they have nothing to do, they will get a dictionary, and they will just read the words. I don't know if they are comprehending, but they just like looking and looking. The visual aids.*

Clandinin (1986) found that imagery of teachers often clusters around metaphors such as "planting a seed" or "making a home" and that these metaphors reveal the complex merger of personal and professional experience and of theory and practice. Another way of thinking about the sources of knowledge for teaching concerns communities which may inform our knowledge base, cultures which may exist in harmony with one another, or may clash and cause tension for the teacher (Gee, 1992). The early metaphors which came out in this study are not specifically metaphors for teaching, they are metaphors for life. Teaching is a part of this life. This longitudinal perspective of generative metaphor gives us information that moves beyond some of the recent studies of metaphors which teachers have formed about teaching. These tend to look at present beliefs without the component of personal and family history.

Comparing and contrasting personal metaphors with institutional metaphors might be a useful means for preservice teachers to develop alternative ways of thinking about teaching, and for considering the ethical implications of holding one or another conception of teaching. The understanding that these personal metaphors are life metaphors arising out of early language experiences fed by experience with books and media is very important. It tells us that work with preservice teachers must go deeper than the creation of new metaphor. These generative metaphors must be uncovered. "It is difficult for me," Maxine Greene (1995, 99) tells us, "to teach educational history or philosophy to teachers-to-be without engaging them in the domain of imagination and metaphor. How else are they to make meaning out of the discrepant things they learn?" We would extend the importance of imagination and metaphor to preservice and inservice methods classes.

Teacher education programs pay too little attention to the importance of having novices make personal beliefs and images explicit. Often this kind of symbolic work with teachers is too superficial. Brunner (1994) creates a thoughtful pedagogy in which preservice teachers problematize their perspectives through what Maxine Greene calls, in the introduction, "informed engagements with works of art." Brunner leads her students to discover for themselves the meaning of critical reading, critical writing, and the claiming of voice. It is clear that any kind of clarification and deconstruction of personal beliefs has to involve the whole of life, not just the classroom, because these beliefs emerge from a total life experience.

In "Poem for Flora" Nikki Giovanni (1975) describes how Flora at Sunday school heard "'bout nebuchadnezzar" and how God was "no color at all," but what she remembered was that "Sheba was Black and comely and she would think I want to be like that" (23).

Myth is a story to live by. Without stories to live by we can gather facts but not discover meaning; we can have goals but not over-arching purposes. Myth situates facts in networks of meaning. Myth grounds ideas and feelings in generative images. Myth connects isolated individuals to family and community. Myth invisibly and powerfully connects us to the meaning and mystery of our lives.

More surely than anything else, we are defined by our stories, the cultural myths we hear from our earliest days. At the same time, we are defined by the way we "rewrite" the myths we hear. Only as old patterns in our consciousness crumble are new patterns possible.

The life metaphors of the teachers in this study seem to provide a mechanism for "remything." Living in the twilight of the twentieth century, we are surrounded by the ruins of myths and metaphors that have lost their power to shape and to animate our lives. All around us, we hear the cracking of old certainties. And yet, in the midst of our confusion and grief, a new mythology is being born. All the teachers in this study are involved in midwifing emergent mythologies. They are transforming their school classrooms into mytho-genetic zones: places where new myths and metaphors are born. They are vessels through which new mythologies are slowly emerging. These teachers faced with the need to recreate common mythologies did so at a young age. This "recreation" happened during a critical reading of what they were learning in and out of school.

As a child in Texas Raúl realized,

We didn't have any heroes to identify with. . . . We had one person, General Zaragoza. The reason that we identify with him is because he was born in an area of south Texas, which is now Goldeanne, and he was the one that won the final battle. The Mexicans didn't want us because we were Chicanos, and Americans didn't want us because they think we're Mexican. So we made this guy our hero.

For Donn, it happened as she learned literacy skills at the same time as she created a fantasy world for herself which was safer than her neighborhood.

Kathryn, through critical writing, was able to break the taboos of silence forced upon her by her abusive home life.

The teachers in this study while creating new mythologies are strongly connected with wisdom of the past which has been passed on through story, lending depth and reverence to their lives.

The words of many of these teachers evoke a strong sense of place. Grover, Cookie Monster, and other puppets; the river; the campfire; the friendly library—places carry the power of story, of myth. Place is connected to life metaphors. The teachers' deep understanding of the importance of place helps them understand the importance of place to the children that they teach. They see the neighborhood of the housing project as important and as rich as other, more affluent neighborhoods.

For Vicki, New York City is a rich treasure for her students to share. Although he lived in an urban neighborhood, Bill found the wilderness which he craved and which he now shares with others.

With great consistency, the words of the teachers in this study show how each individual's generative life metaphor and involvement with art directly affect each person's professional life. The teachers in this study were personally involved with many different art forms. Writing, particularly journal writing, however, was the art form most frequently discussed. Writing, especially journal writing, has also received more support in school curricula. The importance of this is supported by these outstanding literacy teachers who model for children.

"Teachers write with children for themselves. Children can tell if it's fake or not. When teachers write for themselves, children can't wait to write" (Graves, 1994).

The development of the teacher as writer has received much attention during the past decade both in the professional literature and in the work of writing projects across the country (Calkins, 1994; Graves, 1994). This very strong belief that good writing teachers must write is the cornerstone of the development in children of an "authorship literacy" in which the writer claims ownership for and vigorously participates in the processes of writing.

It is not easy for public school teachers to write. They have been afforded neither time nor space within the traditional demands of their roles, and they have often not been taken seriously as writers. Many of these teachers speak of the power of language in speaking the truth, in building community, in giving courage. Naming carries weight and definition. Concepts shift. The new is born.

Kathryn and David described the power of writing from two different perspectives. Kathryn talked of writing as nurturing, even life-saving, personal practice:

It has just always helped me sort out things. I went through a period in my life where I suffered from really severe depression as a result of, I think, a lot of abuse in my childhood, and I was in a psychiatric hospital for a number of months, and writing at that time was part of what saved my life. I remember that I struggled with picking up the pen and beginning to write. Yet, it was absolutely necessary to my survival at that time. I don't think I would have been able to write it if it had not been for my past experience of doing it as a child.

David, who is a professional writer, talked about his writing coming out of listening to others:

So I've had those experiences with people. I feel like the ultimate gift has been that . . . well I'm a big believer that there is some combination of divine intervention of some kind and an extremely complex mental process that gives us our stories and I have been fairly prolific over the past couple years, and I think the reason for that is that I'm just constantly being bombarded with stories, and so they just keep coming and melding into something new.

Tracy voiced the emotions of many of the teachers when she talked about participating in a long-term project which emphasized personal writing.

Many teachers in this book have written or expressed the desire to write a creative work. David has had four novels published and has more in press. Del told us of the book which she wrote for her daughter and how she shares her writing with her students. Drama is also an art form that these teachers use. With some, such as Donn, it began very young as she sang and danced with the characters on "Sesame Street." For many, drama is an important part of their literacy teaching. Mary described creative dramatics in her classroom in the context of fantasy, identification, and voice:

If you can get children to move from their own selves and place themselves in different characters, you can get so much more out of them. It is so affirming for them. Particularly, I will have Southeast Asian students, and some of them are very quiet, a lot of the girls are very quiet. Some of that has to do with traditional roles. Today we read this story about Jane and her new mittens, and I had different people reading the different parts. It was very interesting. This one little girl, Yer, is always so quiet, but when she was the voice of Jane, because Jane was kind of this boisterous person, all of a sudden I heard this voice I had never heard. She was talking so loud and clear, she took on a different role. All the kids noticed and commented on how they could really hear Yer. Yer was just beaming; she was so proud of herself. I think it is always good to clarify to children what is reality and what is fantasy, and I think there are times to use both. But actually, I think fantasy lends itself more towards instilling real creative ability in students. It is a form of higher level thinking which is what we want to move all our students to.

Pamela began her interest in dance as a child, and again it was connected with reading as she read the biographies of dancers. Pamela's artistic sense is an activist characteristic that she uses to enrich her students' experiences as she teaches them dance and creative movement. Donn knows how to guide her first-grade students in visual art because she is an artist. She understands the process, and she gently encourages her students to create. Bill keeps a photographic record of his wilderness journeys

It doesn't matter which comes first—the passion for an art or teaching. Earlier we quoted Achebe (1988). For him, art and education are synonymous:

> I would be quite satisfied if my novels (especially the ones I set in the past) did no more than teach my readers that their past—with all its imperfections—was not one long night of savagery from which the first Europeans acting on God's behalf delivered them. Perhaps what I write is applied art as distinct from pure. But who cares? Art is important, but so is education of the kind I have in mind. And I don't see that the two need to be mutually exclusive. (Achebe, 1988)

Maxine Greene, Diane Brunner, Eliot Eisener, and others have long proposed that teacher education include literature and the arts as a vehicle for reflection. Brunner (1994) adds television and film to these avenues to reflection. However, the only art requirement for most elementary teacher education programs is one beginning level introductory class and one art methods course (Speaker and Peterson,1995). This is clearly inadequate when the importance of art in the lives of these teacher "artisans" is considered. These teachers "do" arts with children, but, more important, art in some form is central to their lives, and this becomes the heart of the gift that they share with children. Their lives are an organic whole.

Most of the teachers speaking here talked about their involvement in creative activity at a young age. Art is being cut from the elementary curricula at the same time that classroom teachers are receiving little or no training. Teacher educators must help preservice teachers and those already in the classroom to express the form of art that is a personal passion and then share it with children.

One frequently recurring theme in the literacy stories of these teachers is that of identification. This occurs between reader and story. Del, for example, talked with great enthusiasm about the adventures of the female characters in the Laura Ingalls Wilder books that she loved as a child. This identification also occurs between teacher and children as they meet over books. Judith described her students' enthusiasm for

"Mrs. Borer's favorite author!" Del described how a book "becomes hot stuff after the teacher reads and mentions it, causing a run on the library."

Most important of all, the inner life, the power of spirit shines through the words of the teachers in this study. Their life metaphors, their art are spiritual expressions. Like an artist, Wayne, who struggles with a handicap, uses his gift of vision and expresses himself through his work with children. He described his work in the context of a book, *A Stone for Danny Fisher*:

> *He had a choice of living or coming back deformed or blind and handi-capped. He chose to die instead of live that way. I can relate to that. If a handicapped kid sees me, they will want to know about the leg because they also have a handicap; we relate right away. It is really a beautiful thing. The Lord has used my handicap for good instead of bad.*

Bill received from reading the visions or dreams that would direct his life. For example, he read books about canoeing and taught himself to canoe. His reading as a young person about the Boundary Waters Canoe Area, especially the books by Sigrid Olson, drove him to go canoeing there.

Staff development needs to be considered more broadly as "person development." A school administrator recently talked about the large number of teachers in his district who voluntarily undertake the extensive control-theory-based training created by William Glasser (1992). Teachers he works with have told him that it is the most mean-ingful staff development program which they have experienced. "I think they like it because of the personal development. And that makes sense. If you have difficulty relating to others in your life you will have difficulty relating to students." It seems, listening to these teachers, that the meaningful, lasting changes that have occurred in their teaching were related to much broader aspects of their lives. Literature is an important part of this spirituality. Writers such as Toni Morrison and Louise Ercrich reflect a spiritual connectedness with the world and help create it in us. They give us the acknowledgement that we live in mys-tery as part of something far greater than ourselves. And they do it all with words. This is important to remember in methods instruction of preservice teachers. If this instruction is to promote lasting change so beginning teachers will not immediately revert to poor practices that are prevalent in their school culture, it must cause change on the spir-itual level through reading of literature and through inward-looking reflection practices like those used by Mary Tacheny as she teaches her primary students:

With C. S. Lewis, part of that is the transcendence. He talks about reflection. There is very much of an inward journey. I think a lot of teaching is that you have to have the students look inward and ask them an evaluation question like, How do you feel about this piece of writing? Have them look inward with the portfolio assessment. The children see their own progression. You need a lot of lofty ideas and inspiration. I suppose that's what C. S. Lewis is to me, an inspiration. He's sort of farther along the journey than I am, but some of his is fantasy, and some of it is experience.

At the beginning of this chapter, we discussed the generative life themes clustered around personal metaphors which seemed related to early reading experiences. We ask you, the reader, to consider this reality in your own lives. What are the metaphors that drive your teaching and living? How are they related to your early experiences, especially with literacy? How are your reading, teaching, and life connected? How is this phenomenon occuring in the unique lives of your students as they develop in literacy both at home and at school.

References

Achebe, C. (1988). *Hopes and impediments: Selected essays.* New York: Doubleday.

Applebee, A. and Langer, J. (1986). *The writing report card.* Princeton, NJ: Educational Testing Service.

Brunner, D. (1994). *Inquiry and reflection: Framing narrative practice in education.* Albany: State University of New York Press.

Calkins, L. M. (1994). *The art of teaching writing.* Portsmouth, NH: Heinemann.

Casey, K. (1993). *I Answer with My Life: Life histories of women teachers working for social change.* New York: Routledge Press.

Clandinin, D. (1986). *Classroom Practices: Teacher images in action.* London: Falmer.

Gee, J. P. (1992). What is Literacy? In Shannon, P. (Ed.), *Becoming Political.* Portsmouth, NH: Heinemann.

Giovanni, N. (1975). *The woman and the men.* New York: William Morrow and Co.

Glasser, W. (1992). *The quality school: Managing students without coercion.* New York: Harper Collins Publishers.

Graves, D. (1994). *A fresh look at writing.* Portsmouth, NH: Heinemann.

Greene, M. (1995). *Releasing the imagination: Essays on education, the arts and social change.* San Francisco: Jossey-Bass Publishers.

Kunitz, S. (1985). *Next-to-last-things.* New York: Atlantic Monthly Press.

Lakoff, G. and Johnson, M. (1980). *Metaphors we live by.* Chicago: University of Chicago Press.

Rummel, M. K. and Quintero, E. (1994). Literacy metaphors in teacher education: A way to reorder experience. Paper presented to the National Reading Conference in San Diego.

Speaker, K., and Peterson, G. (1995). Outcome based goals for admission to teacher education. *Outcomes, 14* (2), 45–48.

White, E. B. (1952). *Charlotte's web.* New York: Harper and Row Publishers.

———. (1954). Natural history: A letter to Katherine from the King Edward Hotel. In *The second tree from the corner.* London: Hamish Hamilton.

18

NURTURANCE PAST AND PRESENT
(SELF AND OTHERS)

With great consistency, the words of the teachers in this study show how each individual's generative life metaphor and involvement with art directly nurture professional life. Bill, for example, used the metaphor of life as adventure to open up wider worlds outside his experience through reading. He actively engages in photography. This art making is clearly a part of his self-nurturance and is something which is part of his teaching as he presents slide shows and brings his students in contact with students from other countries. This shows the interrelated nature of our theoretical model and our findings. Art and/or literature is part of the self-nurturance of each teacher and also becomes a way in which children are nourished. The path that leads from the school into the broader community flows directly from literacy-enriched metaphor and art. "It takes imagination to engage with literature and other art forms," Maxine Greene (1995) tells us. "Encounters of this sort push back the boundaries. . . . They locate learners in a wider world, even as they bring them in closer touch with their own actualities."

Bill Simpson's interview provides an example of this. The connections among his reading for self-nurturance, his adventuring, and his work for children become global:

We started a sister city in Ginger, Uganda, with Stillwater. Then we started a special school project with our school and a school in Uganda. There are three thousand students in this school and no books. So a friend of mine started this program. This month the community and schools in Stillwater are bringing in their favorite new books. And also fifty cents for postage. And then we are shipping them to Africa. So my goal is to go over there and visit this school. It would be nice to set up some kind of exchange program with students.

Other teachers talked about personal reading and art in ways that clearly convey their nurturing power. They used language that calls to mind their metaphors. Their words also illuminated the spirituality that underlies their literate, artistic, and teaching lives. It is the life of the spirit (not necessarily connected to formal religion) which they are describing. The spiritual is best evoked by metaphoric gestures and rituals. These rituals are often connected with reading in a way that nourishes the individual and helps the individual nourish others. Mary talked about connecting stories her students are reading "to a meaning or value." As she described reading to connect herself to worlds beyond, she also talked about reading her children, and thus her teaching is nurturance, connected to worlds beyond.

Over the years I think I've learned a great deal from children. I've learned about the human condition that many children's lives take. Children are not just these sweet little things that come to school and learn. They come with a lot of brokenness and a lot of tragedy. Sometimes these children's eyes are like they are looking at you through the eyes of an adult because of their experiences.

Pam talked about her deep need to write. Judith's reading in spirituality led to her love for the writing of women. As stated earlier there is a need for staff development to reach teachers at these deeper self-nurturing and other-nurturing levels. The spiritual dimension in these teachers' lives, as related to their reading and their teaching, was evident.

Most of the teachers described early reading in terms of mentoring. Reading helped guide them even when, as in some cases, little else in the environment supported this vision. As adults these teachers find their reading a source of wisdom and growth.

Raúl said:

When I got into high school there was a Chicano movement, so I got into that. I got into migrant Mexican American Chicano literature. I did a lot of that type of literature reading. All of my favorite authors were from southern California. Valdez, Sipuedes, all Guerra, más y más. I got very involved. When teachers asked us to write a report I would use our type of literature. I would say, "Why can't I use Mexican American books?" Everybody else did the opposite. But it was good because the teachers started to learn or understand about diversity.

Now he subscribes to *Educator Magazine* and two or three magazines about Mexican Americans and *American Education* and *Psychology Today.*

Kathryn reads "stories about women who are adventurers and that portray women in strong roles." Like Kathryn, many teachers talked about particular authors as important to them. Certain books became guides; certain authors became mentors. Lisa sees authors as mentors:

I feel that I have a relationship with the authors that I read. I feel like they are speaking to me. I have met some professional educational writers, if I like their writing . . . I usually like them and can relate to them as a person.

These teachers bring this sense of authorship into the classroom. Bill talked about the visit of his favorite author, Barry Lopez, to his school. Dell talked about reading and teaching from books by the same author.

Many teachers described reading as a way to discover and to learn and frequently as a way to explore new places. Raul said:

I always did and I still do want to learn about other countries. I majored in geography too. I wanted to learn about different people and would look at the map and say, "I wonder what they do in school?" or "I wonder what they do when they get home from school. What do they do? Do they have a TV? . . . I read about politics, the Republican party, and Democratic party and the Gras Unida party. I wanted to know where it came from; I wanted to know the background.

Vicki talked of her love for reading and how it influenced her career choices, her choice of friends, and her work in schools. "I wanted to read, and I just couldn't get enough."

Most of the teachers described reading as a way to escape, to dream. They would echo these words found on a bookstore T-shirt: "I have often wondered how anyone who does not read, by which I mean daily, having some book going all the time, can make it through life."

The interviews showed us that teachers in this study had some common approaches to pedagogy consistent with and expanding upon the characteristics of "teacher as artisan" (Casey, 1993), which we recognized when we asked them to participate. They all exhibited a belief that it is their responsibility to find ways of engaging all their students in learning activities. They accept responsibility for making the classroom an interesting, engaging place. They persist in trying to meet the individual needs of the children in their classes, searching for what works best for each student. Their basic stance is a continual search for better ways of doing things. An example of this continual search is the involvement of students in learning that transcends curriculum, text-books (often), and achievement tests. None of them talked about testing as a measure of success. They have a predisposition to emphasize students' efforts in defining success. These teachers see protecting and enhancing students' involvement in learning activities as their highest priority. If they run into a problem in doing this they find ways around it. They are able to generate practical, specific applications of theories and philosophies; at the same time, they are able to see the whole picture. Day by day, these teachers are working hard to make schools better. Their teaching is an act of love like that described by Hannah Arendt (1961):

> Education is the point at which we decide whether we love the world enough to assume responsibility for it and by the same token save it from that ruin which, except for renewal, except for the coming of the new and the young, would be inevitable. And education, too, is where we decide whether we love children enough not to expel them from our world and leave them to their own devices, nor to strike from their hands their chance of under-taking something new, something unforseen by us, but to prepare them in advance for the task of renewing a common world. (196)

The teachers in this study also seem to have great physical and emotional stamina. They are involved in some life activity that provides them with a sense of well-being and from which they continually learn. Their lives show us how the things we care the most about are the things that we teach best.

The stories of the teachers in this book are filled with ideas, methods, and approaches to literacy instruction that are a continuance of the personal nurturance they received in the past and still get from reading and the arts (their own literacy). The metaphors and beliefs which drive their approaches to teaching give them a sensitivity to the needs of the child within a particular social context. This awareness of the importance of social context leads them to look at literacy methodol-ogy differently, directing the professional choices that they make. Mary, for example, talked about working with the district to support pre-school readiness and about working with her students' parents.

These teachers use methods associated with that particular cluster of beliefs about children, language, and learning that has been called "whole language." However, their awareness of children's social con-text leads them quite naturally to adapt these methods to the individual needs of children. They already blend skills teaching in a literature-based, wholistic approach to literacy in the effective approach being described by those responding to the current denunciation of whole language approaches as responsible for low reading test scores (Blau, 1995). They would never return to the skill-and-drill approach to literacy which they all experienced and which they all described in the interviews. Instead, they are all committed to teach differently than they were taught and to create positive learning experiences for their students. However, the sensitivity of these teachers to student needs leads them quite naturally to integrate skill teaching into their reading programs. Beyond that, they teach skills directly to students who need them. In the way suggested by Lisa Delpit (1990), they make sure that their students learn what they need to know, "not page after page of skill sheets . . . but rather helping students gain a useful knowledge of the conventions of print while engaging in real and useful communicative activities" (99). The teachers in this study are quite eclectic in their methods.

Although the methods which they use to achieve their goals are many, there are some which are common among all the teachers in this book. Their descriptions of pedagogy show that they understand that all language learning requires performance and interaction, activities that are productive in small groups where familiarity and contact facilitate risk and involvement. They all see their classrooms as communities. For all of them, literature is at the center of their work with children. In general, the approach to pedagogy described in these interviews is a "culturally relevant pedagogy" as defined by Ladson-Billings (1995). The nurturance which they give to students leads to academic success as well as to a developing sense of competence in home culture and the developing of a critical literacy.

Tracy, in describing her use of resources, gave us an outstanding example of these pedagogical practices which are based on beliefs shared by all the teachers in this study.

We've got an open library. We're uncomfortable with reading centers, Manny and I, because we feel like, what do you do for the kids who slip through the cracks? But we also use the traditional approach of pulling kids out on a needed basis. We may do the mini lesson which is focused on a skill or reader response to a book or anything that is related to reading that we feel is important that day. It may be with a partner or we ask questions like, "How did this make you feel?" or "Did you notice the periods?" or "Were you able to read with voices?" or "Wasn't this a great story because . . . ?" or teach mini lessons about five to ten minutes in length. After that we have our reading time when kids have the rest of the forty-five minutes or so to be into reading baskets. Those change weekly; they choose them on Friday, and our library is entirely organized by theme, so we have an animal bin, a transportation bin, seasons and holidays, and poetry bins. While kids are in those baskets, Manny and I will pull kids out; I've got half the class, and he's got the other half.

Some days I'll pull out one child who really needs help on one skill for that day, and sometimes I'll pull out two or three. We'll read books and talk about it, and meanwhile the other kids are in their reading baskets also responding in a reading log. It wasn't always an hour long. We started for ten minutes of reading, and then we worked ourselves up. They really run it themselves. They've got their reading logs which they respond to, and sometimes they don't, and that's okay. We are not very structured in the sense that we tell them exactly what to do or how. It is sort of open-ended, so that everyone has the chance to accomplish what he/she wants to do within that reading.

Mary described the strength and acceptance that is built in these classroom communities:

One thing I have noticed about kids with different backgrounds and diversity is that there isn't a lot of judging. I have seen a lot of empathy grow in children. They rally around each other when someone is low or has had a bad point, and the kids are kind of like, Don't mess with my people, we're all in this together. They are good buddies. I had one boy tell this story from Cambodia. He was talking about how his mother saw one of her children killed, and there was nothing she could do, and she had to keep running with the baby, or she might die, too. This is not something the kids would have seen even on TV. The different ways that the kids respond! Diversity is something I wish that every school had. Even when you are talking about counting. Children come at it from so many different ways. If they are counting in another language they naturally start sharing their language. If you happen to be reading a book with a cultural background and a child has connections they show a lot of ethnic pride. I think diversity lends itself to hopefully, someday, erasing prejudice. We should all realize that we have a lot of things in common and that we all have past histories. What we bring to the present and where we want to be in the future are parts of who we are, but I think we are parts of each others' stories now.

Pam talked about the importance of the children feeling safe in her classroom, about giving them privacy in their writing and also giving them an accepting audience.

Vicki is always searching for books that will help her students of diverse backgrounds feel pride in their own identities and heritage and learn about diversity and the complexity of American society.

Earlier in this chapter, in the discussion of the importance of each teacher's personal involvement in art, we showed how this involvement led them to model for their students. Modeling is central to the literacy programs of these teachers. Tracy transfers her journal work to her work with students. *"Whoa, Tracy has a writing journal; look at my journal!"* she tells them as she ties her own learning to that of the children:

> *I like to know about people in other cultures I think that they need to be surrounded by maps just to let them know the world view, that there is something else out there besides the little place where you live. I think kids like to know about other places and other people.*

The reading and writing which Del does for self-nurturance becomes a driving force in her professional life. Once in a while she reads from her own books when she is looking for a lesson.

The literacy classrooms of these teachers are filled with child-based activity related to books on subjects such as art, dramatic play, puppetry. Enjoyment of experiences related to literacy is a characteristic common to the teachers in this study. Many of them talked about their negative experiences with reading and writing in school and how they want to make it positive for their students. Donn, Vicki, and several others described their lack of connection with the books they read. Donn told us how she

> *had to sit down with that Jane book, and I hated it, and we sat in a semi-circle, and each person had to read a sentence, and what I would do is count the number of sentences and children so I would know what sentence was going to be mine, and we would not know what was going on in the rest of the story, but you know your sentence when it was your turn.*

Support of colleagues is important to sustain these teachers both professionally and personally. Pam discussed a writing group that she had belonged to and the context of literary nurturance in New York. Much of the nurturance as professionals these teachers receive from others relates to reading and literacy teaching. Donn described her mentors, including Pam Russell who teaches in the same school:

> *Pam did these writing workshops the first year that I was here, and it was on children writing their own journals, and it was introducing them to*

literature and author studies, and I said, "That is what I want to do!" It is so much fun to be able to bring these kinds of experiences to the children.

Vicki seemed especially sensitive to the cycles of literacy, describing her reading club called "Brown Women." Vicki provides an example of the wide breadth of the reading of the teachers in this study. It is characterized by the absence of a negative, limiting "political correctness." The teachers interviewed here are courageous and deliberate in their choice of books—some from newer ethnic writers, and some from a more traditional canon. For example, David, an African American who writes novels centered upon African-American characters, is an English major who shares Shakespeare with fourth-grade children in St. Paul. Bill, whose favorite author is Barry Lopez, reads Doris Lessing and Cristina Garcia. Judith told how *Zen and the Art of Motorcycle Maintenance* was important to her growth. Vicki, whose favorite author is Toni Morrison and who searches for all available multicultural literature for her students, talked about reading the Narnia chronicles with third-grade children in Brooklyn. These teachers know what they like and need, and they read for those purposes.

Is it possible that the next step is to evaluate what we have learned from these teachers as we develop admissions criteria for our preservice education programs? These interviews tell us much about what makes strong teachers in a diverse society. The strengths found in these teachers has little to do with admissions test scores and more to do with an expansive, creative approach both to life and to teaching as well as a strong inner life of mind and spirit. Tracy described this quality as the "creative teacher's love of play."

As Haberman (1995) found in his study, *Star Teachers of Children in Poverty,* the best teachers live what they believe. It is not possible to talk about beliefs and commitments apart from behaviors. The reverse is also true. How can this understanding be translated into preservice admissions criteria?

The importance of teachers' self-nurturance is evident in these interviews. In these mean times, how can school administration support this need of teachers? Many of the teachers talked about the importance of the support of administrators. Eileen Jones, an administrator in the district where Tracey teaches, described a school that is supportive of teacher development:

It is a school that is now solidly literature based. We have reading programs, and all of the teachers are involved in one stage or another in the writing process. The early childhood specialist is at school a couple of days a week. She teaches at Teacher's College and is connected with the college one day a week. We also are beginning—just this year for the first time—some early work that Lucy Calkins is doing with what are called "reading centers"—developing reading instruction in kindergarten and first grade, going with more of a center approach rather than a direct instruction approach in reading. We are also involved in school with a primary language record. Both the principal and some of the teachers have gone to Great Britain for training. We work by sitting in groups and doing primary language with prekindergarten, kindergarten, and first-grade classes. It's a school that is involved with a lot of very diverse things. It's on the edge of lots of things.

Do nurturant administrators have the same kinds of literacy experiences as nurturant teachers? Like the teachers she works with, Eileen, as a teacher, changed the way she taught through contact with the work of literacy leaders such as Lucy Calkins.

*Lucy Calkins used my classroom to kind of validate a book [(*The Art of Teaching Writing*] that she was writing. When I started, I did writing process and then instruction for reading. What happened one day kind of interestingly was, I was talking to the children about a book we were reading and the author of that book. One of the children said something like, "Oh, that book has a writer, too?" I never gave emphasis to them that there was somebody—a writer—who had put this book together. I probably couldn't do it with the basal readers which were done by computer. It got us to think about it, the fact that I never connected with a writer and they therefore never connected it either. It made us look at having authorship behind a book and see how it can change the way you teach reading.*

She faces censorship issues that arise in her work with directness and is not afraid of controversy.

I think it is always a little bit scary when someone talks about censorship. We had a big city-wide hoop-la a couple of years ago about a curriculum we called the "rainbow curriculum." It included some books that had to do with gay and lesbian parents, and it really set off the worst in some people. But you know it kind of died down after a while.

Eileen exemplifies the kind of administrator who is open to learning from teachers as they learn from their students. This kind of leadership nurtures teachers in their risktaking and sets the stage for a broad literacy community.

> *I've had to learn a lot. I've had to come to the realization that after having been in the classroom fifteen or sixteen years, that I have a lot to learn. There were a lot years where I went nowhere myself as a learner. There is really never a time where you can feel really, really comfortable in what you are doing. You always have to feel a little bit uncomfortable and then move on and keep on learning. I guess the risk is to admit that I don't know everything about classrooms.*

Reader, reflect now on your favorite teacher or administrator. Are you aware of what that person did outside of the classroom/school to nurture himself or herself? Thinking of the same teacher. What did that person do in the classroom to nurture her or his students? What can the school as an institution do to promote the kind of self-growth that is needed for professional growth? How can the connection between self-growth and professional growth be communicated to educational policy makers and funding sources?

References

Arendt, H. (1961). *Between past and future.* New York: Viking Press.

Blau, S. (1995). Literacy task force at work in California. *The Council Chronicle* 5 (1). National Council of Teachers of English.

Casey, K. (1993). *I answer with my life: Life histories of women teachers working for social change.* New York: Routledge Press.

Delpit, L. (1990). The silenced dialogue. N. Hidalgo, C. McDowell, and E. Siddle (Eds), *Facing racism in education.* Boston: Harvard Education Review Reprint Series.

Greene, M. (1995). Notes on the search for coherence. In J. Beane (Ed), *Toward a coherent curriculum: The 1995 ASCD yearbook.* Alexandria, VA: ASCD.

Haberman, M. (1995). *Star teachers of children in poverty.* West Lafayette, IN: Kappa Delta Pi.

Ladson-Billings, G. (1995). A coherent curriculum in an incoherent society? Pedagogical perspectives on curriculum reform. In J. Beane (Ed), *Toward a coherent curriculum: The 1995 ASCD yearbook.* Alexandria, VA: ASCD.

19

FAMILY HISTORY

As we learned about these teachers' family histories, we saw glimpses of what sociologists and anthropologists call "positive social context" and the effects of this on the adult teachers. In other words, the magic of what families across cultures do best—care for, attend to, and love each other, regardless of conditions—has a lifelong effect. The teachers in this study bring the synergistic effects of their own families to their relationships with their students and to their teaching. They show us how magic is made when educators are informed by families' knowledge: "Knowledge can come from many sources, and alternative ways of knowing can only add to our vision of issues, influences on development and schooling, and understanding of curriculum and pedagogy. It is useful to hear different voices tell their stories about how they experience education or schooling" (Bloch, 1991, 106).

These ways of knowing are being recognized by some policy makers. Oakes and Lipton (1990), California researchers whose work influences educational policy nationwide, explicitly state: "We believe that parents, policymakers, and schools need to look at how children learn naturally. This view will lead to lessons built on knowledge that is important, challenging, complex, related to real life, and rich in meaning. Furthermore, curricula grounded in complex knowledge stand the best chance of stretching the intellectual sense making of all children" (95).

Family knowledge and literacy, according to teachers in this study, are an interwoven fabric of cultural practices. The art of this family knowledge and related literacy practice promotes strength, encourages nurturance, and supports risk taking.

The teachers in this study, like many well-known writers and visionaries (Allen, 1991; Walker, 1990) talked about the importance of the passing on of stories by parents and grandparents. Vicki smiled as she reported that her West Indian grandmother passed on teachings through folk tales. She also spoke at length about her mother's influence on her reading, in terms of modeling, interest, and actually providing trips to bookstores and libraries. Likewise, Pam's mother was in her first memory of reading. Her mother brought home the illustrated book about the ballerina and read it to her. Pam then read it over and over again as a precursor to her reading and her dance. Wayne talked about both grandfather and grandmother. He noted that passing on stories in his American Indian community during his youth was done orally. They would gather around a campfire, and the eldest would talk, often it was the grandmother.

The positive modeling through family, in many cases mother and grandmother, did work to offset bad school experiences. For example, even though Del had a difficult time with reading in elementary school, reading was a central part of her family life and a source of nurturance for her from the time she was very young. Her early school experiences in reading were very negative, yet she was a self-described "book-worm." Her grandma lived with her family, and she read to the children while both parents worked. A similar thing happened with Donn and her stepmother, who encouraged Donn to read. Yet, Donn's school experiences were not positive.

School experiences of many of these teachers did not reflect their families' realities in terms of ways of life, values, or language. Raúl talked about the old basal readers with Dick and Jane family stories. He said he could not understand the situations where Mommy dropped Daddy off at the airport, with a suitcase. Nor could he relate to Daddy always wearing a tie. He said they would go home and say, "My father never wears a tie," and "We didn't know anything about airports." Even the food was out of context for him and his community. There was a breakfast of eggs, milk, toast, and orange juice. The breakfast he knew was cup of coffee and a piece of Mexican sweet bread. They could make no relation between the school and the home settings.

Nor, in many cases, did the schools recognize or use the families' strengths such as sibling support. Bill remembered that everyone in his family read a great deal. His parents read all the time. His mother never graduated from high school, but she read all the time. He already knew how to read when he entered first grade. He remembered a nun at school being surprised. She handed him some letters, and he read them, and then she handed him a book and he read that too. He remembered going to school with his sister, two years older than he is, and he could already read, so it got him motivated and excited.

Donn's career choice was initially affected by her younger brother. She noted that after her brother was born she thought about teaching, because she was twelve and really loved being with him and his little friends and teaching them the alphabet and new songs and watching them grow. And Judith talked about her older siblings reading. Her sister was always getting yelled at because she was hiding in a book instead of helping with the dishes or cleaning. Today in her professional life, Del noted the support of her sister. She said that she and her twin sister talk about books a lot.

Raúl, whose family context was very different from Judith's, described similar experiences with siblings. His story is important because of lack of information about the strengths of poor families in migrant communities. He explained:

We were so many. There wasn't a big house, so there wasn't a lot of space. I would read outside. I wasn't the only one. There were two little ones that I read with. We would play school. I would read inside even though my brothers and sisters would look at me and wonder, "What is he doing?" Well, reading. Or if I had a project to work on for school I would practice a speech or a presentation with them, but they couldn't understand. They would laugh. . . . They didn't understand.

Another family strength that affected the teachers was parents' reading practice. While families did not always read bedtime stories, people read what they were interested in. This reading combined with the relationships among family members seems to be what matters. This often differs from much traditional literacy development advice, which stresses the importance of the "bedtime story." These teachers were affected as children, not in very many cases by storybooks being read to them, but by the positive relationship of the parents and children and the exposure to parents reading what they wanted and needed to read for themselves.

Del talked about her mother and father reading at night, so the children would read with them and try to be like them. Her father would read the newspaper, and her mother would always be reading a novel of some type. Bill also noted that his mother read mostly novels. Both of his parents read the newspaper avidly, so Bill is a newspaper junkie. Wayne said his family did not have many books. But, he read the Sunday newspaper, *Life* magazine, and *Look* magazine. His parents read very little. Raúl said that his parents never read to the children, but they themselves read novels and magazines. They read magazines such as *Superman*, written in Spanish in comic book form. His cousins in Mexico had many magazines (obviously, written in Spanish) lying around. He remembers reading *La Bruja* and many others. Spanish seemed easy to him.

Some of the teachers did have storybook reading at home. Pam told us that her mother, who was an educator, read a lot. Pam saw a lot of books for adults which had characters of color, writers such as James Baldwin and Richard Wright. However, she did not see a lot of children's books with people of color, so she became interested in the adult books and read them.

Tracy reported that her mother always read to her and her brother and her father tucked them in. Lisa explained:

> *Dad associated books with riches. Because after he had read all of his books in his library, he would try to borrow books from neighbors. . . . Before I had reached five years of age there must have been more than five hundred books in the house.*

Raúl pointed out the ambiance of his migrant farmworker family when he explained:

> *Everything was very positive. Your father is there; your mother is there, and your brothers and sisters are there too. You are all working together, and your father is saying good things all day, every day for a long time. I didn't know at that time, but it was a close family unit. They talk about supporting a family now with two incomes. With the migrant families we were doing that long ago.*

The familial cohesiveness—both emotionally and interactively—in support of literacy and learning in general seems to contradict some research regarding the correlation between formal education (a high school diploma) for mothers and school success for their children (Sticht and McDonald, 1989; Teale, 1982).

Another myth perpetrated by personnel in many schools is that minority parents often do not attend school functions, meetings, or special classes because they do not care about their children. Minority parents do care; this myth has been disproved by researchers and educators (Auerbach, 1988; Quintero and Macias, 1995; Weinstein-Shr, 1992). Yet, often minority parents do miss school events. Why?

> Mexican parents, like everyone else, have problems that keep them from attending classes consistently. Drug abuse, child and spouse abuse and extreme poverty—to the point of not having running water, heated shelter, warm clothes or food—are some of the problems faced by the families. Additional problems, which though less severe, still pose obstacles to attendance, are lack of transportation, cold weather, and illness in the immediate or extended family (Quintero & Macias, 1995, p. 181–201).

In almost all of the interviews the teachers talked about the importance of the library in their early literate lives. Pam remembered going to the library. She said:

You know, it is so funny because my friends look at me now and say, "We're not surprised you're a teacher," because I would arrange for the children in my neighborhood to go on trips to the library, and I would go there all the time! Anyone who knows me would say, "Pamela was always a reader." I always used my imagination. Books took me places, and I always enjoyed that.

Raúl also pointed out that the library was not only his "friend" but also a bridge for him to the side of town where the white kids lived. Mary likewise said that she was lucky that the library was on the same side of the street as her house so she could walk there alone, at will, as a child. Lisa remembered in detail going on walks, in her town, to the library. She remembered being told that one of the first words that she said was, *berberdy* which was her word for going to the library.

Access to information is very, very important. If federal and state funds are continually whittled away and libraries disappear, where will the children learn about other worlds of information and how will attitudes grow toward tolerance of the unfamiliar?

As we hoped, the teachers' stories about their families and their experiences growing up showed us a combination of the importance of sociocultural context and images of place in childhood. The teachers spoke of family strengths in a variety of contexts and with a variety of family members. We believe that their stories bring new questions to the forefront of critical discussions about advocating for families. Some critical questions we might ask about the influence of family history on students' lives and how we as educators support this history are: Whose values are reflected in homework assignments? Whose agendas are carried out in parent-teacher organizations? What kinds of family interactions truly enhance a child's literacy development other than storybook reading? What kinds of strategies could teachers suggest to parents who do not speak English in order to share storybooks with their children? How can classroom contexts support the teaching power of siblings?

References

Allen, P. G. (1991). *Grandmothers of the light: A medicine woman's source book.* Boston: Beacon Press.

Auerbach, D. (1989). Toward a Social-contextual approach to family literacy. *Harvard Educational Review,* 59 (2), 165–181.

Bloch, M. N. (1991). Critical science and the history of child development's influence on early education research. *Early Education and Development, 2* (2), 95–108.

Freire, P., and Macedo, D. (1987). *Literacy: Reading the word and the world.* South Hadley, MA: Bergin & Garvey.

Oakes, J., and Lipton, M. (1990). *Making the best of schools.* New Haven, CT: Yale University Press.

Quintero, E., and Macias, A. (1995). To Participate, to speak out . . .: A Story from San Elzario, TX. In Martin, R. (Ed), *On Equal Terms:* Addressing Issues of Race, class, Gender in Higher Education. NY: State University of New York Press, 181–201.

Sticht, T. G., and McDonald, B. A. (January, 1989). *Making the nation smarter: The intergenerational transfer of cognitive ability.* [Executive Summary] San Diego, CA: Applied Behavioral and Cognitive Sciences, Inc.

Teale, W. H. (1982). Reading to young children: Its significance for literacy development. In H. Goelman, A. Oberg, and F. Smith, (Eds.), *Awakening to literacy.* Portsmouth, NH: Heinemann.

Walker, A. (1990). *The temple of my familiar.* New York: Scribner.

Weinstein-shr, G. (1992). Learning lives in the post-island world. *Anthropology and Education Quarterly* 23, (2), 160–165.

20

RESISTING READER/TEACHER

Sleeter and Grant (1991) point out that "ideally, education should help all students acquire knowledge that empowers. This implies that knowledge should include a perspective of history from the students' point of view and be selected and constructed in relationship to the students' desires, visions, descriptions of reality, and repertoires of action" (50).

How do teachers and schools become aware of the students' desires, visions, realities, and repertoires? Greene (1986) notes, "I think of how little many teachers know about their students' diverse lives and thinking processes, how little they can know because of the paucity of dialogue in the classroom space" (80).

We, like Brady (1995) believe that our teachers' stories illuminate three educational issues that are not addressed by Freire or by many critical theorists and must be addressed. These issues reinforce our emphasis on the theoretical triangulation using critical theory, feminist theory, and autobiographical theory. According to Brady (1995) these pedagogical issues involve the following:

1. Teacher authority can be emancipatory when a feminist pedagogy of place is recognized (schools are institutions based on patriarchal philosophy, goals, delivery systems). Feminist pedagogy recognizes the limits that this contextual reality places upon cooperative, noncompetitive learning, production of knowledge, and social realities.
2. Any discussion of authority must be rooted in identity politics that acknowledges the need for people to represent themselves. This is not to romanticize experiences, but that this experience must have the opportunity to speak, be responsible for actions in both the ideological and political sense.
3. Feminist authority must provide the conditions for students to gain control of their learning within a place and in context in which they are not threatened by the implications of what they say.

Brady (1995) points out that in identifying a politics of difference and identity, literacy is a central mechanism for discussing power, subjectivity, history, and experience. Literacy becomes a way to translate issues of politics involving the issues above into pedagogy. According to Giroux (1991), "At its best . . . as a form of engaged practice, critical pedagogy calls into question forms of subordination that create inequities among different groups as they live out their lives" (16). The teachers we interviewed all showed a strength of resistence to subordination for themselves and others that is prevalent in many different contexts of their lives and work. We believe that they would agree with Brunner (1994) that "not questioning, not pursuing education as inquiry into both the knower and the known may also get us killed, metaphorically speaking if not otherwise" (236).

Regarding the issue of genderized classrooms Swadener and Kessler (1991) point out that there is a relationship between "what we teach in school and the unequal outcomes of schooling based on social class, race, language or dialect, and gender" (87). Brunner (1994) acknowledges that it is fallacy to assume that democracy guarantees justice.

Judith had much to say about her feminist beliefs and the contexts of classrooms. She discussed the differences in classroom behavior, the labels applied to girls, and even the language she finds herself using that is probelmatic in terms of gender. However, Del feels that in her classroom "things have changed tremendously." She describes more androgonous characteristics (including reading interests and preferences) both of boys and of girls.

According to Behar (1993) the question of whether feminism translates across borders has lately begun to preoccupy feminist ethnographers who want to learn how to listen and respond to the words of women from other cultural, racial, and class backgrounds. The teachers here inform us of ways some "crossings" have occurred in their lives. Like those of Behar's (1993) Esperanza, many of the teachers' transgressions against patriarchal ideology are tied up in paradoxes. Of course, the question remains: From whose perspective, whose absolute scale of feminist perfection, are their attitudes and actions being measured? Their critique of, and struggle against, the dominant gender ideology, like any such critique, any such struggle, is necessarily ambiguous.

The teachers' autobiographies put into context a way to see feminist issues in everyday contexts and point out the complexities embedded in racial and class contexts. Judith's story illuminates feminist questions in a starkly personal light. She talked about becoming a single parent, raising a daughter, learning about *Ms.* magazine, and starting to analyze everything:

> *I remember a National Geographic special on television in 1976 in which experts talked about the future. They were all men at the seminar. Only one woman was taking notes, and she wasn't quoted. I still count today. When a presenter gets up at a school assembly I count how many boys and how many girls she calls on.*

Del spoke of her own daughter and her hopes for equality for her. Pam remembered her own schooling and the influence of a feminist teacher, Judy Blume's books, and Louise Maryweather's *Daddy Was a Number Runner.*

In terms of resistence against censorship, our teachers, like many literary and literacy figures, are active.

Katherine Patterson, author of *Bridge to Terabithia* (1993) warns: "And if our ideas are right, we do not have to fear opposing ideas. Our arguments may momentarily fail, but time will reveal untruth. Perhaps the worst way to oppose an idea is to seek to suppress it. Banished ideas, like martyrs, have a way of coming back to haunt you. Remember Galileo?" (55). Pam said:

> *It's hard dealing with censorship, especially expressing that it is my point of view. I have a selection of different versions of the Cinderella fairy tales, and so I bring them in a lot. I tell kids that this is my point of view, and you have your point of view, and all points of view are different. We all have different views, and that's okay. It helps to develop critical thinkers instead of just passive listeners. I encourage children to express themselves, and sometimes it gets me into trouble, and sometimes I look and I say, "Why did I try to bring out that in this child? Now this child is just too vocal, too verbal!" The writer in me says that everyone has a voice and they have a right to express it. Everyone's voice counts because you might not like what someone has to say but it may affect someone very deeply that is going through that same experience that may be taboo to someone. I believe everyone has a voice, and they have the right to express themselves, and in terms of working with children it's up to parents to decide what they like for their children to read and not to read and what's okay and acceptable in their homes and what they like to expose their children to. But if a child is anything like I was, they're going to read it anyway. I believe in having children select books.*

Judith said that she worries if she talks about divorce or homosexuality, not because she is afraid to talk to the kids about it, but because of parents' reactions. She does not think books in school should be censored. She thinks censorship comes out of fear. Parents are sometimes afraid that information they feel is harmful can't be kept out of their children's learning.

Donn candidly described what many teachers have experienced:

Honestly, as I've gone through the years in teaching I haven't censored books, but there have been times when I have left certain types of books out, and I guess that is a type of censorship. I feel that we don't have the right to take books off the shelf, but we have the right to choose which books we encourage in the classroom. There are some books that have children calling other children names that I might actually read to the kids, but I won't use the names that they use like stupid. *I might take out certain words, but I think that those books are still good books except for that type of language. There could be that one little part that you disagree with, but the rest of it might be something that you really want to get through to them. Now back to censorship. When they have their time in the front and they see that book that I read, and they see that word and look at me like, "You didn't say that word!" I could get away with that in September, but not now that they are reading. You know, when we start off the year and we go over the rules and talk about respecting each other's feelings and calling each other by their own names, so every moment after that is a teacher's moment.*

Del, as a female reader, responded to the strong female characters in the Laura Ingals Wilder books. This was the basis of her response to the books. She brings in books for children written from social contexts different from her own and different from that represented in the Wilder books. While some people, particularly native Americans, hate Wilder's *Little House on the Prairie* series because of its negative portrayal of Indians, Dell addresses the limitations of perspective in these books and others while using them in the classroom. She guides questioning and discussion that helps even young children to read critically and shares many books that involve many perspectives. The multitext, response-driven pedagogy used by Del and the other teachers in this study provides the opportunity for children to look at life through eyes different from their own. Dell exemplifies Freire and Gadotti's (1995) advice:

One of the things the teacher should do is, for example, understanding culture in a multicultural way, commenting with the students on the differences and point out that this part of the curriculum is not universal. . . . It is also necessary to know how to reinvent language, to understand the diversity of its syntaxes. . . . . Every day one has to recreate one's tactics to overcome the exclusivism of a narrow cultural comprehension. (56–57)

Risk is a positive force and related to resistance in teaching. Tracy acknowledged that teachers take risks every day in terms of which students are reached and which ones are not, in terms of decisions about methodology and classroom mangagment. Both Judith and Tracy also discussed the risks involved in collaboration. Tracy said:

Team teaching is extremely difficult, depending on who you're working with. It was a choice. It's hard because you have to be able to work with someone that you respect, but there are also some kind of limits. It's hard to be with a friend, and Manny and I are friends, and it's been difficult to work with a friend; where do you draw the line?

Donn admitted:

Sometimes though you can't help but feel, Am I doing the right thing by doing all these things that aren't typical? Even though you're praised for it you still question yourself before you do it, because you don't know if the children are going to respond well to it, and you won't know until you try; that's a big risk.

Judith said that she thought the biggest risk is staying open to ideas and people and not being isolated in your classroom.

Pam, too, talked of taking risks often and in many ways.

I've had some struggles in terms of the direction that I like to go and that I find myself going into, and so I've decided that yes I do take a lot of risks. Now I'm just beginning to acknowledge it and say, "I'm taking these risks, and that's it, and this is what I have to do." Any way I can get to the children. A lot of teachers are unfortunately stuck. They are saying, "This is the right way to do it and the only way, and we've been doing it like this for years, and all that fancy stuff is nothing new, and we're not excited about it." Then I come in and I say, "Well I have to do this. I have to show you. I'm going to be in your face showing you this all the time introducing it to you; I've done writing workshops here." Some of the teachers are like, "OK, where do I find the time to do this?" or "Is this woman crazy, she thinks I'm actually going to implement this?" I'm sure that is what they are saying, but I keep doing it because I see the benefits.

Mary's risk taking has become activism in the truest sense. She gives children experiences of leadership and opportunities for real participation such as writing to state senators. She works on a classroom climate that offers children the opportunity to question, where it's okay to make mistakes. In terms of risk taking and curriculum activities, Mary feels it's well worth the risk to go beyond that and to extend curriculum by embracing an integrated approach. She feels strongly about taking risks in the area of assessment because of the benefit to her students. She does a lot of portfolio assessment and avoids what she calls "typical grading." Mary also risks taking the lead in working with parents. She goes to the homes in the housing projects and various other neighborhoods if she is worried about a child.

Bill's risk taking has become activism. He works with junior high students and senior high students in what is now one of the largest programs in the United States: Wilderness Inquiry. The program is based in Minneapolis and now operates all over the country.

Raul's activism began much earlier in his life with his high school teachers and his demands to study his own heroes and continues as he works with the Minnesota Migrant Council and parents in different migrant communities.

Mary's words are straightforward:

I could go home to my nice little quiet neighborhood and just tuck myself in, but I can't now because of what I know about my children's lives and different things about school. [I have] . . . to fight, fight not only for the rights of our particular program but for equal rights for all children. Like right now with the governor and budget cutting in education. I feel I've gotta fight now even for college; he has reduced the college budget by 21 percent. If all anyone ever did was think about what was happening to themselves, collectively nothing would happen. I think we have to have these global eyes, these eyes that the children have, so that we can make a difference. As one person we are not going to, but if these little packs of kids can stand up for each other, we can. I mean, they are going to make the difference, and they are going to be the voice of the future. So, why would we want to squelch their voice now? They've got ideas!

The teachers we interviewed showed us many ways that we as teachers can be resistant and take risks for the ultimate goal of improving learning situations so that our students can become transformative intellectuals. A wise Anishinabe woman once advised activists in the Minnesota community where she lived and worked for decades, "I just have to wake up each morning and tell myself that I'm going to do the best I can to make one small change for the better for my people. And I vow not to let society take the sparkle out of my grandchildren's eyes" (Myers, 1988).

What kinds of voices are heard in literacy classroom activities? From what kinds of classrooms are these voices derived? Who has the right to speak and be heard? What are the political, social, and cultural forces that are affecting the students? Whom shall schools serve? What is legitimate knowledge? What is the teacher's right to intervene and to try to change a student's agenda? What are the tensions between form and freedom in teaching? How do students see what is happening? How do teachers see it? What is the difference?

References

Behar, R. (1993). *Translated woman: Crossing the border with Experanza's story.* Boston: Beacon Press.

Bloch, M. N. (1991). Critical science and the history of child development's influence on early education research. *Early Education and Development, 2* (2), pp. 95–108.

Brady, J. (1995). *Schooling young children: A feminist pedagogy for liberatory learning.* New York: SUNY.

Freire, P. & Gadotti, M. (1995). We can reinvent the world. *Taboo: The Journal of Culture and Education,* pp. 48–61.

Giroux, H. (1991) The politics of postmodernism: Rethinking the boundaries of race and ethnicity. *Journal of Urban and Cultural Studies, 1* (1) 5–38.

Greene, M. (1986). Reflections and passion in teaching. *Journal of Curriculum and Supervision, 2* (1), 68–81.

Myers, R. (1988.) Interview in *A Matter of Culture.* Duluth, MN: Community Video.

Patterson, K. (1993). Tale of a reluctant dragon. In Shannon, P. (1993). *Becoming political.* Portsmouth, NH: Heinemann.

Sleeter, C. & Grant, C. (1991). Mapping terrains of power: Student Cultural knowledge versus classroom knowledge. In Sleeter, C. and Grant, C. (Eds.) *Empowerment through multicultural education*, New York: SUNY, pp. 49–68.

Swadener, E. B. & Kessler, S. (1991). Introduction to the special issue. *Early Education and Development*, 2, (2), 85–94.

INDEX